W9-BUY-606

# Revolutionary Hamburg

# Revolutionary Hamburg

*Labor Politics in the Early Weimar Republic*

RICHARD A. COMFORT



1966

STANFORD UNIVERSITY PRESS
STANFORD CALIFORNIA

Stanford University Press
Stanford, California

Printed in the United States of America
L.C. 66-15297

*To Raymond J. Sontag*
*in gratitude*

# Preface

The emergence of the working classes as a significant social and political force was one of the major events of European and American history in the latter half of the nineteenth century. Not the least important aspect of this development was the great opportunity it offered to those who wished to reform society in one way or another. For here was a force which, if properly channeled, seemed capable of destroying the established order and rebuilding a new world on the ruins.

The extent to which labor has fulfilled the expectations of the various reformers who have tried to lead it is very much open to question. But that their attempts to do so have had extremely important effects can scarcely be doubted.

The Weimar Republic marked a significant step in the political development of the working classes. For it was during this period that one of the first attempts was made to integrate a traditionally Marxist labor movement into a parliamentary democracy. The effort to strike a compromise between liberal political democracy and Marxist social democracy is perhaps one of the most interesting aspects of the history of the Weimar Republic. The failure of the attempt makes it no less significant for many another democratic country seeking a similar solution.

To gain an understanding of the nature of this compromise, and the reasons for its failure, is not an easy task. The issues involved are numerous and complex, and in the past they have not always been dealt with objectively. This study attempts to unravel the tangle of issues involved in the development of the role of labor in Weimar politics by examining the history of Hamburg from late 1918 to the beginning of the period of "recovery" in 1924.

Very little space is devoted here to the seemingly endless doctrinal disputes so much indulged in by Marxist politicians. I have been more concerned with the political behavior of the workers themselves, examining it quantitatively whenever possible in the hope of uncovering the issues and social realities that lay behind the disagreements of the leaders. As a result, there is much here concerning the nature of political conflict in the workshop and on the streets, but very little about political conflict in the local parliament. I have tried to write what is best described as social history—the history of a social class and the development of its role in politics.

The scope of this study is limited to the city of Hamburg, the second largest city in Germany and center of one of that country's most important industrial complexes. In most cases, the adjacent areas which, together with the city, constitute the *Land* Hamburg were not considered, in order to avoid complicating what is essentially a study of urban politics with the special problems of rural areas.

Several rather special methodological techniques were used in this study. One portion of the book is devoted to a statistical analysis of the voting behavior of labor, with the aim of uncovering the effective social bases of the various parties competing for the labor vote. Another portion is devoted to the study of the social characteristics of the leadership and membership of the major parties and trade unions. And considerable attention is directed toward the internal development of the trade unions, their relation to the labor force as a whole, and their importance in political affairs. I have attempted throughout to weave these points of interest into a narrative history of Hamburg during the early Weimar years.

The student of the history of Hamburg, especially if his subject concerns the labor movement, encounters a situation far different from the one he would expect to find at the national level. There are almost no dependable scholarly works with adequate source references; diaries and memoirs are scarce; newspaper files are incomplete and scattered; and the files of the local labor organizations containing correspondence and reports of local conferences were largely destroyed in 1933. To some extent, the gaps in documentary material have been compensated for by the use of statistics, interviews, and literary works. Particularly useful were the novels of Willi Bredel, one of East Germany's leading literary figures, who was a member of the Hamburg Communist Party in the 'twenties.

The archives of the Staatsarchiv contained a huge mountain of documentary material, most of which had not been previously examined for its historical value. Unfortunately, much of the most important material was destroyed in the war, a fact I discovered only after sifting through great piles of uncataloged document folders.

Nevertheless, local history can be a rewarding pursuit, perhaps especially in a country like Germany, where regional and local differences have always played an important role in political and social developments. Germany is not just Berlin, and only when we become completely aware of this fact will we begin to understand some of the most important and basic problems in German history.

I should like to express my appreciation to the following persons and institutions.

Professors Cyril E. Black, Gordon A. Craig, Carl E. Schorske, and Arno J. Mayer, for numerous helpful suggestions and criticisms.

Professors Fred I. Greenstein and Elton F. Jackson, whose assistance with a number of methodological problems was invaluable.

The Senate of Hamburg for granting me free access to the material in the archives, some of which had been officially closed after

1914; and the staff of the Staatsarchiv, especially Dr. Martin Ewald, for their ready cooperation and helpfulness.

Wolfgang Schröder and the personnel of the Zentralarchiv der Gewerkschaften in East Berlin for making it possible for me to use the valuable materials gathered there.

The personnel of the Auer Verlag, the Social Democratic Party, and the Free Unions in Hamburg, who assisted me in the location of many useful sources and who allowed me the free use of the materials at their disposal.

Heinrich Brandler, Heinz and Willi Ruhnau, Gerhard Orgass, Robert G. Livingston, and numerous others in Hamburg, who gave so generously of their time to assist me in my undertaking.

The *International Review of Social History* (Amsterdam) for permission to use material previously published in that journal.

The Penfield Foundation, the Social Science Research Council, Stanford University, and the Hoover Institution for generous financial assistance at various stages in the writing of the work.

My wife.

R.A.C.

*Oakland, California*
*June 1966*

# Contents

# Revolutionary Hamburg

*If Germany does not receive a single national labor movement, she will collapse.*

FRIEDRICH EBERT

*Chapter 1*

# Introduction

At the beginning of this century Hamburg had one of the best organized and most powerful labor movements in all Germany. No other group in the city-state bore as much responsibility for the success of the Revolution of 1918, and none seemed more likely to profit from the new republican institutions. And yet, by 1924 the labor movement had become about equally divided among those who supported the Republic, those who wanted to see it destroyed, and those who did not care much either way. United in support of the Republic, the labor movement could have been a formidable political and economic force. But weak, fragmented, and torn by internal dissension, it offered only half-hearted resistance to its enemies, and hence was ignored with impunity.

To explain these developments, we must first of all form the most precise picture possible of the political behavior of the most important groups within the working classes. Second, we must try to understand the major interests of each of these groups. And, finally, we must inquire how the Weimar political system, as it was manifested in Hamburg, met or failed to meet these interests.

To deal with these matters adequately, it is essential that the "political system" be defined as broadly as possible. Therefore this study is concerned not only with formal political institutions, such as parliaments, laws, and political parties, but also with "informal" political entities, such as trade unions, organizations of the unemployed, and intra-party factions. Similarly, we must include in our definition of the "political system" those political struggles and maneuverings that were conducted within party and union organizations, more often in the factory than in the legislature or the lecture hall. Our choice of subject matter in itself constitutes a degree of interpretation of the history of the Weimar Republic, a fact that should be made clear at the outset. The fundamental assumption here is that political attitudes are formed not in response to specific events, but over a considerable period of time, as a product of a patterning of perceptions about the nature of the political system. The practical significance of this assumption can be seen most clearly with reference to the effects of the various crises on the development of Weimar politics.

For example, it is generally accepted that the astronomical inflation, culminating in the crisis of the autumn of 1923, was a major factor in the loss of faith in the Republic by large segments of German society, especially the lower middle class and labor. The former, it is held, having seen their salaries shrink to near or below subsistence levels and their savings evaporate, became ready recruits for the burgeoning National Socialist movement. Labor, for similar reasons, was drawn to the Communist program. These are plausible hypotheses, but let us look more closely at the assumptions involved.

It is assumed, first of all, that both these groups associated the economic and social events with the government and reacted by rejecting it. It is assumed that these groups either experienced or thought they experienced greater economic hardship than any other group in the society, and that this economic hardship was the primary or decisive element in their alienation from the political system. These are difficult assumptions to document, but they are of considerable importance because they form the core of any interpretation of these major events. To test these assumptions, there are a number of specific questions we might ask. Can we be certain, first of all, that the election results, which indicated a loss of support for the moderate parties and a gain for the extremes, actually represented shifts of individual voters from one party to another? Might not changes in the electoral participation rate of various groups reflect similar returns? Was the reaction of a given group in the society to the inflation significantly related to the degree of economic hardship that group experienced? If not, what other variables were involved?

Questions like these only underline the fact that the determination of the impact of any crisis situation, economic or otherwise, on the formation of political attitudes and on the performance of political action is a highly complex matter. It is not always true, of course, that national crises result in a loss of faith in the political system. A crisis may actually increase national solidarity, or lead to alterations in the system that raise the level of legitimacy. And, in any case, its effects will almost certainly be different in different parts of the society.[1]

The explanation for the variation in the political effects of any crisis is to be found in the manner in which the citizenry perceives and interprets the objective events of the situation. In 1923, for example, many Germans were prepared to accept quite readily the notion that the inflation was caused either by conscious conspiracy or by incompetence on the part of government officials. One must ask, first of all, who were these people? How complete was their information and where did they get it? What sort of preconceptions did they have concerning their leaders, their neighbors, their nation, and the political system that was attempting unsuccessfully to unite them? The effects of the crisis could perhaps be traced to feelings on the part of the populace that everyone was out for what he could get, that political representatives could not be trusted, that the government was uninterested and unresponsive to their wishes and needs. Then the economic crisis itself might have been seen simply as a conclusive demonstration of what everyone knew already.

If the problem is couched in such terms, the historical approach to it must be altered significantly. Our attention is directed less to the specific events associated with the crisis and more to the whole web of associations between government and the people.

We must be concerned with the continuing process through which people's ideas and feelings about their political system were formed. This would include consideration of the many points of contact between the political system and the populace with an eye to discovering the significance of these contacts for the citizen. We would need to form a picture of the entire scope of the citizen's public life in order to discern patterns of action and response.

These are essentially the aims of this study, with special reference to the working classes of Hamburg. Through detailed study of some of the major events that involved the political activity of the working classes, through sociological analysis of the membership and leadership of the various labor organizations, and through the use of some of the techniques of electoral sociology, we shall try to reconstruct as completely as possible the political context within which the various working-class groups were operating. While I do not claim complete success in this undertaking, I do believe that this line of research has led to a fuller, more realistic understanding of the dynamics of labor politics in Weimar Germany.

One of the products of this study has been a general interpretation of the nature of the Revolution of 1918–19. This interpretation is so bound up in the organization and development of this study that it should be made explicit at the outset. Germany, first of all, certainly did experience a major political revolution early in the twentieth century, though it would probably be more meaningful to date it 1914–19 rather than 1918–19. The republican government may be seen as an attempt to objectify this revolution in a totally new political system based upon popular consent in a country accustomed to quite a different kind of political life.

In the course of the preceding half-century, the social and economic life of Germany underwent revolutionary changes. The growth of population, the emergence both of vast new social classes and of intricate new interdependent relationships among them significantly altered the bases of power at every level. The World War itself provides the most striking evidence of this transformation. In this war, it became necessary for the first time in German history to mobilize the energies of the entire population, civilian and military alike. Not only were sacrifices required, but enthusiasm in making them as well.

The war is only a particularly striking example of the changes that took place in almost every aspect of national life. For the first time the wishes and will of the German people had to be taken into account—as consumers of goods, as operators of machines, as marchers in armies. Germany, in other words, had become what has been loosely described as a "mass society," a full-fledged participant in the age of mass communications, public relations, advertising, and—particularly relevant here—the mass movement. Mass participation had become a force to be reckoned with in cultural events, economics, and politics.[2]

In political terms, this is another way of saying that Germany, like many other nations, came to discover that the phenomenon of modern nationalism is a two-sided proposition. On the one hand, it is an instrument through which the power of the ruling authority is enormously enhanced. The nation, insofar as it can rely upon the loyalties of its citizens, becomes capable of carrying out unprecedentedly ambitious national projects, like the wars of the twentieth century. On the other hand, this involvement of the population-at-large in the affairs of the nation is not without difficulties, for it brings with it the necessity either of granting the citizenry extensive participation in the making of national decisions, or of devising complex machinery for the maintenance of loyalties by other means.

One great wave of this so-called "participation revolution" swept over Germany during the war years.[3] The war was not very long in progress before the inadequacies of the old system were obvious. Designed for a less complex age, it had few facilities to cope with the new conditions. The old system was poorly adapted to enlisting the willing support of society as a whole. Its communications channels were hopelessly inadequate. The government was neither able to speak easily to the population, nor able to perceive clearly alterations in popular sentiment. What was needed was a modification of the political system that would facilitate the establishment of contact with Germans in every corner of the Reich and at every level of the social scale. For immediate purposes, the wartime military administration devised numerous expedients for drawing previously ignored Social Democrats and others into the administrative machinery. It seems extremely unlikely that such a process, once begun, could have been reversed. In any case, the revolution was inherent in the creation of responsible ministries and the coming into power of the Social Democrats, the Centrists, and the Democrats. It did not really need the explosive events of November 1918. The revolution was victorious well before the Armistice was declared.

What we have come to call "the Revolution of 1918–19" was not in reality concerned with the obvious issues. For the most part, it was made by enlisted men in uniform, supported primarily by workers employed in large-scale "mass industries." This was a new wave in the participation revolution, cresting before its predecessor had fully broken. The war had given these men their first real sense of national consciousness. They had discovered in a profound way the degree of their involvement. As a consequence, they became a political force—without leadership, without real political experience, and without the training and knowledge necessary to formulate realistic political objectives.

What did these men really want? This was the central question of 1918–19. Fear of "Bolshevism" on the one hand, and enthusiasm for it on the other, were primarily responsible for the wildly distorted answers the question received. It is the contention of this study that the workingmen of Hamburg came out into the streets in 1918, and on several other occasions in the years that followed, chiefly for these reasons: they wanted an end to the authority of the military regime they had learned to know and hate during the war; and they wanted jobs which paid a decent wage and at which a man could work without the necessity of obeying uncompromising, authoritarian mandates from either factory manager or trade-union official.

The trouble was, of course, that they didn't know how to go about realizing these objectives; and their search for leadership and a program created an unknown political force that was highly unstable, susceptible to arguments for the "quick and simple" solution, and impatient with the politics of compromise and moderation. The existence of this new political force posed a formidable problem for the Majority Socialists, so newly come to power. How could these workers be convinced that, in the long run, the republican form of government offered the best hope for the realization of their objectives? A massive job of political socialization, of integrating these workers into the new political system, confronted the organizations of the pro-republican labor movement.

The central focus of this study is on precisely this problem. What attempts were made to integrate the newly awakened working classes of Hamburg into the new political system of the Weimar Republic? How did they succeed or fail? How successful was the SPD, traditionally a Marxist class party, in leading the working classes into a more generalized commitment to a republican political system?

It should perhaps be stressed that ending this study in the year 1924 constitutes in itself something of an interpretation. It seems clear that by that year the political activity of the working classes of Hamburg had settled into a fairly fixed pattern. No significant changes could be observed during the rest of the Weimar period.

One disclaimer should be added. The conclusions reached here will not necessarily be applicable to the study of the German labor movement as a whole. On the other hand, an intensive study such as this, conducted on a closely limited scale, may well uncover important elements that could be missed altogether in a broader view of the national scene. The hope is that this study will add new dimensions to the knowledge we already have concerning the failure of the republican political system in Germany.

*Chapter 2*

# Trends and Traditions in Prewar Hamburg

Approaching Hamburg from the south, the first thing one sees is five imposing towers rising abruptly from the broad North European plain. Behind and below them, a myriad of smaller towers are visible, clustered together in a dense forest slightly to the west.

By the time one has crossed the Elbe, gray-green and littered with commercial flotsam, and entered the industrial outskirts of the city, the vague shapes of the towers have begun to take on definite form. Four of them mark the splendid old Protestant churches of "Old Hamburg." St. Peter's and St. Jacob's, with their powerful four-sided spires that gleam copper-green in the rain, are in the heart of the downtown district; St. Nicholas's, now completely gone except for its ornate stone-tracery tower, is a little farther out. And on the highest ground of the city, overlooking the waterfront, is St. Michael's, the harbor church.

At the base of this friendly old church is St. Pauli, the harbor-workers' district. In 1917, St. Pauli was a cluster of low, sprawling flats. These tired old houses, built helter-skelter over the centuries, formed a picturesque (and unsanitary) maze, rarely penetrated by the representatives of law and order. For generations, children at play in the courtyards, like their fathers close by in the harbor, have heard "Der Michel" measure out the hours of the passing day.[1]

Not far away, rises the last of the great towers, the splendidly ornate Renaissance city hall. Built toward the end of the nineteenth century along the edge of a large, open square, it is impressive, though cold and perhaps a bit vulgar in its blatant announcement that it is the governmental and administrative center of a proud and prosperous old commercial city.

Not much of old Hamburg remains today, and these towers represent the Hamburg that was: the medieval center of North European Christianity and wealthy member of the Hanseatic League. Behind and below them, thousands of cranes line the shores of the harbor. Hamburg is proud of these, too. They represent the Hamburg that is: the largest and most modern port of continental Europe.

The skyline of a city, like the face of a man, reflects a way of life. Hamburg's skyline (especially when viewed with the knowledge that it has twice been rebuilt just as it was before) reveals two important things about the city: it is proud of its traditions and dedicated to commerce. Perhaps the single most striking characteristic of the city is the extent to which the harbor permeates its existence. Until 1943, when Hamburg was nearly eighty-five per cent destroyed by Allied bombers, the city was laced by a complex system of waterways that reached far into the outskirts. Along these canals were the warehouses of the great commercial firms, and fleets of small barges (propelled by long poles, hooked first onto one piling, then the next) shuttled between harbor and warehouse.

A large picturesque lake, the Alster, divides the city at its center. Along its shores are Hamburg's most elegant shops, its finest hotels, and the grand old homes of the leading banking and commercial families. But the sounds and smells of the harbor reach even here, and the gay sailboats must share their playground with dirty iron barges bringing odd boxes and crates from the harbor to inland destinations. The influence of the harbor can be seen in other areas of communal life, in ways not so readily apparent to the casual observer. It has played an important role in shaping the social, economic, and political traditions of Hamburg. These traditions played a significant role in the political turbulence of the 1920's.

A discussion of them, therefore, is a necessary introduction to the problem at hand.

The Hamburg businessman or civic leader prides himself on possessing what is known as the "Hansegeist," the Hanseatic spirit.[2] Obviously, the "Hanseatic spirit" is at bottom a reference to a more glorious past. It refers, perhaps, as much to the golden years of the eighteenth and nineteenth centuries when many of the great mansions were built, as to the thirteenth and fourteenth centuries when Hamburg thrived as a member of the Hanseatic League. It is an essentially conservative spirit that wishes to see Hamburg kept as it was at the time of its greatest prosperity.

But the Hanseatic spirit has its other side. While the true "Hanseatic man" espouses a determined conservatism on most social, economic, and political issues, he knows that to maintain and extend Hamburg's world position, constant attention must be paid to the improvement of the harbor and its facilities and to the other means by which the commerce of the city is conducted. Thus the "Hanseatic spirit" looks to the past for its model, but looks to the present for economic development. It is to this dualism that one must look for an explanation of many of the odd paradoxes in the history of the city.[3]

Hamburg, for example, was widely known as one of the world's leaders in the field of city planning. Even before the end of the nineteenth century, the city inaugurated extensive slum-clearance projects to make way for a new and efficient commercial center in the heart of the city.[4] At about the same time there was evidence that the city's drinking-water had become contaminated. But from 1872, when a medical collegium declared the water "harmful in every respect," until 1893 when a filtration system was finally installed, the issue was passed dilatorily from committee to committee.[5] In 1892, while the Hamburg government was still arguing about the desirability of installing water meters, the second cholera epidemic in less than fifty years struck the city. Over eight thousand residents died of the disease in a few weeks.[6]

This is not to suggest that the city's leaders cynically neglected a vital civic need while actively supporting ambitious projects that suited their own interests. On the contrary, there is considerable evidence to show that a humanitarian impulse was a strong motivating factor behind the slum-clearance projects.[7] Rather, it is to point out that in matters which do not touch directly upon the commerce of the city (such as the drinking water), the basic conservatism of the Hanseatic spirit is likely to take hold, and change, if any, will be gradual in the extreme.

Another aspect of the Hanseatic spirit is a certain local chauvinism and a corresponding reticence to identify with the German nation as a whole. These qualities are reflected in the official title of the city, "The Free and Hanseatic City of Hamburg." The important word here is "free." Hamburg became a free imperial city by a decree of Emperor Maximilian I in 1510, and was admitted to the diet of the Empire in 1770. The status of the city remained virtually unchanged, except for the period of French occupation during the Napoleonic wars, until 1866–68, when it was incorporated into the North German Confederation.* This apparently drastic alteration in Hamburg's 350-year-old status was carried out with surprising ease. To be sure, the citizens grumbled a bit over the loss of the traditional flag, the Hamburg post office, and the privilege of conducting independent diplomatic relations.[8] But, generally speaking, opposition was sporadic and confined to a few special-interest groups.[9] The initial steps having already been taken, the transition, in 1871, to a member-state (*Land*) of the German Reich was accomplished virtually without protest.[10]

Hamburg's incorporation into the German nation was not absolute: in one major respect her traditional free-city prerogatives were left virtually untouched. Although Bismarck and others considered the Customs Union an integral and necessary part of the new union of the German states, the constitutions of both the Confederation and the Reich explicitly gave Hamburg the right

* The history of Hamburg's entry into the Confederation and the Reich is closely paralleled by that of Bremen. The negotiations outlined here may be taken as also applying to Bremen.

to decide whether or not she would enter the Customs Union.[11] For there was one aspect of Hamburg's free-city status that was considered eternal and inviolable—the right to import and export goods duty free. "As long as one allowed Hamburg its economic freedom of movement," wrote one observer, "its particularistic tendencies were satisfied."[12] The far-seeing, of course, might have guessed from the beginning that incorporation into the Reich would ultimately mean curtailment of this freedom, but little was said about this possibility during the "honeymoon years" of 1866–78.

In spite of the broad cultural gap between Prussia and Hamburg, relations between them were relatively cordial. In 1873, for example, the first official celebration of the Kaiser's birthday was held in the city, and the officers of the local Prussian detachment mixed sociably with the Bürgermeister and his colleagues.[13]

This "era of good feelings" came to an abrupt end in 1878 when Bismarck announced his new protective-tariff proposals, which included, almost as a footnote, certain restrictions on Hamburg's tariff-free zone and suggestions that more were to follow.[14] Hamburg reacted with cries of outrage to this "declaration of war between Hamburg and the Reich."[15] And in the negotiations that followed, Hamburg's latent distrust of Prussia (i.e., the Reich) was fanned into a glowing ember that has never completely cooled. The National Liberal majority, which had developed in Hamburg in support of Bismarck and his policies, disappeared in a flash as all parties joined together to heap opprobrium upon the head of the chancellor.[16]

Ultimately, the conflict ended in a compromise. In 1888, both Hamburg and Bremen became members of the Customs Union. Each, however, was allowed to construct (for the most part with Prussian funds) a large area in its harbor that was thenceforth to be a special "free area"; goods could be imported and re-exported from this area without tax or tariff. The conflict over Hamburg's status as a free-city did have lasting effects: the National Liberals never recovered their status as a majority party, and a residue of animosity and distrust toward Prussia was left behind to play an important role in future relations between Hamburg and the rest of Germany.[17] The word "free" in the city's title serves as a constant reminder of Hamburg's reservations concerning her status as a member-state of the German Reich.

These reservations were considerably reinforced by the nature of Hamburg's international orientation. "For the residents of this city," wrote a French visitor, "there is only Hamburg and the world."[18] His observation constitutes about as neat a statement of the nature of Hamburg's so-called "traditional cosmopolitanism" as one could wish for. However, this cosmopolitanism had certain special features that are worth comment.

Since the middle ages, Hamburg had lived in a state of continual hostility both with her neighbor to the north, Denmark, and her neighbor to the west and south, Hannover.[19] This hostility led Hamburg into the Prussian camp at the time of the Prusso-Danish war of 1864, and provided the city with a certain vested interest in the creation of a unified Germany.[20] But neither then, nor later, did the city show much interest in continental matters. Hamburg's external interests were formed instead by its centuries-old trade connections with England and, more recently, with North and South America. This spirit of cosmopolitanism, reinforced by animosity toward Prussia, made it difficult for Hamburg to become involved in the political and international issues that concerned the rest of Germany.

Another factor that contributed to the Hamburg resident's conception of his city as distinct from other parts of Germany is the notion that his city possessed an unusual "liberal tradition." Probably, this idea stems from the fact that Hamburg scarcely experienced feudal rule, and has been governed for most of its history by some sort of elected council. Citizens of Hamburg like to point to the fact that the city has always been "democratic," but, as we shall see, this was true only in a very special sense. In any case, it is a source of great civic pride that no nobility, Danish or German, has ever played a major political or social role in the city. And so far as is known, no political party in Hamburg before World War I —whatever its orientation—dared not call itself "liberal."[21]

Interestingly enough, Hamburg residents like to point to the laxness with which Bismarck's "antisocialist law" was applied in the city as a recent example of Hamburg's liberal predilections.[22] This law, which created severe difficulties for labor organizations of any sort, and forced the Social Democratic Party virtually to disband its national organization, came into effect in 1878, the same year that saw the beginning of Hamburg's conflict with Prussia over the free-harbor. Many felt that refusal to support the law gave them an effective stick with which to beat the hated Bismarck. The law was vigorously attacked in the Hamburg press, and anyone who tried to enforce it was accused of "Prussian servility."[23] Indeed, though perhaps only coincidentally, the period during which the law was in effect was also a period in which the Socialists gained support at the polls.[24] Many of these votes may well have been votes against Bismarck rather than votes for the Socialists.

Although Hamburg's half-hearted attempts to enforce the "antisocialist" law were undoubtedly due in part to anti-Prussian feeling, it is also a fact that most Hamburg businessmen and city leaders, up to the turn of the century, had rather liberal attitudes toward the labor movement. It was generally felt that the workers, too, would recognize the connection between their own livelihood and the uninterrupted flow of commerce, and that they would not, therefore, unreasonably disturb it.[25]

One other instance must be taken up to indicate the scope of Hamburg liberalism—the discussion concerning the founding of a university that ran from about 1900 to 1913. The debate was heated and at times even vicious. The intensity and passion of the arguments involved reach across more than fifty years to impress the reader with the idea that this conflict somehow struck at the heart of the city. The basic argument against the university, removed from its background of invective, is not an unreasonable one. It was believed that the academic community, with all its virtues, would nevertheless tend to be generally antimaterialistic in outlook. Materialism had made the city what it was, and materialism was, understandably enough, what the city believed in. A university, it was argued, would be an alien institution in Hamburg. Why should the businessmen of the city spend good money to create an enemy in their very midst?[26] As it turned out, they did not have to. The interests of the commercial community triumphed, and the proposal was killed.[27]

The most striking element in all these manifestations of Hamburg's so-called "liberal tradition" is the tacit commitment to the cultural hegemony of the city's dominant business elite. Danish and German aristocrats, Prussian military men, and university professors were seen as essentially foreign to the "Hanseatic culture" of the city. The leaders of Hamburg's commerce were confident, moreover, that they spoke for all of the inhabitants of the city-state, and could scarcely imagine that others might, in good faith, disagree.

It is important to note here that the chief advocates of the formation of a university were the Progressives and the Social Democrats. Their disagreement with the establishment on this matter provided one of the most striking confrontations of the old and the new in pre-World-War Hamburg. The issue itself continued to play a role in Hamburg politics throughout the Weimar period. Later, we shall see that the conflict between the ruling elite and the Socialists involved far more than obvious economic and social disputes. It was a conflict deeply rooted in the culture of the city.

## POLITICS AND GOVERNMENT

Before the First World War, the government of the city-state of Hamburg was an almost perfect embodiment of the Hanseatic spirit: it gave predominant weight to the forces of conservatism and the interests of commerce.[28] The central organ in the government was the Senate, which performed the principal executive functions. Eighteen senators were elected by the representative arm of the government, the Bürgerschaft, for life terms, each senator serving as the head of some branch of administration. In effect, the government consisted of committees chaired by an elected senator and composed of Bürgerschaft members and other leading citizens. These committees were the principal source of legislation; often they were able to command the services of experts from various fields to help them draft new laws.

Even though the right to initiate money bills technically belonged exclusively to the Bürgerschaft, in this area as in others that body was most often in the position of approving or rejecting legislation presented to it by the Senate. Control by the Bürgerschaft over the Senate was not extensive. There were certain formal methods by which the Bürgerschaft could protest any Senate action, but since these were never used, what control there was was exercised by a kind of watchdog committee and by the various Bürgerschaft members who were also members of Senate committees. Typically, it was felt that the *bürgerliche Tradition* was a sufficient safeguard against Senate abuses.[29]

The most important and controversial aspect of this form of government was the manner in which the members of the Bürgerschaft were elected. In Hamburg, as in Prussia and several other states of the German Reich before 1918, two very different forms of political selection prevailed at the same time: one for the election of deputies to the national parliament, and a totally different one for the election of deputies to a state parliament. The constitution of the Reich specified that deputies to the Reichstag were to be elected by universal manhood suffrage, but since the constitution did not specify the manner in which state elections were to be conducted, there were wide variations from state to state. The elections to the Bürgerschaft in Hamburg were conducted by a variation of the "three-class system." This system eliminated about two-thirds of those qualified to vote in national elections from participation in the local contests. To qualify for the exercise of either "active" (voting) or "passive" (candidacy) political rights, one had, first of all, to obtain a "letter of citizenship," the prime requisite for which was the payment of the taxes on an income of

1,200 marks (or more) for five consecutive years. This group of "citizens" was then broken down into three categories. Of the 160 members in the Bürgerschaft, half were in the first category, "citizens," and were elected by all those exercising the rights of citizenship; forty were members of the second category, "landowners," and forty belonged in the third category, "notables." The representatives of the second and third categories were elected only by members of their own citizenship category. A further distinction, added to the system in 1906, was a division of the "citizens" (in a slightly different manner) into two groups divided by a taxed income of 2,500 marks. The nature of this rather complex system can best be understood by examining its operation.

In the various elections held in Hamburg between the years 1910 and 1913, 152 representatives were elected. In the "general election," 83,187 citizens cast their ballots. About 48,000 of these had incomes of less than 2,500 marks and elected 24 deputies; 28,479 earned more than 2,500 marks and elected 48 deputies; 8,731 landowners elected 40, as did the 954 notables. A further peculiarity of the system was that both the landowners and the notables could vote in the general election as well as in their special elections, and since many of the notables were also landowners, quite a number of them voted three times in any given election.[30]

With such an electoral system, it is not surprising, then, that the government of Hamburg was conducted, for the most part, by the more substantial members of the community. Indeed, the system was frankly designed to insure that this would be the case. After the turn of the century, the Social Democratic Party began to make such imposing gains at the polls that it was felt that the three-class system, as it then existed, would no longer protect the wealthier elements from being swept right out of their own city hall. The law was accordingly altered in 1906, replacing single-member constituencies with proportional representation and adding the new distinction at the 2,500 mark level, in an effort to hold the Socialists to a "reasonable" representation.[31] The effort was a highly successful one. Although since 1890 all three deputies from

Hamburg to the Reichstag have been Social Democrats, the Socialists held only 20 out of 160 mandates in the Bürgerschaft that was sitting at the outbreak of World War I.[32]

It is perhaps all too easy, after considering this system of government, to smile a bit cynically at the Hamburgers' pride in their "liberal republicanism" and "traditional democratic tendencies." But in all fairness, one must take into account the fact that these men had little conception of the kind of politics that was soon to render them obsolete. A political party, to them, did not represent a specific social class or group, but was a very loose, informal organization that represented certain general economic interests. One could shift easily from party to party. There was no question of loyalty, one voted with the party that represented one's views on a particular issue. The parties, after all, really only existed at election time, none having a formal organization to preserve its existence between elections. It was difficult, therefore, for these men to understand the aggressiveness and pugnacity of the new Social Democratic Party. It alone of the Hamburg parties had a permanent staff that conducted a perpetual drive for members and votes.[33] When the Hamburg politician spoke of democracy, he meant it for "reasonable men," that is, men like himself who were in fundamental agreement about the interests of Hamburg, and who were ready to compromise on their differences.

The threat posed by the continued growth of the Social Democrats was a very real one. Although the cards were stacked against them even before the electoral law was altered in 1906, they seemed to be on the verge of overwhelming the traditional parties. In requesting legislation to restrict the Social Democratic fraction in the Bürgerschaft, a group of senators and other leaders prepared a petition to the Senate in which they outlined their fears:

> Certainly it could not be the goal [of the legislation] to withdraw their voting rights from the workers. . . . There is nothing to be said against the representation of their interests in the Bürgerschaft . . . , but this representation should not be such that it completely excludes or renders ineffective the representation of other equally important interests.[34]

And in the original Senate proposal for electoral reform: "One did not want to declare war against Social Democracy, but one could see in its continued growth a threat that would ultimately lead to complete politicization."[35]

These quotations are important because of the very revealing insights they provide into how these men conceived of politics and government. In the first quotation (and throughout the statement from which it was taken), it is assumed that something called "interests" deserves representation, and it is implied that the representation should somehow be in accordance with the importance of each "interest." Nothing is said about the representation of individuals. In the second quotation, the writer indicates that the major threat is that of "complete politicization." He is apparently referring to the new and different way in which the Socialists conducted politics, their adherence to and belief in the party as the most important element, and their uncompromising demands for certain far-reaching objectives.

These two ideas, the representation of "interests" and the nonparty conduct of politics, lay at the center of the traditional political system in Hamburg before the First World War. They indicate a conception of political life that was well adapted to the kind of "modernizing oligarchy" by which the city was governed.[36] The city-state was seen primarily as an economic organism, and the continuation of a "free enterprise" condition depended upon the maintenance of the balance between the various economic interests composing it. Leonard Krieger has pointed out that the German conception of political freedom generally centered on the freedom of the state from outside interference rather than on the freedom of the individual.[37] The ruling groups in Hamburg shared this view, not only in regard to interference from outside, as was indicated earlier, but also in regard to forces from within that threatened the development of the city's commercial interests.

It would certainly be incorrect to conclude that the absence of organized political parties meant that there was little political activity in prewar Hamburg. On the contrary, there was a great deal of activity, but the really important political matters were dealt with under less formal circumstances, in the meeting rooms of businessmen's clubs and at the social gatherings of Hamburg's commercial elite.[38]

In this context, it is clear that the ruling circles in Hamburg quite rightly evaluated the Social Democrats as "revolutionary." Even if one did not take into account their social and economic objectives, the Socialists still posed a decided threat to the accepted manner of political conduct. At the core of Social Democratic political activity lay a demand for the rationalization of the political system, and for its reorganization on the basis of the "rights" of individuals. The electoral reform of 1906 was specifically designed to counteract these demands. According to the political ideas of Hamburg's ruling elite, the new electoral law merely restored the balance among interests and thus preserved traditional democracy.

But there was a contradiction inherent in the various objectives pursued by the businessmen of Hamburg. For the balance they wished to restore could not be a static one. It was in fact changing with startling rapidity, and it was Hamburg's own economic success that was in large measure responsible for the change.

### INDUSTRY AND LABOR

Hamburg, beginning in about 1890, was inundated by the great wave of industrialization that was rolling over all of Germany. Accustomed to a steady and undramatic expansion of shipping and commerce, the city was surprised to find itself transformed into an important industrial center almost overnight. The industrialization of Hamburg followed a somewhat different course from that of other industrial areas in Germany. Since the city-state was without significant deposits of raw materials, the development of industry was neither encouraged nor directed by the materials at hand. Instead, new industry was deliberately developed whenever it seemed that a market for some product or other existed. The Hamburg businessman would then locate a market where he could purchase the necessary raw materials, and establish a plant in the city (or the free-harbor whenever possible) to produce from the imported materials the desired article.[39] As a result, the industry of Hamburg was extremely diversified, and tended to emphasize "quality" products such as special sorts of rubber goods, asbestos, food products (especially coffee and tea), and manufactured goods requiring special materials.[40]

The most important boom came in the shipbuilding industries. The enormous growth of transoceanic shipping during those years stimulated a very rapid development in all those industries associated with the building and repair of ships. The shipyards themselves quickly outgrew their accustomed location in the free-harbor area and spread out for several miles along the shore of the Elbe. By the eve of the First World War, some 30,000 workers were employed in the yards or in industries directly related to them.[41] Some of Germany's greatest warships—the *Vaterland,* the *Moltke,* the *Bismarck*—were built in Hamburg's shipyards; Germany's build-up of naval arms in the years before World War I contributed substantially to Hamburg's new prosperity.

In general, the industry of Hamburg falls into three principal categories. The most important group consists of shipbuilding and related industries (metalworking, machining, etc.); second are the manufacturing industries, which transform imported raw materials into various products to be distributed throughout Germany and the world; third are the processing industries, which refine or otherwise improve a raw material for re-exportation. This last group of industries was especially profitable because it was possible to establish a refinery (for oil, sugar, etc.) in the free-harbor and import, refine, and re-export the goods without having to pay any tax or duty.

In terms of the occupational distribution of the labor force, the industry of Hamburg was quite similar to that of Dresden and Berlin. About 60 per cent of all workers in Hamburg were employed in the metalworking and machining industries; about 15 per cent were in various foodstuff industries; about 10 per cent worked in the clothing industries, and there were smaller percent-

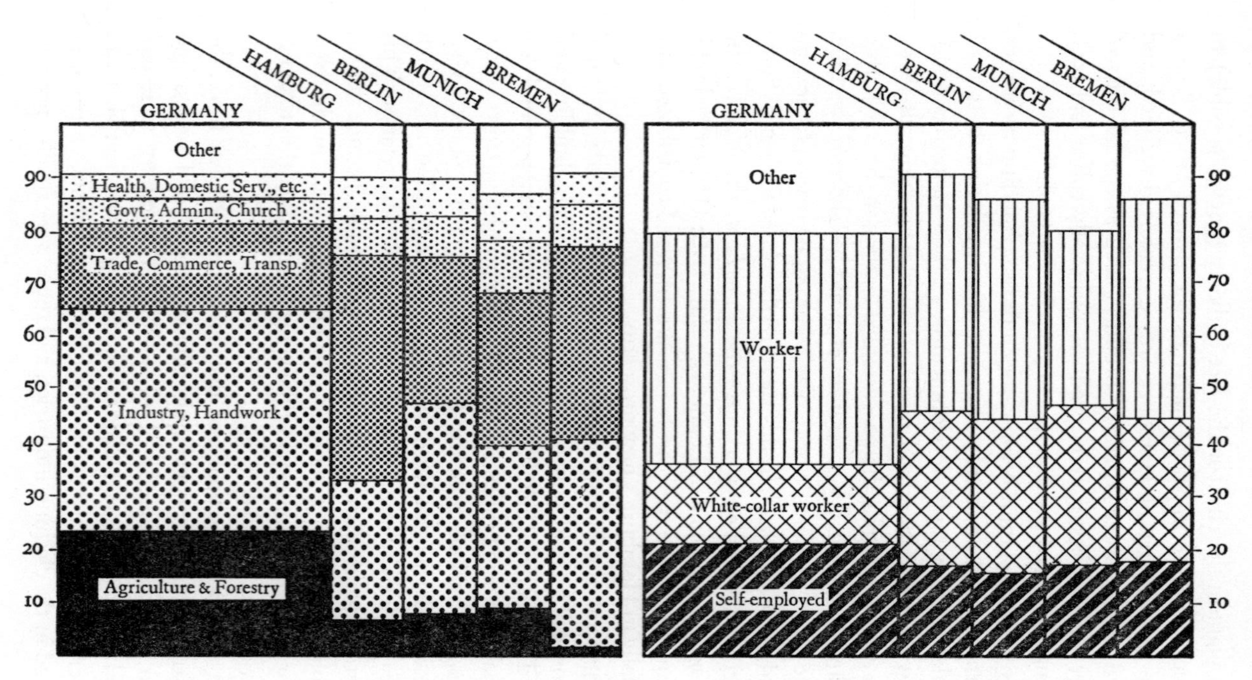


FIGURE 1 The Socioeconomic Composition of the Work Force: A Comparison of Hamburg with Germany and with Three Other Major Cities

ages employed in woodworking, textiles, chemicals and leather-working.[42]

The industrialization process, of course, wrought many major changes in the life of Hamburg. Coming as it did on the heels of Hamburg's strongly contested entry into the Customs Union, the wave of prosperity did much to placate those who still opposed Hamburg's position in the Reich. Their old target, Bismarck, was in any case soon gone from the scene, and Berlin's encouragement of colonial trade, together with its orders for Hamburg shipyards, was enough to melt the hearts of even the most recalcitrant Hamburgers. Much of the old hatred and distrust was to return with the hardships and disappointments of 1918. But, in the meantime, the growth of a certain amount of national sentiment could be observed, and more interest was taken in the affairs of the Reich.[43]

Industrialization was accompanied by an explosive growth in the population of the city. In 1890, some half-million people lived in Hamburg. Only twenty years later, the number had doubled, and continued to grow at the rate of about 20,000 per year.[44] New residential areas were quickly developed to accommodate new residents, and the city was suddenly presented with a whole series of problems concerning housing, sanitation, transportation, police, and so on.

A large proportion of these new residents were men who worked with their hands; they had been attracted to the city by the easy availability of jobs and the promise of good pay. At first, the largest influx was of those in the building trades—carpenters, masons, and so on; there was a heightened demand for skilled workers of almost every kind.[45] But it soon became obvious that this new industrial growth was not just limited to the traditional industries. New industries were developing, and they all had one very important characteristic in common: they depended upon machines. And their most pressing need, after the machines themselves, was for men to run them. The work these men had to do frequently could be learned in a few weeks or months instead of the years necessary in most traditional apprenticeships. No longer would they work together in little groups of two or three; instead, they would be brought together by the hundreds or thousands into great sheds, where each would perform his limited share of the industrial process.

One result of these developments was a profound alteration in the nature of the work force. There was, first of all, a relative increase in the number of industrial workers in the society.[46] This increase was accompanied by major changes in the relationships of the workers to one another, to their jobs, to their employers, and to society in general. The end result of these changes was the emergence of labor as a major factor in the political, social, and economic life of the city. The chief instrument through which this transformation was brought about was the labor movement—the complex of political parties, trade unions, and other organizations in which workers joined together to further their special interests.

Almost from the beginnings of the German labor movement, Hamburg held a special place as one of the "fortresses of Socialism."[47] Home of one of Germany's greatest labor leaders, August Bebel, Hamburg was viewed by much of the Socialist world as the model of thorough and efficient labor organization. As early as 1880, the Hamburg organization of the Social Democratic Party held one of the city-state's three seats in the Reichstag. Three years later, Bebel won the second. And in 1890 the Socialists took the third.[48] Since then none of these seats has ever been held by another party. Similar though less dramatic victories were also won by the Socialists in the local Hamburg elections.[49] The electoral successes of the Hamburg SPD were, for the most part, the result of an effective and imaginative cluster of subsidiary organizations (youth groups, singing clubs, etc.) which provided the party with an ever-widening network for recruitment and the dissemination of propaganda.[50] One of Germany's most outstanding Socialist dailies, the *Hamburger Echo,* was founded in Hamburg. It became the property of the local organization in 1891.[51]

Hamburg was also the birthplace of an imposing cooperative structure. The Grosseinkaufsgesellschaft für die deutschen Consumvereine (known as the GEG) was founded in Hamburg in 1894. As the leading purchaser and producer for cooperatives all over Germany, the GEG rapidly became one of the largest and most important institutions in the German cooperative movement.[52] Five years after the founding of the GEG, Hamburg's own consumers' cooperative, the Produktion, was formed.[53] Boasting 74,328 members by 1914, the Produktion was one of the leading cooperatives in Germany; it operated warehouses, retail stores, and apartment buildings throughout the city. Hamburg's position as the capital of the German cooperative movement was finally assured by the organization there, in 1904, of the Zentralverband deutscher Consumvereine, the central organization of labor-oriented consumers' cooperatives.[54]

It is difficult to categorize the cooperatives neatly as a part of the labor movement. The cooperatives in Hamburg were created by the joint efforts of businessmen and labor leaders.[55] Very early, however, the trade unions took an interest in these organizations, and began to play an active role in their leadership. Moreover, a large proportion of the cooperatives' membership came from the working classes. The Socialists, at first opposed on principle to the cooperatives, also came around to active support of the movement.[56] This development was of some importance because the cooperatives consistently expressed a very conservative, business-oriented political viewpoint.[57]

The existence of the entire labor movement depended to considerable extent upon the existence of a powerful, well-organized trade-union movement. In largely Protestant Hamburg, the main strength of the trade unions resided in the local units of the so-called "Free Trade Unions," which were organized on a national basis under the General Commission of German Trade Unions (ADGB). The Free Unions, as opposed to the "Christian Unions," were an integral part of the Socialist movement. Their aims and objectives were for the most part the same as those professed by the SPD. Indeed, the policies of the SPD were to some extent directed by the Free Unions.[58] In Hamburg, as in the rest of Germany, membership in trade unions began to increase quite rapidly around the turn of the century. In 1891, the Hamburg Free Unions had 21,793 members; the number had grown to 37,364 by 1900, and to 143,338 by 1913.[59] This was, of course, a much larger membership than that of the SPD, which in 1904 had 9,226 and in 1913, 49,422.[60]

Before World War I, the most important unions in Hamburg were the more traditional craft unions. Members of the building trades, tobacco workers, and printers seem to have played the leading roles in the movement.[61] Members of these unions were most often to be found in leadership positions, and the unions themselves were probably the most influential in the formulation of policy.[62]

It should be pointed out, in this connection, that in Germany the local unions have had far more importance than, for example, in the United States. The German unions were for the most part organized from the bottom up, and the city-wide federations of local unions were the most powerful centers of union activity. In Hamburg, the federation (Gewerkschaftskartell) controlled a large strike fund and was in a key position to determine union policies in the area.

The Hamburg labor movement, when compared with the German labor movement as a whole, was well organized, quite wealthy, and relatively right wing.[63] The 1903 program of the Hamburg SPD organization, which remained in effect until the end of the war, provides an accurate picture of the party's interests and orientation. The following demands were presented:

(1) General, free, equal, and secret suffrage.
(2) End of the privileges of the landowner and notable classes.
(3) Introduction of proportional representation.
(4) End of lifelong Senate terms.
(5) Creation of a unified school system.
(6) Creation of labor offices.
(7) The eight-hour day.[64]

These demands may be considered as the Hamburg equivalent of the national party's Erfurt Program of 1891. Each point listed here was either mentioned or, in the case of those referring specifically to Hamburg, implied in the national program. What is revealing about these points, however, is what they do not include. No mention is made in the Hamburg demands of free medical aid, a progressive income tax, or the abolition of tariffs and excises, all of which are included in the Erfurt Program.[65] Indeed, with the exception of the eight-hour day, there is not a word in the Hamburg program about social and economic reform. The demands of the Hamburg SPD were almost purely political in 1903, and were to remain so throughout the Weimar period.

Good reasons for the economic and social conservatism of the Hamburg SPD are not difficult to find. It is highly unlikely, first of all, that the Social Democrats in Hamburg derived their support entirely from the working classes. It has been estimated that the national party derived about twenty-five per cent of its electoral support from middle-class groups.[66] It is reasonable to expect that this proportion was even higher in Hamburg. The growth of the party during the Bismarck period, seemingly at the expense of the National Liberals, suggests such a conclusion, as does the absence of an important Catholic party that might have competed for the support of democratically oriented middle-class voters. Suggestive, too, is the fact that Hamburg, the "fortress of Socialism," had an extremely high proportion of white-collar workers, while the proportion of working class was about the same as the national average.[67] In any case, it is certain that the Hamburg SPD was greatly interested in winning increased middle-class support, and there is little reason to doubt that they had some success in doing so.[68]

But it is very unlikely that any Hamburg party could have hoped to win substantial middle-class support, or even tolerance, with a program of radical economic and social reform. The Hanseatic spirit could not accommodate such experimentation; even the merest suggestion of a downward revision of harbor duties was apt to set off an explosion of opposition.[69] Social Democracy in Hamburg was clearly much more democratic than socialistic.

Although it is true that at least the articulate portion of the labor movement in Hamburg subscribed to the policies of the SPD up to 1918, one must be careful not to equate the SPD with the labor movement in general, concluding, therefore, that labor as a whole in Hamburg was more conservative than elsewhere. There was another element in the Hamburg labor movement that was growing rapidly and beginning to pose serious problems to the more established movement. There was a rather large group of workers, at first in the harbor but later in other areas as well, which was not adequately represented in the trade-unions, cooperatives, or party organizations. These workers had a certain penchant for unauthorized strikes that were frequently conducted with extreme bitterness. In the years shortly before the World War, strikes of this sort followed closely behind one another in a manner that strongly suggested the anarchists' conception of "mounting revolution."[70] It was largely in this area, which the usually efficient Hamburg organizations failed to penetrate, that the traditions of radicalism were kept alive. The origins and nature of this radical element in Hamburg will come in for detailed examination in the chapters to follow.

All considered, the outlook for the labor movement in Hamburg on the eve of the First World War was distinctly favorable. The organizational structure had expanded steadily, the coffers of union and party alike were far from empty, and day by day, labor was gaining recognition in new areas. This is not to say that there were no problems: the unions had yet to win the legal right to carry on organizational activities without restrictions; there were many workers who were still not represented by a union; and a means had to be found to control the dangerous strike weapon.

To the SPD, distracted by mounting internal dissension, the achievement of equal political rights still seemed to be a long way off. On the other hand, there were signs of a weakening of resistance by the Hamburg Government. Changes in the constitution of the city were at least being considered.[71] And a number of leading citizens had begun to show signs of a willingness to negotiate with the Socialists.[72]

There can be little doubt that at the outbreak of war in 1914, Hamburg was on the verge of fundamental political changes. The Social Democrats, with ever-increasing authority, demanded full membership in the political system. And as their numbers increased, so too did the threat they posed to the established order. But one thing was certain. The demands could not much longer be ignored. For as time passed and major reforms did not appear to be forthcoming, workingmen called for increasingly radical political and social changes. This clamor was not likely to lessen. As the profound economic and social upheaval that had begun in Hamburg in the latter part of the nineteenth century continued, the demands for corresponding changes in the political system were bound to become more insistent.

But the prevailing Hanseatic spirit guaranteed that none of these changes would be accomplished swiftly. The fact that the years before the war were quite prosperous ones for Hamburg gave increased weight to the conservatives' argument that there was no need for change. Finally recognizing the dangers inherent in the rising labor movement, the civic leaders of Hamburg had reacted with a firm resolve to preserve the world as they knew it. Perhaps they were right in believing that nothing short of a world cataclysm could loosen their hold on the reins.

*Chapter 3*

# The Revolution of 1918–19 in Hamburg

For the Bürgermeister of Hamburg the evening of November 5, 1918, began quietly, with the pleasures of a cigar at his fireside. Earlier that day he had been mildly disturbed by reports of strikes in the shipyards. However, these were merely "local matters" and not cause for serious concern.[1] But the rest of this evening did not pass as pleasantly for the Bürgermeister. He was soon interrupted (a rare occurrence) by messengers bringing rather muddled reports of some sort of "trouble" in Lübeck. Not long after, he heard the first reports of disturbances in his own city. The reports kept coming in throughout the night, but it was not immediately clear what the nature of the disturbances was. In any case, neither the Bürgermeister nor the police chief considered the reports serious enough to warrant any special police measures.[2]

The Bürgermeister was not the only citizen of Hamburg to have his sleep disturbed that night. From time to time, the quiet of the city was broken by shouts, the sounds of running feet, and once by bursts of gunfire from the harbor. Unknown to all but a very few, the revolt that had broken out among the sailors at Kiel, and was soon to spread all over Germany, had reached Hamburg that night. The Revolution of 1918–19 had begun.

The tumultuous events that followed were, at the same time, local and part of a larger pattern encompassing all of Germany. The people of Hamburg did not operate in a political vacuum. Their actions were frequently determined, or at least conditioned, by the national leaders in the capital. These leaders, on the other hand, could sometimes do little more than give formal acknowledgment to facts already accomplished in the provinces. The revolution began earlier and, in one sense, ended later in Hamburg than it did in Berlin. And although the Weimar Constitution, in establishing the form of local government throughout Germany, later negated many of the decisions made by local politicians, the manner in which these decisions were reached remains an important matter. In the winter of 1918–19 most citizens of Hamburg still believed that they would continue to determine the form of government in their city. Moreover, the decision of the national government in this respect would, to a considerable extent, ultimately depend on the various solutions reached in Hamburg, Bremen, and other prominent cities.

The two basic ingredients in the outbreak of revolution in Hamburg were: a spontaneous manifestation of disappointment and hostility directed primarily toward the military authorities and others identified with the conduct of the war; and the total absence of other legitimate unifying entities that could restore order and provide goals for the future.[3]

Certainly, the failure of the government to keep the people adequately informed about the course of the war was largely responsible for their shocked reaction to the news of defeat in November 1918. But dissatisfaction with the conduct of the war and disenchantment with those in charge had been clearly in evidence for some time.

Although Hamburg, because of her position athwart the main supply lines, probably suffered fewer food and fuel shortages than the rest of Germany, these shortages were serious enough. And in August 1916, there had been a whole series of mass demonstrations, riots, and strikes protesting the manner of distributing food. Stores were plundered, and, ultimately, army units had to be brought in to quell the uproar.[4] Throughout 1918, there were strikes, demonstrations, and peace meetings that occasionally were met with force by the authorities.[5]

Toward the end of the war, even the authorities in Hamburg began to realize that the situation was getting badly out of hand, and that something other than the shortages themselves was involved. In July 1918, the War Provisions Office in Hamburg reported to the district army commander:

It must be recognized that *as a result of our policies or those of our army,* we can expect even greater disaffection on the part of the people at home because of food shortages. The almost complete lack of potatoes, the absence of fruit and vegetables, *and the conviction that these circumstances can be traced to inadequate administration* have, together with the unstable political situation, created a mood in society that is not conducive to courage or firmness in regard to the war. Only in this way can one account for the fact that in spite of apparently sufficient wages, and in spite of the efforts of the large factories to improve the food situation of the workers, there are still strikes in the shipyards, *for reasons even the workers themselves cannot explain....* Similar signs of unrest may be observed also in the usually peaceful segments of labor.[6]

One has only to add to this picture the sudden news that all the sacrifices had indeed been in vain, and the outbreak of violence in some form seems almost inevitable.

A revolt against military authorities, however, does not necessarily mean a revolt against civil authorities, unless, as was the case in Hamburg and almost all of Germany, the two are identical. It is important to note that in 1918 the government of Hamburg was almost entirely in the hands of the local army commander. When his control was removed, as it was almost at once, Hamburg did not revert to its pre-1914 condition, but to a confused, anarchical state of affairs in which no one was quite sure who was in charge.

The fact that the government of Hamburg had been almost entirely in the hands of the military during the war years accounted for much of the hesitancy displayed by the traditional ruling elite in their initial dealings with the revolutionaries. The senators were not entirely certain that they were once again in possession of the executive power in Hamburg. It was widely believed that the military would soon intervene to restore order.* Many citizens did not welcome this prospect. They felt that it would be wiser to wait until the Prussians had gone for good before setting out to re-establish orderly government in the city-state. The traditional antipathy toward Prussia and the German Army had been revitalized during the war years.[7] The proud old senators had not relished their secondary position[8] under the military administration, and the local detachment had made few friends among the citizens of the Hanseatic city.[9]

An indication of the civilian leaders' abdication of governing responsibility in Hamburg was their failure to make sufficient preparation for the war's end. Not until October 9, 1918, did the Senate appoint a committee to study the problems likely to result from demobilization.[10] Even though the German people were not, for the most part, aware of the weakness of their military position in 1918, one could easily have foreseen long before October that the war was likely to come to some kind of conclusion in the near future.

The pre-1914 political system did not disappear with a rush and a cheer in 1918. Its weakness and unsuitability had been demonstrated early in the war, and it had been displaced, for all practical purposes, by a centralized military regime. Defeat in the field, and revolution in the city, swept the military men from the stage. The revolution, then, had to devise a substitute. The crux of the confusion and turbulence following November 1918 was that there were no existing institutions strong enough to fashion a new political system. Not one of the political parties of prewar Hamburg was in a position to perform this function. The various conservative and liberal parties, which had been at best only loosely structured organizations, had deteriorated badly during the four-year political moratorium imposed by the "civil peace." The old "Left" and

* In fact, however, the Commander of the IX Army Corps left Hamburg with his unit on November 6. Walther Lamp'l, *Die Revolution in Gross-Hamburg* (Hamburg, 1921), p. 12. Cf. Ruth Fischer, *Stalin and German Communism* (Cambridge, Mass., 1948), p. 56.

"Right" parties were just then in the process of regrouping, but the political situation was so unclear that the formation of new parties was not yet practicable.[11] Only the SPD came through the war with some of its organizational structure intact.

In Hamburg, as in Germany, the party was split into two wings: the SPD, or Majority Socialists, who stood for a more or less "patriotic" consummation of the war; and the USPD, or Independent Socialists, who supported the war with reservations if, indeed, at all. In additon to these two groups, there was an articulate and important radical segment that generally subscribed to a more "international" Socialist view.

One of the major postwar difficulties faced by Socialist leaders was that of determining the seriousness of the split in the movement which had brought about the formation of the USPD in 1916. In Hamburg, as in Berlin, it was clear that some of the movement's most talented leaders had left the SPD to join the new organization. But since the USPD was forbidden to hold mass meetings, and no city election had been held since 1912, the Socialist leaders were unable to form a very accurate picture of the USPD's Hamburg membership. Now that the chief cause of the split in the movement—support for the war—was no longer an issue, the future of the movement seemed to be uncertain. Many leaders in both the SPD and the USPD were strongly in favor of a reunification of the party. But until they could find out how their respective memberships felt about this, it was extremely difficult for them to think concretely about the future development of the party and its program.

The attempts of various groups in Hamburg to find solutions to the problems of the moment, and at the same time to draw up an acceptable blueprint for the future, forms the central theme of our study of the revolution. In the early attempts to aggregate interests, to formulate specific policy alternatives, and to marshal bodies of popular support, we can see the roots of the later party structure and of the evolving political system. For the purposes of analysis, this process may be seen as having occurred in three stages.

During the first phase of the revolution, which extended for about a fortnight after the outbreak on November 5, 1918, the most important event was the abdication of the city's military administration. Apparent control was exercised by those who in fact controlled the streets—the representatives of the hastily formed "Council Government." Both the ruling elite and the SPD leadership were so unprepared for revolution that their opposition to the Council Government was confused and insignificant. In reality, a kind of political vacuum existed.

By mid-November, the opponents of the Council Government had begun to rough out some counterstrategies, and the status of the revolution altered significantly. In this second stage, as day-to-day problems of government and administration became increasingly important, control over the streets became relatively less important, and power came more and more into the hands of those prepared to deal with such problems—the traditional ruling groups and the leaders of the SPD. Until the first national elections were held in mid-January 1919, these groups agreed that some kind of "holding action" was called for, at least until Hamburg itself could settle down, and until certain fundamental national decisions could be reached.

Once these basic decisions concerning the future political structure of Germany had been made, and order had been more or less restored, the really difficult problems of applying these principles to specific situations and of marshaling popular support behind them became of primary importance. In the evolving party structure, the SPD emerges as the primary standard-bearer of the Republic, and the first concern of the party becomes the fitting together of elements that will allow it to build a broad coalition in support of its particular conception of the significance of the revolution.

### "ALL POWER TO THE WORKERS' AND SOLDIERS' COUNCIL"

The first reports of the sailors' revolt in Kiel appeared in Hamburg's morning papers on November 5, and had an effect, according to one observer, "like a thunderbolt."[12] Before noon, a strike, completely unauthorized by the trade unions, had broken out in one of the shipyards, and spread like brush fire to one yard after another. By the early afternoon, representatives of the harbor workers were meeting in the large hall of the trade-union building, calling for a general strike in support of the revolt at Kiel, and demanding the abdication of the Kaiser.[13]

The leaders of the established labor movement were taken completely by surprise by these developments. Representatives of the Majority Socialists were present at the meeting, but they could offer no plan of action to the excited crowd. They could only try to gain some time by introducing a motion calling for a postponement of any further action until a meeting of all labor representatives could be held two days hence. The motion passed by a bare majority.[14]

The narrowness of the SPD's margin of control over the meeting was shown by the fact that no sooner had the one motion passed, than a second, this time in opposition to the wishes of the SPD leaders, was accepted. This second motion included demands for the abdication of the Hohenzollerns and for the institution of immediate and far-reaching democratic reforms. The reforms asked for were considerably more revolutionary than those demanded by the sailors at Kiel, and went a great deal further than the SPD was at that time prepared to go.[15] The Majority Socialists, it must be recalled, continued to serve in Prince Max's cabinet until November 8.* They felt that until a coherent policy could be worked out on the national level, it would be wise to avoid a spontaneous formulation of policies from below.

If the Majority Socialists believed they had obtained a breathing spell with the acceptance of their motion by that first revolutionary gathering, they were disabused of this notion several hours

* Prince Max of Baden, who, in October 1918, had formed a government which was responsible to a Reichstag majority and which included three Social Democratic ministers. See S. William Halperin, *Germany Tried Democracy* (New York, 1946), pp. 56–64.

later, when the Independent Socialists held their first open meeting in Hamburg. Some five to six thousand workers took part in the tumultuous gathering. Wilhelm Dittmann, the USPD leader from Berlin who was soon to play an important role in the first republican government of Germany, was the leading speaker. Frequently interrupted by the cheers and shouts of the workers, he spelled out the demands of his party: "Down with the old Socialist Party and its pro-war policies! Down with the false democracy of Prince Max and his colleagues! The Hohenzollerns must abdicate! Long live the Workers' Socialist Republic!"[16] He urged the workers to lay down their tools and join in a general strike that would open the way for a great socialist revolution in all Germany.[17]

In this meeting, what one may call "the spirit of revolution" was clearly evident. Elated by the war's end and ebullient with the release of pent-up emotions, the excited participants filled the hall with cheers and shouts as groups of sailors from Kiel and various escapees from military prisons leaped upon the stage to urge their comrades to action. The Independent leaders, who had called the meeting, did not create this spirit. They could only hope to channel it for the accomplishment of concrete ends, something the Majority Socialists had so patently failed to do that afternoon. With great difficulty, the USPD leaders were ultimately able to bring the meeting to a vote on a series of specific proposals: workers' and soldiers' councils must be formed; no functionaries of the trade unions or cooperatives should be allowed to participate; the workers of Hamburg should at once go out on a general strike in support of the socialist revolution. These proposals were adopted unanimously.[18] But revolutions are not made solely by the adoption of revolutionary demands, and the USPD leaders, in their turn, were deprived of their initiative by the onrush of events.

Friedrich Zeller, a young sailor with a rather checkered background, was on his way back to Kiel to rejoin his naval unit.[19] His trip was interrupted in Hamburg. Trains were no longer running to Kiel because of the revolutionary disturbances. Descending from his compartment, Zeller caught sight of a little knot of sailors, some of whom he knew. They quickly described the events of the day in Hamburg. Zeller felt his "call." Ordering some sailors he had found in the train station to follow him, he marched off for the harbor, leading a growing band of excited shouting men. In the harbor, they found a torpedo boat of the German Navy, manned by only a few enlisted men. The crew was easily cajoled or overpowered, and Zeller found himself in command of an armed vessel of war. With the weapons found in the first boat, including a heavy machine gun mounted in the bow, the band seized one after another of the small naval vessels in the harbor. Resistance was neither severe nor prolonged. A few shots sufficed. The crowd, now armed, rode roughshod over the guards at the harbor entrance, commandeered a streetcar, and clanged triumphantly off to the Trade Union Hall, which they promptly declared their own. Later, a detachment was sent to occupy the main train station.[20]

It is highly questionable whether a determined police effort at some point during the night of November 5–6 would have made any significant difference in the final outcome of the revolution. It seems reasonable to assume, however, that the sheer ease with which a not particularly purposeful or disciplined group of sailors was able to take over a large city contributed to the rising momentum of the more radical revolutionary elements. The police of Hamburg, in any case, made no such effort. By morning, news of Zeller's exploits had spread, and a huge gathering filled the streets around the Trade Union Hall. The most important military concentration in the city, the barracks of the Seventy-Sixth Regiment, was soon taken over, although this time not without a serious exchange of gunfire and a loss of several lives.[21]

The course of the revolution was now largely in the hands of Zeller and the one or two USPD leaders who had appeared at the trade-union building that morning.[22] It was already clear to the SPD leaders that their maneuver to gain time had failed. The general strike they had hoped to prevent was to considerable extent in effect.[23] Before leaving for Berlin to consult with the party chiefs, the leaders of the Hamburg SPD organization, Otto Stolten and Heinrich Stubbe, had left orders that the SPD newspaper, the *Echo,* should be put in the service of the movement if it seemed that the SPD was losing control, probably with the idea that it would be seized anyhow.[24] This was accordingly done, and the first revolutionary handbill appeared on the streets shortly thereafter.[25] The demands stated were essentially the same as those adopted by the USPD meeting the night before. The handbill is most interesting because it was signed by Ferdinand Kalweit (USPD) on behalf of the "Workers' Council," and by Zeller for the "Soldiers' Council." The principal institutions of the revolution of 1918–19 were, at least on paper, in existence.[26] Their development from this point forward forms the core of the history of the revolution.

By noon of November 6, an enormous crowd (estimated at 40,000) had gathered on a large field at the edge of town in response to a call by the USPD.[27] A USPD speaker, modestly suggesting that the *Echo* should be taken partially out of SPD hands, was greeted by an overwhelming response in favor of taking it away entirely.[28] The meeting culminated in a demand for the proclamation of the Socialist Republic, after which the workers marched through the streets singing and shouting. At one point, they were greeted by a hail of bullets fired from the windows of buildings lining the street. A number of workers were killed, and the movement had its first martyrs. By evening, the picture of revolution was complete. The crowds milling about in the streets frequently had to make way for cars sporting red flags and trucks full of armed troops rushing here and there about the city. Little bands of armed men, strips of red cloth fastened to their arms, patrolled the streets. The ships in the harbor flew the red ensign, as did the railroad trains and streetcars.[29] No revolutionary government, however, had yet come into existence.

The representatives of the old order in Hamburg were apparently singularly unimpressed by the tumult and shouting around them. November 6 was a Wednesday. The Bürgerschaft had met every Wednesday evening for over a century. It met this evening as well. The noises from the street did not reach the hundred or so dignified men in City Hall, who were solemnly discussing the establishment of a labor office, a long-standing demand of the SPD.[30] At this meeting too, the Mixed Commission of the Senate reported on its months of work concerning the revision of the constitution. It concluded that certain of the electoral categories should be altered and the tax requirements for voting lowered.[31]

Clearly, what was lacking in these deliberations was a realistic sense of the present. The present was brought home in a quite unexpected way as the great oak doors of the hall suddenly burst open to reveal a band of men, replete with arm bands and red flags, and dressed in the baggy corduroy trousers and small short-billed black caps typical of the Hamburg workingman.[32]

But the confrontation was more than just picturesque. The legally constituted government of Hamburg was forced, at that moment, to declare its attitude toward the new revolutionary institutions. Would the Senate deal with these men who had come to demand its help in negotiating with the military commander of the city? It would. And in concluding the night's business, the Senate went so far as to declare itself "ready to serve the new times and the new conditions."[33] These statements, which were made to USPD leader Hugo Haase and some comrades who identified themselves as representatives of the Workers' and Soldiers' Council of Hamburg, must be considered highly significant.* These negotiations, which were not made under force of arms, would seem to constitute no less than *de facto* recognition by the executive branch of the Hamburg government of the revolutionary institutions. And indeed, this was the general interpretation at that time.[34]

* Haase, who like his colleague Dittmann, was soon to take part in the revolutionary government in Berlin, quite by chance found himself in Hamburg when the revolution broke out there. On November 8, both Dittmann and Haase returned to Berlin, thus depriving Hamburg of the benefit of their intelligent, sensible leadership in the critical days that followed.

The Senate, having recognized the Workers' and Soldiers' Council as a body with which it would negotiate, and having implied at the same time its subservience to the Council, did not give up its powers and functions. On the contrary, the Senate and Bürgerschaft went about their business exactly as before. From November 6 on, Hamburg had two governments; each recognized the existence of the other, and each continued to operate as best it could. The confusion of the situation is perhaps best illustrated by the November 6 proclamation of the Workers' and Soldiers' Council, which announced somewhat equivocally that "...the *major portion* of the political power" was in its hands.[35] This dual situation was to continue in Hamburg until the end of the Council Government.[36]

Having two governments, Hamburg in fact had none. Neither the trade-union building nor City Hall was able to exert sufficient authority to restore order to the city. Looting was becoming a serious problem.[37] For these reasons, and because they wished to legitimatize their newly won position as quickly as possible, the revolutionary forces were anxious to create a full set of revolutionary institutions. Zeller and Kalweit accordingly called for the election of workers' and soldiers' councils (which thus far had existed in name only) to begin the following day, November 7, and to continue for three days. These councils were to form the basis of the revolutionary government. The election of the councils and the subsequent formation of the revolutionary government was the single most decisive event in the revolution in Hamburg, as it was elsewhere in Germany.

In deciding upon workers' and soldiers' councils as the foundation for Hamburg's revolutionary government, Zeller and his colleagues were following a pattern which had already been established in a few German cities by November 6, and which was to become standard throughout Germany during the revolutionary period.[38] Derived in part from the experiments of the Russian revolutionaries in 1905 and 1917, and in part from the German Government's practice of establishing workers' councils in factories during the war, the "council system" was felt by some to be the ideal political form for establishing political and economic democracy.[39]

Elections to the Workers' Council, which were completed in Hamburg on November 10, were held in various plants in the city and surrounding countryside, each plant electing delegates in accordance with an intricate system of proportional representation. These delegates, who together constituted the Workers' Council, were then to come together with the delegates elected by the various military units in the area (the Soldiers' Council) to elect the Executive. The Executive, in turn, would elect from its membership the Presidium, which would then assume the executive powers of the government. Questions of basic policy were to be decided by a joint meeting of the members of the two Councils.[40]

The Majority Socialists in Hamburg, like their fellows in Berlin, strongly opposed the idea of establishing the councils. The revolution, from their standpoint, was already all but over. The Senate had already shown its willingness to recognize the "new conditions"; all that remained to realize the SPD's objective of a parliamentary democracy was to elect a new Bürgerschaft on the basis of "free, universal suffrage." There was, therefore, no need for a system of councils. A very temporary provisional government would suffice for the purpose of conducting the new elections. These were to be held as swiftly as possible.[41]

The Independents, on the other hand, while generally in agreement concerning the establishment of a parliamentary democracy, wished to postpone the elections for a time. In their eyes, the revolution had scarcely begun, not having become as yet a "social revolution." The councils were to provide the leadership during the subsequent stages, which would include the socialization of large segments of industry. Only when these social objectives had been achieved, should the new parliamentary system be established. This was essentially the same argument that was being fought out on the national level concerning the calling of a constituent assembly. There were, of course, some Independents (especially those in the party's left wing) who envisaged a continuing dictatorship of the councils. In November, however, these were a very small minority.*

The issue concerning the formation of workers' and soldiers' councils provides a clear example of the difficulty of the Majority Socialists' position. On the one hand, it was apparent that there was considerable enthusiasm among the working classes for the council idea—so much that it seemed impossible simply to ignore the movement altogether. On the other hand, the SPD could have little to gain from the formation of such councils. The parallels that could be drawn between the Hamburg revolution and the Russian might well frighten the conservative middle classes. Moreover, on the basis of its earlier electoral successes, the party could reasonably expect that Hamburg would vote heavily in its favor in a normal democratic election. But the outcome of a council election, especially one conducted primarily by the USPD, seemed far less certain. And if the USPD were to gain control of the councils, that party would be in a position to strengthen its support among the workers, and perhaps ultimately gain complete control of the socialist movement.

The most striking proof of how popular the "council idea" had become is that in spite of all these disadvantages, the Hamburg SPD leaders consented to take part in the formation of the councils. Returning from a conference in Berlin with national party leaders, Stolten and Stubbe met with representatives of the USPD on November 7, and indicated their willingness to participate in the elections.[42] They demanded, however, that the Executive be formed on the basis of "parity," by which was meant that one-quarter of the members should be chosen from each of four lists put forward by the USPD, SPD, Free Unions, and the so-called "left radicals," respectively.† This arrangement would have re-

* It is difficult to ascertain the views of individual local leaders since they rarely set them down in pamphlets or articles. The best estimate can be reached through a comparison of votes at various meetings. Compare Eugen Prager, *Geschichte der USPD* (Berlin, 1921), pp. 179–95.

† The term "left radical" is a vague one. Most often, it refers to those who belonged to the left wing of the USPD. Here, it apparently also refers to all those standing to the left of the Independents, including assorted syndicalists, etc.

sulted in an Executive equally divided between the two wings of the labor movement: the Free Unions and the Majority Socialists on one side, the USPD and left radicals on the other.[43]

Rejecting this solution as one that would lead to hopeless party division within the Executive, the USPD leaders insisted on a compromise in which the factory delegates directly elected eighteen members to the Executive and each of the four organizations elected three, making a total of thirty.[44] The result was an Executive in which the leftists held a majority of about seventeen.* The Executive, at its first meeting on November 10, proceeded to elect a Presidium that was, again, dominated by the USPD and left radical representatives.[45]

Thus the worst fears of the SPD leaders were realized. In agreeing to the compromise, they had hoped that the factory representatives would be predominantly of their party. "This," as the report of the SPD points out, "was an illusion."[46] The Majority Socialists, who had to considerable extent built the Hamburg labor movement to its present strength, suddenly found themselves a minority in the first "workers' government."

No sooner had the elections been completed than the SPD and Free Unions, regretting their consent to the compromise, began petitioning for new ones. At the same time, they continued to demand the immediate election of a new Bürgerschaft. It is undoubtedly true that the opponents of the councils were justified in claiming that the elections of November 8–10 had in some instances been badly conducted. Some plants had scarcely had time to hold some sort of meeting, let alone carry out an orderly electoral process.[47] The feebleness of the SPD's protest, however, would seem to indicate that the party did not really believe that another election held on the same basis would yield substantially different results. The fact of the matter was that the SPD's decision to cooperate with the councils had been no more than a barely concealed political maneuver. Having failed to gain control of the

* This majority varied from time to time and from issue to issue. Since the members are not identified by party, this figure was obtained by tracing the important votes in the Executive.

councils, as they had hoped, the Majority Socialists promptly returned to their earlier opposition, becoming more vigorous as their party solidified its position in Berlin.

Opposition to the Council Government (from all sides) was considerably exacerbated by the Presidium's choice of a chairman (the chief executive of the government), Dr. Heinrich Laufenberg. Laufenberg was an understandable though in some ways unfortunate choice. At this point in his political career, he was acting as the leader of the left wing of the USPD. It is extremely difficult to form a very exact idea of what his goals were at this time; in his own account of the revolution in Hamburg, Laufenberg scrupulously avoids any reference to his own ambitions or long-range policies.[48] It is certainly clear, however, that he was a convinced advocate of council government. Later, as a leader in the Communist Workers' Party (KAPD), and as spokesman for the policy known as "National Bolshevism," he came to evaluate the councils as the only institution that could save the working classes and Germany as a whole. He came to share the syndicalist view that the old order should be toppled by a mounting wave of mass strikes.* We know that in 1918 he was no friend of the trade unions or other traditional working-class institutions, and it seems that his experiences in the revolution made him move even further to the left.

Insofar as one can find the man under the mountain of criticism and abuse heaped upon him from almost every side, Laufenberg emerges as an intelligent and well-educated man, a persuasive public speaker who was certainly well equipped to lead Hamburg's labor leaders. However, like so many intellectuals in the socialist movement, he tended to make rather doctrinaire evaluations of political problems, and was certainly ill chosen from the standpoint of the unity of the labor movement. Laufenberg had long been a

* For Laufenberg, see Otto E. Schüddekopf, *Linke Leute von Rechts* (Stuttgart, 1960), p. 108n; and Ruth Fischer, *Stalin and German Communism* (Cambridge, Mass., 1948), pp. 92–93. Schüddekopf mistakenly associates Laufenberg with the outbreak of the revolution in Hamburg (p. 100). He also maintains that Laufenberg was a "National Bolshevist" from the outset, but cites a pamphlet of 1920 as verification (pp. 100, 107–20).

leader of the left wing of the Hamburg SPD, and was involved in a number of controversies in connection with his recent editorship of the *Echo*. He had, at one time or another, managed to come into conflict with every leading Hamburg Socialist. He was, therefore, the last man in whom they were likely to place any degree of confidence.[49]

In general, the establishment of a set of governing institutions was a source of encouragement for the Hamburg revolutionaries. Moreover, news from Berlin was similarly heartening. The revolution there was apparently a success, and on November 9 Scheidemann had proclaimed the establishment of the German Republic. A similar proclamation was made in Hamburg shortly thereafter.[50] Confused as the situation was, it seemed clear that Hamburg would have a Socialist government. The way seemed clear for further action.

At an explosive meeting of the Presidium on November 12, Laufenberg proposed that the Senate and Bürgerschaft be dissolved, their places to be assumed by the organs of the Council Government. In spite of the heated opposition of the Majority Socialists, he was able to carry his motion, and a commission, with Laufenberg at its head, was accordingly dispatched to inform the Senate of its fate.[51] With considerable ceremony, the Workers' and Soldiers' Council of Hamburg took up new quarters in City Hall that same afternoon, after the previous tenants had moved out in something of a rush. The red flag waved proudly from the top of the building. Hamburg, it seemed, had entered a new era.

But what sort of new era? The apparent control of the revolutionary government over City Hall was to be very short-lived indeed. For the first time since the revolution had begun in Hamburg on November 5, the forces of the established order showed their power—briefly, decisively, and in a manner thoroughly "Hanseatic."

### THE DECLINE OF THE COUNCIL GOVERNMENT

Just four days after the dissolution of the Senate and Bürgerschaft, Dr. Laufenberg received a group of distinguished visitors in City

Hall. Led by Max Warburg, director of one of Germany's most powerful banking and financial empires, these men represented the leading banking and commercial firms of Hamburg. Their business was unequivocal. It was clear, they pointed out, that the government of a city-state of over one and one-half million souls could not be conducted without funds. Already such necessary administrative arms as the police were suffering from an inability to pay wages. Moreover, Hamburg's credit abroad had virtually disappeared. No one would lend to a city torn by revolution at the end of a disastrous war. Their personal credit, they emphasized, had not suffered in a similar way. They generously offered to provide the necessary funds. Since, however, they were to take such large personal risks in the interests of Hamburg, it seemed only fair that they should have a certain voice in deciding how the funds were to be spent.[52]

Of immediate and pressing importance, Warburg pointed out, was the problem of provisioning the city. He explained how the structure of the government of the city-state was related to this vital matter.

> He [Warburg] indicated that the major banks of Hamburg, Berlin, Frankfurt, etc. were just on the point of obtaining a huge import credit from America. [Laufenberg et al.] were aware of the distrust aroused by exaggerated rumors among all men of finance. If a council and assembly of citizens were to appear from Hamburg instead of a Senate and Bürgerschaft, this distrust would lead to grave uncertainties, and Hamburg's credit would be endangered.[53]

This important visit was followed very shortly by a new proclamation by the Workers' and Soldiers' Council. It had been decided to re-create the Senate and Bürgerschaft on a temporary basis, as administrative organs of the councils. Certain Hamburg businessmen had been appointed to serve as members of an "Economic Advisory Council," which, together with the revolutionary government, would handle Hamburg's financial matters. All of this, the proclamation stressed, was being done because of pure financial necessity and solely in the name of the councils, which would retain the veto power in all matters. Almost as a footnote, the proclamation announced that a new Bürgerschaft was to be elected by April 1, 1919.[54]

Oddly enough, the various accounts of the revolution in Hamburg do not pay much attention to the proclamation of November 18.[55] And yet it seems clear that it marked the end of the first phase of the revolution, in which the establishment of a workers' and soldiers' government in Hamburg had been a real issue. To be sure, all parties concerned emphasized that, *legally,* the governing power in the city-state resided in the Workers' and Soldiers' Council. But, there can be no doubt that, in fact, much of the real governing power in Hamburg resided exactly where it had always resided—in the hands of the leaders of business, finance, and the state bureaucracy.

Although the Executive theoretically retained the veto power, there is no evidence to show that it was widely applied. It was to be exercised by a number of "controllers" assigned to the various government departments. But these men, most often, could understand little of the complicated administrative operations. Not only was information consistently withheld from them, but, on some occasions, business was conducted totally without their knowledge. The Executive received some unpleasant surprises in the form of documents of which it had no knowledge, but which bore the official stamp of the Workers' and Soldiers' Council.[56] In general, it seems that all agencies of the government continued to function "just as before . . . without being directly hindered by the councils in their decisions or measures."[57]

In agreeing to the election of a new Bürgerschaft, Laufenberg had in effect guaranteed the continued existence of Hamburg's traditional governing body, although it is not certain just what role he had in mind for it. There is no evidence to show that this subject was discussed in detail at the meeting on November 16. Probably the precise nature of the "new" Bürgerschaft was purposely left ambiguous in order to facilitate agreement. No doubt Warburg and his colleagues intended that the new form of government should be very like the old, modified by liberal, democratic reforms. Laufenberg may well have entertained the idea of a parallel set of institutions—the Workers' Council to deal with economic and social policy, and the Senate and Bürgerschaft to conduct the administration of the city-state and handle other matters. In this, he would have been working toward the compromise finally embodied in the Weimar Constitution: a system of economic councils to function alongside the political institutions.

In any case, it is difficult to escape the conclusion that Laufenberg was consistently unrealistic in evaluating the nature of the revolution and his role in it. For Laufenberg, the only conceivable alternative to the showdown of November 16 would have been to seize the resources he so urgently needed for the continuation of his government, and to force the cooperation or submission of those who controlled them. Unwilling or unable to do this, Laufenberg had no alternative but to accede to the irrefutable logic of the businessmen.

In addition to the financial problem, the Council Government in Hamburg also had to face another central problem of the revolution: the lack of trained manpower to take over the administrative machinery. Even during the period when the Senate and Bürgerschaft technically did not exist, Laufenberg continued to make use of the established "ministries" and their bureaucratic staffs.[58] And even if it had been possible gradually to build up a new administrative system from scratch, Laufenberg would probably not have been willing to take the risks such an experiment entailed. Moreover, he did not command sufficient military strength to suppress the opposition that would certainly have arisen. The USPD would doubtless have been faced with a very similar problem if it had come to power on the national level.

The situation in Hamburg after November 16 was a curious one, and can perhaps best be understood in terms of the power potential of the various groups. In general, we can say that the political power consisted of three basic elements: economic power, military power, and the power derived from the support of the populace.

The economic power of the leaders of business and finance had never really been called into question in the revolution. At the crucial time, they had wielded it effectively to protect their interests, and were able to do so from then on. At the same time, there was a stalemate in the military sphere. If the conservative elements had had sufficient military power, they would have undoubtedly used it to try to roll back the revolution. If the Social Democrats and their republican allies had been militarily strong, they would have been able to oust Laufenberg, and conduct at once the democratic elections which, they were confident, would put them in power. If Laufenberg himself had controlled such power, he might have been able to force the businessmen to cooperate without giving up so much of his ruling power; perhaps then he could have gone about the business of social reform. But as it was, Laufenberg lacked the power to carry out his objectives, and his opponents lacked the power to remove him. In his lack of concern with this aspect of power, Laufenberg shared the failing of many radical reformers. At it turned out, it was a fatal shortcoming.

Since the primary contenders for political power in Hamburg shared a belief in democratic ideals, popular support was also a highly important factor and was closely related to the military problem. If Laufenberg had not been such a popular figure (especially among the working classes), his opponents would have undoubtedly attempted to force him out of office entirely on November 16. Although they robbed him of most of his governing power, they still could not risk arousing the popular outburst a complete ouster might have entailed. The opponents of the Council Government believed that the radicals would lose their support as their inability to rule became increasingly obvious.[59] And it was generally believed that the Majority Socialists would be able to regain control over the workers before Laufenberg and his colleagues could do any serious harm. Because of this belief, the Social Democrats found themselves receiving increasing support from conservative quarters that, in the past, had not been noticeably sympathetic to the labor movement.[60]

Laufenberg placed his hopes on power derived from popular support. But he surely must have realized that his popular support came from a relatively small segment of the population. Perhaps he believed that he could broaden his base of support before the proposed April elections—if not enough to stay in power, then at least enough to force through some social and economic reforms. Even though his governing power after November 16 was slight, there was one branch of the government where the radicals remained in effective control: the new Labor Office. Through this office, Laufenberg was in a position to intervene in disputes between labor and management. He could thus appeal to the workers at a very effective level, and in a context that was doubtless far more meaningful than any political slogans or abstractions about government.[61] His activities in this direction were to have important repercussions in the years to follow.

The Social Democrats in Hamburg, understandably enough, did not relish this disadvantage in competing for the sympathies of labor. And even after their party was securely in control in Berlin, and the chances for a radical victory in Hamburg seemed very slight indeed, it remained a matter of the utmost importance to them to gain control of the Executive of the councils.

Blocked for the time being from exerting much influence through the Workers' Council, the Majority Socialists (like their counterparts in Berlin) concentrated their attention on the Soldiers' Council. There they were able to work together with Democratic Party leaders and others desiring the establishment of a liberal, democratic republic.

Frederick Baumann, a returned army officer with little sympathy for the labor movement, recounts how, upon his return to Hamburg on November 8, he offered his services to Senator Petersen, Democratic leader in Hamburg.[62] The latter expressed himself "full of optimism concerning the political situation, since he would easily be able to reach an understanding with his 'old friends the Majority Socialists,' " and added that he did not have a very high estimate of the capabilities of the radical movement.[63] Baumann, apparently a rather clever and personable individual, became a member of the Soldiers' Council at once and soon found himself in a position of authority. He considered himself the chief agent of the Senate in the revolutionary government.* His instructions, as he describes them, were to do all in his power to "pack" the Soldiers' Council with Majority Socialists.[64] He was apparently quite successful in this enterprise, eliminating the radicals step by step from all positions of control over military and police matters.

The plans of the Majority Socialists and their friends were nearly upset when, on December 6, a counterrevolutionary plot was uncovered. The local free-corps, the Bahrenfelder, in cooperation with other military men in Hamburg, had made plans to arrest those members of the Workers' Council who also served on the Executive, and whisk them off into "investigatory imprisonment." The nominal leader of the revolt was that inveterate revolutionary Friedrich Zeller, who was apparently put out by his failure to achieve a leading role in the revolutionary government.† The importance of the plot arose from the fact that several leading Majority Socialists and trade unionists were believed to have had previous knowledge of the projected coup without informing the Executive.‡

One result of the so-called "Zeller Putsch" was a revitalization of support for the Council Government.[65] The Majority Socialists found themselves in the embarrassing position of having to participate in demonstrations in support of the Councils.[66] Another result was that Laufenberg was made acutely aware of the weak-

* He did not, however, receive his expense money from the Senate, but from a banker friend of Petersen's. See Frederick-Segal Baumann, *Um den Staat: Ein Beitrag zur Geschichte der Revolution in Hamburg* (Hamburg, 1924), pp. 39, 49; and Richard Bünemann, "Hamburg in der deutschen Revolution von 1918–19" (Hamburg, 1951), p. 128 (unpub. dissertation).

† Paul Neumann, *Hamburg unter der Regierung des Arbeiter- und Soldatenrats* (Hamburg, 1919), p. 39. Although it seems very likely, there is no evidence to prove that the abortive putsch in Hamburg was connected with the similar plan to arrest the Vollzugsrat in Berlin on the same day. See Arthur Rosenberg, *A History of the German Republic,* pp. 54–55.

‡ It remains uncertain whether they actually had such knowledge or not. See Baumann, p. 69 and Paul Neumann, p. 45.

ness of his military position. He ordered the formation of a Red Guard to protect the government. The responsibility for organizing the Guard, however, fell ultimately into the hands of Baumann, who made sure that it existed in little more than name.[67]

The momentary burst of confidence in the Councils was short-lived; it faded fast as food and fuel shortages became increasingly acute and the numbers of the unemployed mounted day by day. The decision of the National Conference of Workers' and Soldiers' Councils, which met in Berlin in December, to hold elections for a national constitutional assembly in January further weakened the Council's position. And confidence in the SPD rose as that party solidified its position in Berlin.[68]

The final crisis in Hamburg closely paralleled the crisis that took place in Berlin during December 1918 and January 1919. The struggle between the People's Naval Division and the Potsdam Guards in Berlin on December 24 had its counterpart in Hamburg three days later. On December 27, a crowd of sailors stormed the *Echo* and forced the printing of a handbill calling for a mass meeting on December 29 to protest against the Ebert-Scheidemann Government and the "counterrevolutionary policies" of the Hamburg SPD.[69]

The SPD, bursting with new confidence, immediately proclaimed their own meeting for January 1 to protest this violent action.[70] For the first time since November 6, the Hamburg SPD was ready to risk a showdown. In fact, their confidence proved not to be misplaced. When the two demonstrations (one called by the USPD and the other by the SPD) finally took place on January 1, the former attracted something over 10,000 participants, while the latter attracted nearly 30,000.[71] The attendance at mass meetings, taken alone, is not a very suitable criterion for judging the strength of parties. Organization, propaganda, and so on may make important differences in the turnout. In labor politics however, such meetings are considered highly important, and the Socialists claimed a major victory.

As Spartakist week and its aftermath raged in Berlin, Hamburg (although it had almost no Spartakist movement) became the site of one mass demonstration after the other, as the two wings of the labor movement moved into the final stages of the struggle for control of the government.[72] The Majority Socialists hammered away at the food shortages, the unemployment, and the perpetual strikes and demonstrations, which, they said, amounted to little short of anarchy, and laid the blame at the feet of the Laufenberg Government. The radicals called their own demonstrations in return, and the mobs gathered in City Hall Square, shouting, waving banners, and occasionally shooting.

On January 9, a crowd that had assembled in front of the trade-union building to demand the removal of union leaders ended by raiding and plundering the *Echo* building.[73] The following day saw a counterdemonstration by the Majority Socialists, during which Dr. Laufenberg himself was spirited away by some security police and held under arrest for several hours.[74] On January 11, there was still another demonstration, at which Laufenberg was forced to promise a re-election of the councils, thus conceding to one of the SPD's major demands.[75] Ultimately, at the Executive meeting of January 19, Laufenberg turned in his resignation as chairman of the Presidium. His place was taken by a Social Democrat, and all that remained was the purely formal step of turning over the governing powers of the Council Government to the newly elected Bürgerschaft on March 26.[76] That same day, the red flag was quietly removed from the roof of City Hall.[77]

The immediate cause of Dr. Laufenberg's resignation was almost certainly the pressure exerted on him by the Soldiers' Council, which was controlled by the Majority Socialists.[78] Both Laufenberg and his colleague, Dr. Carl Herz, the Minister of Justice, stressed in their resignations that they could not continue in office because they no longer had control over the military and police power. All manner of arrests and other police measures were being carried out by persons unknown to them and completely without the authorization of the government. The crowning touch was the arrest of Laufenberg himself on January 10. "The Workers' Council," Herz wrote, "is powerless. Hamburg is under the dictatorship of the Soldiers' Council."[79]

It was probably more than a coincidence, however, that Laufenberg and Herz chose to resign on the very day the elections to the National Assembly were held. If the Council Government enjoyed wide support in Hamburg, the election results did not reflect it. The Majority Socialists won over 51 per cent, and the Independents something less than seven per cent, of all the votes cast in the city. Such a result would have made it virtually impossible for the Council Government to retain power, unless Laufenberg and his colleagues had been prepared to set up an outright dictatorship. This they were neither willing nor able to do.

On the other hand, a certain amount of caution is necessary in evaluating the results of the election of January 19. They do not really provide a very realistic picture of the extent of Laufenberg's support in Hamburg. It is conceivable that many who would have supported Laufenberg in a Hamburg election voted for SPD delegates to the Assembly. The party lines were not yet as sharply drawn as they were to be a year or two later, and the Majority Socialists enjoyed an advantageous position in the conduct of the election. Their candidates were better known, they had a large and efficient campaign organization, and they probably benefited from the Communists' decision not to take part in the election. But even so, the election certainly showed that the Council Government was supported by a relatively small minority of the population, and lacking the authority to administer and finance the city-state or to control the activities of the police, there was little it could do but resign.

The history of the Council Government in Hamburg provides little evidence to substantiate Laufenberg's claim that it was brought down by the betrayal of the Ebert-Scheidemann Government in Berlin.[80] Laufenberg had been forced to concede failure long before the SPD in Berlin was strong enough to do him much harm. Berlin, moreover, had continued to recognize the Council Government as the ruling authority in Hamburg throughout

November and December, and only ceased to do so when the Majority Socialists were in control in Hamburg.* By then, it was well known that the sovereign power would shortly be returned to the Senate. Laufenberg himself, through his failure to build up a dependable military force, gave the Majority Socialists in Hamburg their opportunity to take control. He also failed in his attempt to win the support of the major portion of the working classes. The period between November 18 and January 19 was a difficult time for a ruling party to try to increase its support. Also it would seem that the continuing demobilization of the army during this period provided rather more SPD supporters than Laufenberg had thought likely.

Laufenberg, with his somewhat doctrinaire, idealistic approach to politics, did not make much of an attempt to cooperate with SPD leaders, unless, of course, they renounced their entire program and adopted his. Numerous attempts to work out an alliance between the two parties were made. Early in the revolution, the presence of Haase and Dittman in Hamburg provided a real opportunity for a move toward unity. These two men, of all USPD leaders, were outstanding in their desire for reunification of the labor movement, and their willingness to compromise.[81] But whatever progress had been made was lost when Dr. Laufenberg became chairman of the Presidium. Both parties continued to express their desire for cooperation, committees were formed, and so on, but it is extremely doubtful if either really believed there was any chance of success.[82] Even if they had not achieved a reunification of the labor movement under the SPD banner, the Majority Socialists had reason to be pleased with the success of their policies since November. By January 19, 1919, the threat posed by the Council Government had been largely eliminated,

* Laufenberg, for example, did represent Hamburg at the Conference of the German States in Berlin, November 27, 1918. Walther Lamp'l, *Die Revolution in Gross-Hamburg* (Hamburg, 1921), p. 23. But at the second conference, in January 1919, the Senate sent a representative. See Germany, *Reichskanzlei* (Bundesarchiv) "Akten betr. Hansestädte," R431/2268.

and it seemed relatively certain that the continued development of the revolution would be controlled by the SPD.

And yet, one must use considerable caution in evaluating the strength of the Majority Socialist position in Hamburg in early 1919. The party's political activities since November 1918 had been almost entirely concerned with the re-establishment of order and with the maintenance of the "solidarity" of the labor movement. The SPD had not yet presented its blueprint for Germany's future. Thus the Majority Socialists had been able to attack the governing abilities and some of the methods of the Laufenberg Government without becoming involved in ideological disputes concerning its nature and its long-range plans. The SPD leadership found it possible to organize numerous demonstrations against the Laufenberg Government, and on other occasions to organize demonstrations in its support, without apparent contradiction. In every case, the SPD proclaimed itself the advocate of orderly processes and good government.

The actions of certain radical groups had actually helped to make this ambiguous position possible. The attack on the *Echo* building in January, for example, had provided the SPD with an opportunity to protest against an outrage perpetrated on one of the Hamburg labor movement's most prized institutions. The protest, of course, did not fail to make the point that the Laufenberg Government was apparently unable to defend the labor movement against such outrages. The SPD, then, was able to claim to represent the integrity of the labor movement, and to attack the radicals for divisiveness and weakness, without having to come to grips with basic issues. As the SPD leaders had predicted, the ineffectiveness of the Laufenberg Government made more direct attacks unnecessary. But with its demise, the Social Democrats were confronted with the much more difficult task of providing positive leadership for the job of construction that lay ahead.

*Chapter 4*

# The New Regime

On March 24, 1919, the Majority Socialist chairman of the Presidium of the Workers' and Soldiers' Council of Hamburg mounted the podium of the Bürgerschaft chamber and solemnly declared, "The Workers' and Soldiers' Council hereby places its political power, which it has exercised on the basis of the revolution, back in the hands of the Bürgerschaft [Bravo!]."[1] The announcement was enthusiastically cheered by almost all of the 160 citizens present. The revolution, they believed, was at long last over.

The Social Democrats emerged from the revolution in a surprisingly strong position. For the first time, they appeared to have the opportunity to realize some of their party's long-term goals. On March 16, the people of Hamburg had gone to the polls to elect their new "Constitutional Bürgerschaft." All residents of the city-state over twenty years of age, both men and women, were able to cast ballots for their representatives in the local parliament. Over 80 per cent of those eligible did so. While this percentage represented a substantial drop from the 91 per cent participation in the National Assembly elections two months before, it was still an impressive turnout. The Social Democrats, along with the other parties that had wholeheartedly supported the Republic, suffered a slight loss, while the Independents showed an increase over their January total. Nevertheless, with 50.5 per cent of all votes cast, the Majority Socialists won 82 of the 160 seats in the Bürgerschaft. With this majority, the SPD was assured of a decisive voice in the drafting of the city-state's new constitution.[2]

The objectives toward which the Hamburg Socialists directed their new power were essentially those set down in the party program of 1903. That program, as indicated earlier, was a reflection of the so-called "reformist" ideology that came to dominate German Socialism after the turn of the century. According to the "reformists," the Socialist Party should, first of all, work to achieve full political rights for all members of society, especially the working classes, within the framework of a modern democratic republic. The theory was that the continuing development of the German economy and society would then make it possible for the working classes, joined by some middle-class groups, to overwhelm the vested bourgeoisie at the polls, and vote the socialist revolution into effect. The immediate problem of the Hamburg Social Democrats, consequently, was the creation of democratic political and social institutions and the encouragement of appropriate patterns of political behavior. To achieve these ends, the party needed support, or at least toleration, from a substantial proportion of the population and, of course, a government that could maintain civil peace. Therefore the SPD went about the job of reforming the Hamburg constitution with moderation and with an obvious desire to avoid antagonizing important sources of power.

The first step in the reform process was the passage of the SPD-sponsored "Law Concerning the Provisional State Authority" on March 26, 1919. Only the right-wing German National People's Party (DNVP) and the Independent Socialists voted against it.[3] This law, in providing for an interim government, set down the basic principles upon which the new constitution was to be formed. The heart of the document lay in the statement, "The exercise of the highest authority in the state resides in the Bürgerschaft as *the representative of the people of Hamburg*."[4] The old constitution was simply to be altered wherever it contradicted this principle.

In spite of the Bürgerschaft's enthusiastic beginning, it was some time before a constitution was actually drafted. It was necessary, first of all, to wait until the Weimar Constitution came into effect (August 14, 1919), for the national constitution contained certain provisions affecting the form of state governments.[5] Then there were the customary disagreements and other delays, so that the new Hamburg constitution did not actually come into effect until January 1, 1921.[6]

The old three-class system of voting was done away with; suffrage (in accordance with the provisions of the Weimar Constitution) was now to be "universal, equal, direct, and secret ... in accordance with the principles of proportional representation."[7] The second basic change in the system of government was the creation of a "responsible" Senate, a body of eighteen men which was to be chosen by the Bürgerschaft, and which was to exist only so long as it had the support of the majority in that chamber. Unlike the independent Senate of prewar days, this new organization was potentially an eminently political body. This possibility was a source of considerable consternation to the members of the more conservative parties, who put forth a number of proposals designed to strengthen the hand of the Senate.[8] But the Socialists, with the support of the Democratic Party, held firm, and the Senate was formed according to their pattern. Theoretically, the new Senate was excluded from any role in the lawmaking process, but in fact its committees continued to submit drafts of legislation much as they had done before the war.[9]

The manner in which the new Senate was formed, however, provides a striking example of the close relationship that existed between the SPD and some of the more right-wing groups during the revolutionary period. The new Senate, first of all, did not have a Socialist majority, but was made up of nine members of the old Senate and nine Social Democrats, on the basis of an agreement concluded between the Hamburg SPD and the old Senate early in November 1918.[10] In keeping this agreement, the Social Democrats were in fact the first to violate the very principle they had fought so hard for during the constitutional discussions—the principle that the Senate was to be responsible to a majority in the Bürgerschaft. In addition, when Otto Stolten, chairman of the Hamburg SPD, as head of the largest party, was offered the position of First Bürgermeister, he refused it because he believed that the position should be held by "a man who also had close connections with the old Hamburg families."[11] This important office was ultimately given to Senator Diestel, a nonparty man who stood somewhere between the Nationalists and the People's Party. A firm advocate of financial orthodoxy, Diestel was by education and temperament the personification of the prewar ideal of the "Hanseatic man."[12] One wonders, however, whether the SPD's concessions to the old order were really necessary or advisable under the circumstances. For example, the Senate, with Diestel at the head, could never become much more than a striking symbol of counterrevolution to many working-class citizens.

The Majority Socialists' handling of the so-called "socialization question" must also have been a great disappointment to many workers. Although the Hamburg constitution contained no specific provisions concerning socialization, the National Socialization Law gave to the states the power to take over private property for the public welfare.[13] The Social Democrats, accordingly, formed a committee to discuss the matter. Although certain industries were conspicuously investigated, no significant steps were taken. The party was not, in truth, very optimistic about the possibilities of successful socialization. "No individual state . . . can establish a socialist economy in the midst of capitalism," it was explained, "especially a state like Hamburg with its vast and important worldwide economic connections."[14]

The attitude of the Hamburg SPD leaders toward socialization was characteristic of the economic outlook of the party. To be sure, vague references to a distant "socialism" may be found in abundance in the speeches and writings of the Majority Socialists. But it was always stressed that "the highest possible development of production" was a precondition for this state.[15] All but very moderate wage demands were strongly discouraged.[16] And as for the idea that the workers should be in a position to control production, the SPD pointed out that this would be realistic only after the workers had had a great deal more training and experience.[17] The Hamburg Majority Socialists, in other words, "were anything but revolutionary and closely resembled the type of bourgeois democrat who dabbles now and then in social problems."[18]

Progress was made, however, in the reform of the school system, the establishment of a Labor Office (for the third time since November 1918), and the founding of the long-contested University of Hamburg.* It was necessary, too, to revamp the system of taxation, largely because of the national government's numerous incursions into tax areas previously reserved to the states.[19]

Perhaps the most striking of the SPD attempts to merge the old with the new, the left with the right, was the disposition of the Workers' and Soldiers' Council, which, though bereft of its political power, somehow continued to exist. Its form, however, had been considerably altered.

The incessant petitioning of the Majority Socialists and their allies in the Free Unions for new elections to the Workers' Council had finally borne fruit early in January 1919. Under the pressure of an imposing SPD demonstration, Laufenberg consented to new elections. But he was not prepared to give in to the Majority Socialists on the manner in which the elections should be conducted. Claiming that any other method would substantially alter the nature of the Council, Laufenberg insisted that the elections be held in the plants.[20] But by the time the plan for the re-election was presented to the Council on February 22, the Majority Socialists were solidly in control and could demand that the new Council be elected by the populace-at-large.[21] The elections were held on March 23, 1919, one week after the Bürgerschaft elections. The new Council was elected on very nearly the same basis as the new Bürgerschaft and resembled it in composition.† The Majority Socialists alone held a comfortable majority, and with their usual allies, the Free Unions and the Democrats, could control well over two-thirds of the votes.

* The Majority Socialists were ill paid for their efforts on behalf of higher education. No sooner was the University established than it became a center of rightist opposition. See *Echo* (March 12, 1920), p. 2.

† Of a total of 400 members, there were 239 SPD, 14 ADGB, 37 USPD, 31 DDP, 25 left radicals, 10 DVP, and 44 nonpartisans. See Arbeiterrat Gross-Hamburg, *Jahresbericht 1919–20* (Hamburg, 1921), pp. 5, 87–88.

The new "Workers' Council of Greater Hamburg" was a curious institution. For some months, its most difficult problem was finding something to do, most of the active committees and other organizations created by Laufenberg and his colleagues having been allowed to wither after January 19. No one seemed to have a very clear notion of just why the new Council was elected to begin with, or just how it was supposed to fit into the overall administrative pattern.[22]

The problem was ultimately solved by making the Workers' Council one of the five representative bodies in the Economic Council (Wirtschaftsrat). Hamburg was the only German state that had such a council, even though the Weimar Constitution provided for the establishment of these organizations throughout the country.[23] The Weimar Constitution envisaged a hierarchical system of economic parliaments, or councils, paralleling the political parliaments. At the base of the system were the plant councils (*Betriebsräte*), organized in factories, offices, and other places of employment. The plant councils were to elect representatives to a district economic council, made up of representatives of management and consumers as well as employees. The district councils, in turn, were to elect representatives to a national economic council, which was to act as the source of economic and social legislation and as an advisory body to the Reichstag.[24]

Some have seen the economic-council system as the single most interesting and important idea to come from the German revolution.[25] But because of what was apparently a general lack of interest in the councils in this form, the system was never to become much more than an idea. The Reich Economic Council, its scope and functions inadequately defined, did not play an important role in the lawmaking process.[26] The district councils were never established, and the plant councils, as a result, came to be something quite different from the kind of organization the planners had envisioned. The disagreement concerning the nature of the plant councils, incidentally, became one of the major issues in labor politics, and will be treated in detail in another connection (see pp. 96–108 of this book).

The Hamburg Economic Council, too, was considerably different from the kind of district council outlined in the Weimar Constitution, but its importance was by no means minor. It was originally organized not by the advocates of the council system in the left wing of the labor movement, but by some of the most important and powerful men in Hamburg—the leaders of commerce, finance, and industry. Before the war, the leading entrepreneurs in these three fields had been organized respectively in a Chamber of Trade, a Chamber of Retail Business, and a Chamber of Industry. In the old system, these organizations had often been powerful enough to influence governmental policies.[27] In November 1918, the leaders of the chambers came together with the new Chamber of Consumers and formed the Economic Council.[28] An indication that the new Economic Council wielded considerable influence is provided by its first political act: the forcing of the compromise from Laufenberg on November 16, 1918.

This system of councils was, as the saying went, "anchored" in the Hamburg Constitution by the SPD-dominated Bürgerschaft elected in 1919.[29] Some working-class critics of the Workers' Council considered this a peculiarly apt expression, since in their view, the Council would clearly make little forward progress.[30] Their pessimism undoubtedly grew out of their awareness that the Workers' Council, in spite of its title, had little connection with the labor movement. Later on, it began to take on tasks of a general welfare nature: erection of monuments, free streetcar passes for wounded war veterans, and so on.[31] Nevertheless, it would probably be a mistake to write the Council off as a transparent attempt to achieve continuity with the revolution at a cheap price. The Economic Council, to be sure, amounted to little more than an officially authorized continuation of the prewar system of Chambers under a different name. But the inclusion of representatives of the labor movement was new, and represented the extent to which the traditional Hamburg leaders were prepared to recognize the "new times and new conditions." The Economic Council might have been at least a beginning in the evolution of institutions for the peaceful settlement of economic and social issues among labor and other groups in society.

A survey of the reformation of the government of Hamburg in the early years of the Republic provides some interesting insights into the historical role of the SPD. Unencumbered by the requisites of coalition politics, the Hamburg SPD was able to proceed more or less as it wished. One can see in the composition of the new Senate a striking example of Social Democratic rule. The Senate was headed by Diestel, and many of its key positions were held by representatives of the old regime. The Social Democrats clearly wanted to maintain the continuity of institutions and personnel in the city-state government, altering them only insofar as was necessary to give the Socialists proper participation.[32]

Unfortunately, we do not know a great deal about the terms of the Socialists' agreement with the traditional ruling groups. But, as we have seen, there is considerable indirect evidence to indicate that at least a tacit agreement was reached very early in the revolution. The old Senate, and the forces it represented, was prepared to support the Majority Socialists in their struggle against the left-wing revolutionaries in exchange for a continuing role in the government.

The attraction of the SPD for the business and commercial powers of Hamburg, of course, was based upon the apparent ability of that party to appeal to the working classes in a way that no other party could. The more perceptive members of the Senate were able to see, even before November 1918, that the days of the old system were numbered, and that with the end of the "civil peace," the Social Democrats would doubtless hold the dominant position in Hamburg politics. Having failed to defeat the SPD, the Senate very sensibly attempted to incorporate it into the already existing establishment. Their reasoning is clearly exemplified in a communication from the Senate concerning the projected reform of the electoral law in May 1917:

During the war, Hamburg Social Democracy has demonstrated a worthy and patriotic [*vaterländische*] stance in its general bearing, in its handling of the working population, and in its publication, the *Hamburger Echo.* It has honorably upheld the civil peace and has successfully striven to maintain the tranquility of the population.... That our working population has remained peaceful and reasonable can be, in great measure, ascribed to the efforts of the Social Democratic leadership.... Those Social Democrats now sitting in the Bürgerschaft are thoroughly moderate, and for the most part belong to the furthest right wing of the party. The Senate, accordingly, is directing its efforts toward maintaining the influence of the present leadership over the working population.[33]

One cannot help wondering whether the SPD leadership sufficiently appreciated the irony of their acceptance by the old Hamburg ruling groups. For men like Warburg, Diestel, and Petersen, it was clearly a marriage of convenience. It is hard to imagine that men such as these had suddenly developed a deep affection for the labor movement or its leaders. The Social Democrats were useful and necessary allies. If they ceased to be such, they would (as they were in the late 'twenties) be replaced by others.

On the other hand, it must have been a heady experience for many an old Social Democrat, reared in the tradition of intransigent opposition, to find himself invited into the councils of the great, and consulted on affairs of state. Although it is impossible to determine the exact extent to which the Socialists were influenced by their new intimacy with the Hamburg bourgeoisie, it does seem extremely likely that some of their attitudes, especially toward the radical left, must have been affected. The central fear of the wealthy groups was, of course, "Bolshevism." It was this fear that had chased them into the arms of the Social Democrats in the first place. The Social Democrats, undoubtedly aware of this fact, must have perceived quite clearly how their new position would have been endangered by any flirtations with the far left. This combination of circumstances made the SPD leaders somewhat impatient toward their colleagues on the left, and somewhat intolerant of their aims and methods. The situation was an ironic one. In attempting to reassure their new middle-class allies, the SPD, deliberately or not, moved further away from the left. In so doing, they came to lose control over large segments of the labor movement, thereby decreasing their usefulness as allies of the establishment.

### THE SOCIAL DEMOCRATS' DILEMMA

The spirit of conciliation and peaceful compromise that prevailed behind the leaded windows of City Hall was deceptive. Outside, on the streets and squares of the city, quite a different spirit ruled the hearts of ever-increasing segments of the working classes—a spirit of dissatisfaction, frustration, and violence.

Violence in the streets is not always of great significance to the observer of political events. It may indicate little more than the existence of a small dissatisfied minority, or perhaps only an inadequate police force. But in Hamburg, in the early years of the Republic, the actions of crowds could and did tip the political balance. The problem of how, and by whom, the streets of Hamburg were to be policed led to one of those confrontations of irreconcilable opposites that were to destroy the SPD's efforts at conciliation.

The working classes of Hamburg had little affection for the police or the military. On several occasions before the war, army units had been brought in to cooperate with the Hamburg police to quell disturbances associated with strikes and other industrial disputes.[34] Probably with some justice, many labor leaders believed that both organizations were strongly antilabor, and not at all reluctant to use force and brutality to back up their views. The workers' experiences as enlisted men during the war only reinforced these beliefs. As a consequence, reform of both the military and the police in "democratic directions" had been one of the primary demands of the revolutionaries in 1918.

The Socialist plan for the reorganization of the military was outlined in a decree of the Ebert Government in Berlin on December 12, 1918.[35] It called for the formation of a volunteer citizens' army (Volkswehr). This force was to be formed along democratic lines for the purpose of guarding the frontiers and maintaining the civil peace. Officers were to be elected, insignia of rank abolished, and the whole army was to be firmly under civilian control.[36] It was no mere coincidence that one of the most prominent advocates of military reform, Walther Lamp'l, was a Hamburg Social Democrat.[37] For in Hamburg, as we have seen, the army was the symbol of *"Preussentum,"* of the Prussian domination that could destroy Hamburg's ancient privileges and traditional identity. Antipathy to the traditional military establishment was uncommonly strong in Hamburg. The organization of a local Volkswehr unit was one of the first tasks undertaken by the Hamburg revolutionaries in November 1918.*

In organizing new military and police units, therefore, the Social Democrats had to deal with the longstanding fears and hatreds of the working classes on the one hand, and with the traditional resistance of Hamburg to the process of national centralization on the other. The SPD was, from 1919 on, the party of order and the party of national unity. Only to the extent that it could demonstrate to its constituents that continuing support of the national Republic offered the best opportunity for realizing their various objectives could the party hope to retain their loyalty. The events of 1919 and 1920 in Hamburg provided a severe test of this endeavor.

Although the reins of government had passed into the hands of the Social Democrats with the transfer of the leadership of the Executive of the Workers' and Soldiers' Council on January 19, 1919, the restoration of order remained an extremely difficult problem. Many citizens of Hamburg had good reason to be dissatisfied. In the midst of continuing economic and political insecurity, the numbers of the unemployed mounted steadily, reaching a record-breaking 74,612—nearly 10 per cent of the total work force—in January 1919.[38] And supplies of food and coal remained very scarce indeed during the winter of 1918–19.

* The Soldiers' Council claimed to represent all the military forces in the city. These consisted of the Sicherheitsdienst, or Volkswehr, formed in the early days of the revolution, the IX Reichswehr Regiment, and the police. The various chains of command were confused and uncertain. See *Familienarchiv Lamp'l,* Nr. 9, "Bürgerschaftsuntersuchungskommission betr. sog. Sülze Unruhen, 1919–20." (Hamburg State Archives.)

The Hamburg Independent Socialists, unlike their colleagues in Berlin, had not withdrawn from the government, even after its policies had become largely controlled by their opponents, the Majority Socialists. Laufenberg and the other Independents and left radicals stayed on in the Executive of the Workers' Council as untitled members, with the idea of achieving as satisfactory a position as possible for the councils (and perhaps for themselves) in the future parliamentary government. The leftists, perhaps for the first time, were now aware of the enormous importance of police and military forces, and were prepared to conduct a last-ditch struggle to gain control over them.

The Majority Socialists' control over the Soldiers' Council, while strong enough to force Laufenberg to resign the chairmanship, was not strong enough to give them effective military control over the city. Although the SPD was technically in control of all military and police units in the city, leftist elements continued to have powerful influence in the Volkswehr. To simply disband the Volkswehr and form a new, dependable force, however, might unnecessarily antagonize many otherwise loyal Independents. Moreover, the continued presence of Laufenberg and his colleagues in the Soldiers' Council seemed to offer opportunities for the gradual reshaping of the Volkswehr through compromise and negotiation.

The relatively stable situation in Hamburg was shaken when, toward the end of January 1919, it became known that the Berlin Government was about to send a division of Reichswehr troops into Bremen to "re-establish law and order." In Bremen, the Majority Socialists had been completely excluded from the revolutionary government, and a handful of left-wing radicals, supported by what was apparently a very narrow segment of the working-class population, were attempting to retain control of the city. The result was almost continual chaos.[39]

The news of the Reichswehr's projected action in Bremen exploded like a powder keg in Hamburg. To many, it seemed extremely likely that the Reichswehr units might also occupy Hamburg.[40] And the presence of the Reichswehr in Hamburg would surely disrupt all SPD plans for the systematic reform of the military establishment. The leftist elements in the Volkswehr would undoubtedly oppose the Reichswehr's entry by force of arms, and the Hamburg Socialists would be forced into a position in which compromise would no longer be possible. With the lines so clearly drawn, the Majority Socialists would be forced to take sides with the "Prussian militarists" against a portion of the labor movement, for the Republic. This, they wanted desperately to avoid.

The first reaction of the Hamburg SPD leaders to the imminent Reichswehr action in Bremen was a striking attempt to circumvent the situation. Firmly grasping the banner of Hanseatic patriotism, they took their stand against "Prussian militarism," and, at the same time, against their own party leaders in Berlin. The *Echo,* under full control of the local leadership, was unequivocal:

> One has the feeling that he [Noske, the SPD Defense Minister in Berlin] has increasingly deserted . . . proletarian revolutionary ideas under the clever influence of the militarists. And what is so frightening is that we are now faced with this unhappy development: the danger that Prussian militarism is again on the point of receiving the power with which it can strangle the entire revolution.[41]

The following day, February 1, Laufenberg introduced a motion in the Executive calling for military mobilization (which included the arming of the proletariat) so that Hamburg could move in "support of Bremen with all military means."[42] The resolution was passed with a solid majority, and deputations were sent to Berlin and Bremen to evaluate the situation and prepare for the coming struggle.[43]

But the Social Democrats seem to have greatly miscalculated the intensity of their constituents' revolutionary ardor. The first blow was the open opposition of some of the very groups from which the SPD hoped to win support, the officials of the railway, postal, telegraphers', and telephone-workers' unions. At a full assembly of the Workers' Council to which the proposals for action were presented, a representative of a committee formed by these unions presented an ultimatum: "We want to support the Government in Berlin under any and all circumstances.... If our wishes are not respected... all wheels will stop." Any movement of a corps of Hamburg troops in defense of Bremen would, therefore, be impossible.[44]

In spite of this hostility from so important a segment of their supporters (not to mention the logistical problem thus created), the Social Democrats went ahead with their plans to oppose the Reichswehr in Bremen. On February 4 the Gerstenberg Division of the Reichswehr occupied Bremen in a bloody battle that cost both sides many lives. The Executive in Hamburg responded with a telegram to Noske threatening intervention if the troops were not removed.[45] But the Berlin Government, its hands full with outbreaks all over Germany and with serious separatist movements in Bavaria and elsewhere, was not in a position to be tolerant of this momentary aberration on the part of the usually loyal Hamburg Social Democrats. Noske's answer, crisp and to the point, showed quite clearly the extent of the Government's commitment to the Bremen action, and carried with it the implication that interference would be treated as high treason. "If troops of the IX Army Corps [Hamburg] are led against the Gerstenberg Division," it read, "all those involved will be held strictly to account."[46] The SPD majority in the Hamburg Executive, confronted with a choice between submission and treason, decided against declaring war on Berlin. The mobilization orders were cancelled.[47]

The end of the plan to defend Bremen against the Reichswehr also marked the end of the first and last serious manifestation of separatism in the Hamburg SPD. Indeed, after the decision to submit to the occupation of Bremen was made, the Hamburg Socialists had little choice but to become increasingly bound to their party's national policies. In spite of themselves, they had been forced to take sides; there was now no turning back.

Taking full advantage of the situation, Laufenberg dramatically proclaimed his intention to defend the workers of Bremen if he had to walk there to do so, and called upon the workers of Hamburg to support him.[48] On February 6, a crowd of workingmen filled the great square in front of City Hall protesting the (apparently) imminent invasion of Hamburg by the Gerstenberg Division. They demanded that the working classes of the city be armed and organized into additional Volkswehr units to repel the invaders. This was a particularly dangerous demonstration because many of the workers were already carrying arms, and a number of soldiers were scattered throughout the crowd. After a number of others had tried and failed to quiet the demonstrators, Laufenberg was finally able to do so by promising them that a new military force would be formed, and that the Reichswehr would "never come within Hamburg's walls." In the confusion, shots were fired and a number of lives were lost.[49]

Afterward, the question of how the demonstrators had obtained their weapons was raised, and it was discovered that they had been issued them (apparently by Laufenberg and his colleagues) in contravention of the agreement reached at the time of the mobilization. Against the protests of the leftists, the Executive decided to attempt to retrieve them, and to form the new Volkswehr units in a more orderly fashion.[50] Noske appointed Walther Lamp'l Commandant in Hamburg, and Lamp'l began the task of reforming the city's military institutions.[51]

It soon became apparent, however, that the Reichswehr was not on its way to Hamburg after all, and it was possible, for the moment, to avoid a serious crisis over the military situation. But the continuing turbulence in the city, and the mounting impatience of its citizens with the resulting disorder and violence, indicated that it had only been postponed. The Bremen crisis had given the leftists an opportunity to point out the differences between themselves and the Majority Socialists, and an excuse to distribute arms to their followers.

A little more than a month later, on April 15, a demonstration of the unemployed suddenly got out of hand. A crowd stormed the meeting hall of the new Workers' Council. The Council, then in session, was held under arms to listen to demands for increased unemployment benefits. From there, the demonstrators, some of whom were armed, moved into City Hall Square. During the next two days, excited mobs plundered stores throughout the city; riots broke out again and again. The forces of law and order—the Volkswehr and the police—were once more about equally divided: half wanted to subdue the rioters, half wanted to join them. For the second time in two months, Hamburg was placed under martial law.[52] And, once again, the situation was finally brought under control by local forces.

Even though they had been able to avoid a final military showdown at the time of these so-called "Easter Riots," the Majority Socialists had been placed in the extremely awkward position of having to bear arms against unemployed workers. On all sides, there was a rising bitterness. Workers had been killed and wounded—absolute proof of the "treachery" of the SPD.[53] And the party's middle-class allies were beginning to lose faith in the SPD's ability to find a peaceful solution to the city's problems. The liberal Senator Petersen, so calm and even tempered in November, reflected the mood of many of his colleagues when he expressed the opinion, after the Easter Riots, that probably only the intervention of the Reichswehr could solve Hamburg's problems.[54]

Nonetheless, plans were set in motion which, it was hoped, would create a military force in Hamburg capable of dealing with the situation without outside help. Major Danner, previously a General Staff officer in the Gerstenberg Regiment who had been transferred to Hamburg shortly after the occupation of Bremen, established a new military unit, the Einwohnerwehr (Citizens' Army).[55] The main difference between this unit and the Volkswehr was that the personnel of the new organization were to be carefully screened for political beliefs, every effort being made to exclude Communists and other radicals of the left. The core of the Einwohnerwehr was formed from the local free-corps, the Bahrenfelder, which then numbered about 300 men.[56] At the same time, Senator Petersen was made Director of Police (*Polizeiherr*).

He at once began a campaign to "clear the undependable elements" from the police force.[57]

But before the effects of either of these reforms could be felt, Hamburg was faced with the most serious crisis of the revolutionary period. It is indicative of the emotional state of the populace that this crisis was sparked by a controversy over the contents of a certain brand of jellied meat, or *Sülze*, a staple food-product in certain parts of Germany, especially among the working classes. On the morning of June 24, 1919, the citizens of Hamburg were treated to an unusual spectacle—a parade of wheelbarrows in the center of the city. The wheelbarrows were followed by a large group of angry men and women. In the lead barrow sat the owner of a large meatpacking concern, one Herr Heil. The others were occupied by working girls from the plant, each of whom brandished a cow's tail, a dog's head, a rat, or some other unsavory item, which, it was believed, had been used in the preparation of *Sülze*. Herr Heil was then ceremoniously deposited in the blue waters of the Alster. The crowd next produced the director of the War Provisions Office, who was to be forced to answer for his alleged sins at City Hall Square.[58] The detachment of Volkswehr assigned to guarding City Hall, perhaps enjoying the fracas, made no move to interfere.[59]

The new Commandant in Hamburg, Walther Lamp'l, immediately evaluated the situation as a dangerous one (rightly or wrongly, it is difficult to say), and ordered a detachment of the Bahrenfelder to occupy City Hall. This was done, but not without the use of machine guns and the loss of several lives. By nightfall Hamburg was in a state of civil war. The City Hall (and the Bahrenfelder within) was under siege; throughout the night City Hall Square resounded with bursts from rifles, machine guns, and hand grenades.[60] The fight continued into the following day until, as a result of an almost unbelievable blunder, the Bahrenfelder were taken by surprise, disarmed, and marched off through the city to the accompaniment of shouts and jeers from the crowd on City Hall Square.[61] At that point, nineteen of the Bahrenfelder, and probably that many or more "rioters," had been killed.[62] With the withdrawal of the Bahrenfelder, the streets became much quieter, although groups of armed men still roamed about.[63]

On June 27, Hamburg was shocked by the announcement that Noske was sending Reichswehr troops to occupy the city. Full-scale martial law was declared in effect.[64] Unaccountably, the Reichswehr commander chose to send first only a small detachment of apparently inexperienced soldiers to establish the occupation. These, by means of threat or cajolery, were promptly disarmed and sent back from whence they had come.[65]

Again, the city reverted to a state of relative peace. June 28 passed "without special incident," and the various administrative offices and security agencies went about their business unhindered.[66] The following day, the occupation of Hamburg was announced once again. Forty-eight hours later, General von Lettow-Vorbeck appeared in the city at the head of an almost ludicrously excessive force: 350 officers, 9,600 men, 30 cannon, 100 heavy and 137 light machine guns, 14 mortars, a column of tanks, and a flotilla of torpedo boats. This was more than half of the total mobile military force then at the disposal of the Republic. Hamburg greeted all this with silence and empty streets. Thus was begun an occupation which, legally, lasted until December of that year.[67]

The "*Sülze* Riots" in Hamburg raise several important questions, questions which might well be applied to similar disturbances that broke out all over Germany in the spring and summer of 1919. First of all, the riots had none of the earmarks of a Spartakist or Communist uprising.* The early stages of the outbreak have been recorded here in some detail because they show quite clearly the obviously spontaneous nature of the initial demonstration. The crowd of June 24, though angry, still showed signs of a kind of rough good humor. There were no serious attempts to harm the

* They were, however, described as such in those German newspapers that received their information from the Wolfschen Telegraphenbureau. See *Senat,* Cl. VII Lit. Me. Nr. 12, Vol. 24, Fasc. 11b, "Unruhen in Hamburg, 1919–21." (Hamburg State Archives.)

director of the factory or the director of the War Provisions Office. At the outset, the demonstration was surely no more than the outburst of a frustrated and hungry people against an authority in which they had lost all faith during the years of war and months of tumult.

Such crowds, of course, can soon become ugly and dangerous if not restrained, but one must severely question the appropriateness of the action taken by the Commandant. It is hard to conceive of anything more directly provocative than presenting the excited demonstrators with a body of heavily armed troops, for the most part made up of ex-army officers, many of whom were undoubtedly still clad in their field-gray uniforms.[68] If, indeed, the outbreak had been Spartakist or Communist inspired, certainly someone would have been prepared to make capital of it. No leader appeared at the head of the movement; when control was finally established it was by a "Committee of Twelve," which claimed to represent the factory councils, the unemployed, and the Volkswehr. To be sure, this committee consisted largely of representatives of the various left-wing organizations in Hamburg.[69] But even after the Bahrenfelder had been disarmed and removed from City Hall, and "the way was free for a revolutionary government," as Danner puts it, "there was no one there to take it over."[70] Instead, the "revolutionaries" seemed interested only in re-establishing law and order.

On the morning of June 25, two days before the first occupation of the city, the Committee of Twelve, in negotiation with the Senate, presented the following demands, none of which were particularly revolutionary: (1) lifting of martial law, (2) withdrawal of the Bahrenfelder from the City Hall, (3) maintenance of order by the Volkswehr under the supervision of the factory councils.[71] By the afternoon of the same day, the Committee, in cooperation with the SPD, had begun restoring order in the city.[72] The proclamation issued by the Committee early that evening is indicative of its intentions:

The Bahrenfelder have been marched off, and, accordingly, the principal cause of the unrest has been removed. Moreover, the Commandant . . . has declared that Reichswehr troops from outside will not be brought into the city . . . if the workers of Hamburg can succeed with certainty in re-establishing order. . . . Workers and Comrades! The unfortunate disturbances are not a political action. Under no circumstances shall more blood be spilled. Therefore, workers, watch out for troublemakers, support the police.[73]

As this document shows, the workers' fear and hatred of the military lay at the heart of the disturbance. When the Bahrenfelder had been removed, the city became quiet and the process of disarmament was begun.[74] When the first detachment of troops from the Corps Lettow-Vorbeck arrived, excitement stirred again. It receded quickly after the detachment left the city. There was, of course, no question of opposition once Lettow-Vorbeck had arrived in force.

All this does not mean that the radical left had suddenly reformed, and lost interest in taking over the government. However, that particular moment, with the Reichswehr ranging about Germany crushing one leftist movement after another, was hardly the appropriate one for any revolutionary attempts. All parties of the left, including the Social Democrats, could see in a possible Reichswehr occupation of the city only harm to their prospects.

Social Democratic leaders, of course, had realized this all along, and until the last possible moment made every effort to forestall the occupation.[75] But in this crisis, unlike the Bremen crisis, they received little help from their allies to the right, most of whom had since come to consider a Reichswehr occupation an "unpleasant necessity."[76] Paradoxically, it was Frederick Baumann, now special assistant and confidant to the new Bürgermeister, who took the lead in urging that troops be sent for and who was sent off to Berlin to make arrangements with Noske. He subsequently served as a special adviser to Lettow-Vorbeck.[77]

The reaction of conservative elements in the city to the June disturbances is revealed in the report of the president of the Senate to Lettow-Vorbeck on July 18: "It can hardly be doubted that they [the disturbances] were artificially stirred up in order to serve as a means of overthrowing the present political system." The report concludes with an appeal to the general to maintain martial law at least until the participants in the disturbances had been tried for high treason. The Extraordinary War Court (which could function only under martial law) would be highly suitable for this purpose, since "the matter could be conducted with the desirable swiftness."[78] The fact that the War Court was never able to uncover any evidence of high treason adds increased weight to the conclusion that the conservative politicians of Hamburg had been badly frightened by the bogey of Bolshevism. Unable, or perhaps unwilling, to come to grips with the immensely difficult problems of the day, they automatically pointed to "Communist incitement" as the cause of the trouble. They confused the absence of armed workers on the streets with a settlement of the problem, and failed to realize that a forceful solution, though seemingly simple, could be an enormously costly one.

Certainly, the SPD suffered more than any other group from the *Sülze* Riots. Once the troops were there, the SPD, having made its decision back in February, had to cooperate with them. In the process, the party became identified by all who had grievances against the troops with the cause of Hamburg's troubles. The troops were not popular in Hamburg; on several occasions they took forceful action in settling labor disputes and controlling demonstrations.[79] It is not certain that the leftists were deliberately provoked, but no doubt many agreed that "if the radicals wanted a battle, it would be better if it came while the troops were camped in Hamburg."[80] The prohibition against open meetings, accordingly, was not always enforced.[81]

The most important overall result of the occupation of Hamburg was that it forced the city to face an issue that had been a major factor in Berlin since early in November—the relationship between the SPD and the military forces. The effects of this issue upon the labor movement were much the same in the Hanseatic city as they were elsewhere in Germany. The connection of the SPD with the free-corps, and later the army, became one of the major—and probably most successful—talking points of the Communists. Certainly, the occupation of Hamburg was not the direct cause of the growth of the Communist movement there. Numerous other issues figured in that development. But armed conflicts leave very deep scars, and few of the workers who faced the guns pointed at them by the agents of the SPD in June had any further doubts about who their real enemies were.

The full impact of the *Sülze* Riots and the subsequent occupation of the city was not really felt until March of the following year when Hamburg had its own version of the so-called "Kapp Putsch."[82] The two events were very closely connected.

In June 1919, the Volkswehr was disbanded and replaced by the Ordnungspolizei, which was to be the major police force of Hamburg throughout the Weimar period.* The Ordnungspolizei was organized on the direct "recommendation" of General von Lettow. Free-corps organized under the General's command were to form the core of the organization, and the new commander of the "Orpo," Major Völckers, was put forward by the General as a suitable man for the job.[83]

The moderate pro-republican leaders of Hamburg, who had been so intent upon wresting the control of the military from radical hands, soon discovered that they had lost control of it themselves. Even before becoming commander, Major Völckers demanded and was granted the right to deal directly with the head of the Hamburg Government. There were to be no civilian intermediaries to interfere with the efficiency of military actions.[84] And as the months passed, it became increasingly apparent that Völckers was in fact engaged in constructing a private military island

* This force was at first called "Sicherheitspolizei." The name was changed and its armament considerably reduced as a result of French and American protests about such forces in June 1920. See SPD-Hamburg, *Die Sozialdemokratie in der verfassungsgebenden Bürgerschaft* (Hamburg, 1921), pp. 85–87; and Lothar Danner, *Ordnungspolizei Hamburg* (Hamburg, 1958), pp. 9–30.

in Hamburg. The Government found itself rarely consulted on military matters, and any inquiries it made in this direction were ignored.[85] Finally, in December, Völckers' audacity led to a direct conflict with the Senate, and he was replaced by a new man, a Colonel Meyn from Cologne.[86] But the change brought no significant alteration in military policy. Völckers had placed men he could depend upon in key positions. Meyn also found these men generally to his liking, and merely augmented them with the substantial group of his own cronies that he had transferred to his new post. The Senate continued to be excluded from the decisions of the military commander.[87]

The effects of the policies of Völckers and Meyn were acutely felt when, on March 13, 1920, the Ehrhardt Brigade marched into Berlin and sent the legally constituted Government of Germany packing off to Dresden. No sooner had news of these events reached Hamburg, than the security forces disintegrated into three factions. There was a large and important faction—made up primarily of Bahrenfelder and Reichswehr troops led by Völckers' lieutenants—which supported the rebels. A group of these men marched on City Hall on the night of March 13, with the intention of replacing the Hamburg Government with one loyal to Kapp.* There was a still larger segment that remained confused and virtually useless to anyone throughout the days of the disturbance. Finally, there was a segment, augmented by hastily armed civilians, which remained faithful to the Republic, and which, under the leadership of Major Danner, promptly retook City Hall early on March 14.[88] Colonel Meyn's position during the "putsch" could very generously be called "ambiguous."[89]

After the Kapp Putsch, the Ordnungspolizei was reorganized once again, this time under the leadership of Major Danner. It was for the most part purged of the reactionary elements that had been introduced by Völckers and Meyn, and civilian control was reestablished. But it was still a far different force from that envisaged by those who had made the revolution in November 1918. It was

* Wolfgang Kapp, head of the rebel government.

clearly a professional, not a citizens', fighting force and was led largely by ex-army officers.[90]

The effects of the Kapp Putsch and the accompanying general strike on the labor movement will be taken up in Chapter 5. Here, it is enough to say that the effects were similar to those of the *Sülze* Riots. The extremes of both left and right became more bitter, and stronger, as a result of it. And, as we shall see, an important segment of the working classes moved over into opposition to the Republic, never to return to the ranks of pro-republican labor.

It is clear that the organization of the military and police power in Hamburg was one of the central issues in this stage of the revolution. The Hamburg SPD leaders had correctly evaluated it as one of their toughest problems, and had hoped to solve it without permanently alienating important segments of popular support. The occupation of the city by the Reichswehr put an end to their hopes. Once the various opposing groups had been brought face-to-face, weapons in hand, the fundamental basis of mutual trust upon which successful conciliation must be founded was destroyed. It is not at all surprising that after the initial confrontation, the conflict escalated into the civil-war situation of the Kapp Putsch. By then, friends and enemies had been quite clearly identified.

The central question to be asked, then, is whether the occupation could have been avoided. Without becoming involved in an attempt to evaluate the policies of the Berlin Government in this connection,[91] it is safe to conclude that, had the Hamburg Government been able to maintain a reasonable degree of order, the occupation would not have been ordered. At that time, the leaders in Berlin had enough problems without creating new ones. And the group of pro-republican politicians in Hamburg, represented by Senator Petersen, who ultimately came around to requesting the occupation, would certainly have preferred to forgo the experience if they had believed it feasible or safe to do so. But the SPD apparently could neither control the working classes themselves, nor create a police force to do it for them; and they did not appear to be making significant progress in the accomplishment of either objective.

It seems clear that by the time Danner began the formation of the Einwohnerwehr, and Petersen began his reforms after the Easter disturbances, it was already too late. Only two months had elapsed before the matter came to a head in the *Sülze* Riots, hardly time enough to build a new military force from the bottom up. And Commandant Lamp'l, who had been at work since at least February, seems to have accomplished remarkably little. To his surprise, the Volkswehr proved unreliable in April, and again in June.[92] Probably, Lamp'l was simply not a very fortunate choice for the job, as the party leaders finally realized.[93] But the fact that it took until June to discover this leads one to believe that in Hamburg, as elsewhere, the Majority Socialist leaders were not sufficiently informed about, or interested in, the military problem to give it the attention it deserved. For the Republic, it was a tragic oversight.

On the other hand, one must recognize the very great difficulty of the SPD's position. The Hamburg SPD leaders believed, rightly as it turned out, that the military and police problem was a very delicate one, and that any lasting solution would have to be carried out very gradually and carefully. What they could not anticipate was the extreme volatility of large portions of the working classes. The Social Democratic leaders were clearly surprised by the frequent and apparently spontaneous gatherings of large, angry crowds who appeared to be more or less ready for anything. And they were just as surprised by their own inability to calm or control them. The electoral results of 1919 gave the SPD leaders every reason to believe that their popularity was wide and growing. The events in the streets proved beyond question that the party also had many bitter opponents among the working classes. Had the Majority Socialists foreseen the latter development, they might have more urgently sought to establish a firm military support.

The very fact that the SPD leaders were taken by surprise by the frequent eruptions of violence is, of course, some indication that they were perhaps not as close to the voters as they might have been. Indeed, it seems likely that a lack of contact between the SPD leaders and certain segments of the working classes could also have been one of the major causes of the violence.

Having observed the failure of the SPD to develop the means to control outbreaks of violence in the streets, let us now turn to an examination of the roots of the violence itself, and the SPD's inability to deal with the dissatisfactions of the working classes before they became matters to be handled by force of arms.

*Chapter 5*

# The Rise of the "Left Opposition"

Although the SPD had begun as a Marxian labor party, its leaders made a serious effort, during the early years of the Republic, to meet the new requisites of republican politics. In many instances, as we have seen, the party was able to make the necessary adjustments and compromises. In the process, of course, any clearly recognizable "Marxian world-view" was substantially modified. But traditional modes of thought, especially in the area of the most basic assumptions, are not discarded easily. Certain of these traditional basic assumptions concerning the nature and conduct of political action tended to act as blinders, limiting the vision of the SPD leaders so that they failed to see some of the more formidable obstacles that confronted them. One such assumption was that the "normal" situation was one in which the working classes stood closely united in pursuit of common economic and political goals. Thus the disunity existing among the working classes was considered "abnormal," and there was a tendency to blame it on demagogic leaders, particular economic crises, or other temporary and incidental causes.

Throughout this troubled period there was considerable opposition to the policies of the SPD and the Free Unions. The specific issues upon which this "left opposition" was based sometimes changed, as did the leaders, but the opposition itself was always there.* The constancy and virulence of this opposition from the left might lead one to suspect that its origins were to be found not in temporary conditions, but in matters that deeply concerned the workers involved. In this chapter, we shall examine some of the origins of this opposition, and observe the manner in which it became a political fact of vital importance to those who wished to preserve the Weimar Republic.

In Hamburg, as in all of Germany, the most striking (and perhaps the most important) changes brought about by the war and the revolution were those that affected labor and industrial relations in general. In Imperial Germany, labor had been considered a force dealt with most effectively by means of efficient police measures. In Weimar Germany, labor had come to "stand under the special protection of the Reich."[1] Labor unions, once bitterly fought by business and government, were now protected and even encouraged by various constitutional and legislative provisions. German business, almost without exception, was ready to deal with the unions as the recognized representatives of the labor force. By 1919 the trade unions had become far and away the "largest mass organizations in Germany"[2] with a total membership of over six and one-half million.[3]

The so-called "November Agreement" of November 15, 1918, adhered to by all of the leading trade unions and most of the employer associations, contained a major portion of the labor provisions that later found their way into the Weimar Constitution.[4] Although negotiations for the agreement had begun in November 1917, some of the most important industries were not ready to join until October 1918.[5] Undoubtedly, the obvious unrest of the working classes and the beginnings of the revolution strengthened the hand of the unions and facilitated agreement.

The November Agreement was, in effect, an attempt to carry

* The term "left opposition" is used in the literature with a variety of meanings. Frequently, it refers to a specific opposition group within the KPD. Here, however, it refers to the entire spectrum of left-wing opposition to the majority positions of the SPD and the ADGB.

over into peacetime the techniques of industrial relations developed during the war. The necessity for a high degree of industrial efficiency during the war had led the German military authorities to discover what was until then a little-appreciated aspect of labor unions. In attempting to establish uniform wage and working-condition agreements for whole industries, the military soon found that the unions, when made a party to collective agreements, could be transformed into a most effective instrument for controlling the labor force. The unions, with their insatiable desire for expanding "organization" and their emphasis on "labor discipline," had a vested interest in seeing that such agreements were kept, since the very fact of agreement implied that the unions were recognized as the proper representatives of labor.

The result of this wartime alliance between the state and the unions was an unprecedented industrial harmony. The exceptions, since they occurred largely in industries where the unions were weakest, tended to prove the rule.[6] In the interests of the war effort, the various restrictions on union activity were relaxed, conditions and wages improved, and the unions given an important voice in the determination of industrial policy. Committees were set up in every plant to enforce adherence to the collective agreements, and, most important, the unions achieved recognition in many new industries, including some that had long and stubbornly resisted organization.[7] The employer associations, because they recognized the advantages of such a system, or foresaw the tumult that might follow the end of hostilities, or simply realized the impossibility of undoing what had once been done, were prepared to agree to a continuation of this "community of interests" approach to industrial relations in November 1918.

The November Agreement provided for the establishment of industry-wide contracts that would guarantee uniform wages and working conditions throughout the country. A board consisting of representatives from the unions and the employer organizations was to conduct negotiations and see to the enforcement of the agreements. In every plant employing fifty or more workers, a "works committee" was to be established to negotiate with management on local problems and to enforce the contract in detail. Machinery for arbitration and mediation was also set up, as were specific methods for dealing with breach of contract and so on. "Yellow" or company unions were specifically outlawed, and the eight-hour maximum working day was established.[8]

Most of the provisions of the November Agreement were later embodied in the Weimar Constitution. The Constitution, of course, could not demand the conclusion of collective agreements, but it could and did recommend them, and gave the force of law to such provisions as the eight-hour day, the outlawing of "yellow" unions, and the mediation and arbitration boards. The "works committees" mentioned in the November Agreement also found their way into the Constitution, but, as we shall see, in a form considerably modified by the events of the revolution. The Constitution set an important precedent in establishing the principle of federal and state responsibility for the maintenance of the unemployed.[9]

As a result of the November Agreement and the provisions of the Constitution, labor unions (especially the Free Unions) were immensely strengthened in their relations with business and the state. They were also strengthened internally: in many industries a worker could not participate in the new institutions unless he joined, or at the very least cooperated with, the union. And since his pay and working conditions were likely to be set by the unions whether he belonged or not, there was ample incentive to join.[10] As a result, union membership skyrocketed. The Free Unions alone had more than doubled their 1913 membership (2,574,000) by 1919; and by 1921, it was a staggering 7,138,000.[11] The increasing strength of the unions brought with it increasing prestige and power. Unions played important roles in political parties and in the councils of state. The trade unions, for example, were directly represented in such governmental agencies as the Reichsbank, the Post Office Board, the Electricity Board, the National Railroad Board, and, in Hamburg, the Economic Council.[12]

This imposing structure of union strength was misleading. It had one flaw: it could stand only so long as the unions were able to exercise effective control over their memberships. The employers, of course, in signing the November Agreement, expected in return that the unions would cooperate in maintaining industrial peace, restraining wage demands, and so on.[13] Furthermore, the employers were interested in the union leaders only so long as they could claim to speak for the bulk of the working classes. Union strength, therefore, depended quite directly on the size of union membership, and on the ability of the leaders to marshal this membership in support of their policies. This was a far from easy task. For there was a large and important segment of the trade-union membership which consistently opposed the "community of interests" approach to labor relations embodied in the November Agreement, and which conducted a vigorous and unrelenting opposition to the leadership of the Free Unions.

There were two major issues involved in the opposition within the Free Unions at the end of 1918. One concerned the nature of the ADGB itself, and the other its relations with the labor political parties. The two issues, which became more and more closely related, played a fundamental role in the development of labor politics during the period.

One of the opposition's major demands was that the ADGB be reorganized to give proper representation to the large industrial unions.[14] Even though the industrial unions were growing very rapidly during this period—especially in the transportation and metal industries—the basic organizational form of the Free Unions had not changed since the early days of trade unionism. The most important leadership positions were most often passed along on the basis of seniority, and as a result they tended to remain in the hands of the traditional craft unions.[15] In Hamburg, for example, almost all of the top leadership posts were occupied by members of such unions. And of the fifty-two secondary positions on which information is available, only nine were held by members of industrial unions during the period covered by this study. But during this same period, the industrial unions accounted for over forty per cent of the total ADGB membership in Hamburg.[16] The craft unions' control over the ADGB was greatly increased by the growth of a large union bureaucracy. Some of the most important jobs in trade unionism demanded full-time attention, and paid officials were hired to fill them. As a result, there was a growing feeling among some trade-union members that the unions were being taken increasingly out of their control, and placed in the hands of paid administrators.[17]

The ADGB had a highly centralized organizational structure. Local federations, for example, could not in most cases authorize the expenditure of strike funds. Each strike, therefore, had to be approved at the national level.[18] Local leadership councils were frequently appointed by the national leadership, the local membership not always having even the opportunity to approve or disapprove of the choices.[19] In addition, the ADGB seemed reluctant to form new national industrial unions, preferring instead to create synthetic local organizations by merging a number of well-controlled craft unions.[20] All of these factors, then, had contributed to the growth of opposition in the industrial unions. The industrial unions felt that their large unions were in some ways subject to the policies of the much smaller craft unions, that they had far too small a role in choosing the leadership in the ADGB, and that strike policies were often decided on the wishes of the relatively well-off workers in the craft trades without consideration for the problems of the industrial workers.[21]

Resentment against the organizational form of the unions took several forms. There were frequent demands for the organization of more truly "industrial" unions, and for the reorganization of the federation in such a way as to give these unions more scope. Powerful local unions demanded certain decentralizing measures, and there was a widespread movement in favor of "increased trade-union democracy," which meant placing numerous appointive offices on an elective basis and extending the democratic process to the selection of provincial and local officials.[22]

The second major problem confronting the Free Unions in 1918 concerned their position in regard to the labor political parties, especially the SPD. The relationship between the Free Unions and the SPD had altered considerably since the early days of the German trade unions.[23] The most important milestone in this relationship, for our purposes, is the "Mannheim Resolution" of 1906. This resolution of the SPD congress reasserted the unions' "autonomy" in relation to the party. In practice, this meant that the unions renounced the political "neutrality" they had claimed since the 1890's, and became committed to the support (and to some extent control) of the right or "reformist" wing of the SPD.[24] This arrangement had worked splendidly for the unions until 1917, when the Independents broke away from the SPD. This schism raised the danger of a similar split within union ranks, an eventuality the unions wished very much to avoid.

There was an important connection between the problems arising from the internal organization of the ADGB and the problems concerning the relationship between the Free Unions and the SPD. The primary issue in dispute at Mannheim in 1906 was the use of the strike weapon. Was it to be used as a political weapon in the form of a "mass" or general strike? Or was it to be used as an economic weapon, by the trade unions alone, to force certain specific demands from employers? As might be expected, the Free Unions, along with the Majority Socialists, favored the latter use.[25] But a number of unions, especially the large industrial unions, desired a much broader strike policy. Indeed, one of the major factors in the ADGB's unwillingness to encourage the growth of the industrial unions was the tendency of these unions to hold frequent and rather violent strikes.[26]

One of the clearest examples of the interrelationship of the two problems was the great metalworkers' strike in the Hamburg shipyards in July 1913. The ADGB opposed the strike and withheld strike funds. Nevertheless, the strike went on, ending in a severe defeat for the workers. One result was a violent upsurge of demands for the termination of the national organization's right of veto in such matters, and for an increase in the autonomy of regional organizations.[27]

The perhaps almost coincidental merging of the left-wing opposition in the trade unions was carried one step further during the war. The split in the SPD over the party's war policy was accompanied by opposition in the unions to the ADGB's wartime policies.[28] In Hamburg, most of this opposition came from workers in the harbor and in the transportation industries.[29] The harbor has played such a vital role in the Hamburg labor movement that it might be wise to consider briefly its special characteristics.

The harbor, first of all, clearly embodied all the important aspects of the problem of industrial unionism. Harbor workers were frequently overworked and underpaid. Workers in a number of different trades were employed there, and jurisdictional disputes were frequent.[30] The largest and most important union in the harbor, the German Metalworkers' Union (DMV), was also the leader of the opposition movement.[31] The harbor workers of Hamburg, clearly distinguishable by their distinctive dress and language, generally saw the world as divided into two groups—themselves and everybody else. During the Weimar years, the harbor situation grew worse. Because almost anyone with sufficient strength and endurance could perform many of the jobs there, it became a gathering place for the disinherited. When a man lost his job in Hamburg, he went to the harbor to find work. Since many Hamburgers lost their jobs in the 'twenties, the harbor rarely had work enough for all on any one day. Even so, the train stations of the city were crowded with displaced workers who slept on the hard benches at night, and day after day made the predawn trudge to the harbor in search of a few hours' employment.[32]

The combination of large-scale industries employing workers of many trades and a large element of poorly paid "occasional" labor made the harbor highly resistant to union organization.[33] All of these factors made the harbor a tinderbox, likely to be ignited by the first sparks of violence or revolt. As long as the war was in progress, however, the various currents of opposition had to remain underground. The activities of opposition groups were severely limited by the wartime restrictions on "political activity," and the integration of the unions into the war effort made the formation of opposition unions virtually impossible. Furthermore, many labor leaders were gone from the scene during the war years.

With the cease-fire in November 1918, all the old grievances were resurrected, and a few new ones added. Many workers blamed the war and its domestic effects on those who had supported it. In the wave of revolutionary fervor that swept over Hamburg in November 1918, the Free Unions frequently found themselves associated with the "old" that needed sweeping out.

Although there had been a number of incidents in the last years of the war that gave some evidence of the unrest just below the surface, the storm that broke at the beginning of the revolution on November 5 was a surprise to almost everyone.[34] It was immediately apparent that the unions had very little control over certain segments of the working classes. The strike that broke out in the harbor and spread swiftly through the city on the first day of the revolution was conducted entirely without the collaboration of the unions. Moreover, the unions' urgings to return to work went largely unheeded.[35] Later that evening, at the meeting called by the Independent Socialists, the crowd was barely prevented from seriously harming one of Hamburg's leading trade-union officials, who had simply stopped by to see what was going on. Cries of "traitor" and "warmonger" greeted him from every side.[36] The meeting, it will be recalled, then went on to pass a resolution demanding, among other things, the formation of workers' and soldiers' councils. The wording of this resolution tells us exactly how the revolutionaries felt about trade-union leadership. "No official of the trade unions or cooperatives," it stipulated, "shall take part in the formation of the councils."[37] No mention was made incidentally, of excluding the Majority Socialist leaders as such.

There is no evidence to show that the union leaders were terribly worried about this show of opposition. Apparently, like most

Majority Socialists, they believed that the radicalism was the expression of a very small group and would soon pass.[38] Therefore the unions took no steps to change the policy they had held since the split of the SPD—opposition to the Independents and support of the Majoritarians.[39] Unfortunately, it is rather difficult to form a very clear picture of the unions' political activities during the revolutionary days. In Hamburg the SPD leadership and the union leadership was to a considerable extent identical, and it is certain that the Social Democrats did not make a single important policy decision without consulting the unions.[40] Most often, as on November 5, 1918, the executive committees of the party and the unions held joint sessions, with a vote for each member present.[41] All of the important SPD proclamations were cosigned by the leaders of the Hamburg ADGB.[42] In these discussions, as in those surrounding the election of deputies to the Workers' Council, all concerned considered the ADGB and SPD members a single group.[43]

But during the winter of 1918–19, it became increasingly apparent that the revolution was affecting the SPD and the ADGB in very different ways. As was pointed out earlier, the defection of certain working-class elements from the SPD was compensated for in several ways. First of all, the very inability of the Laufenberg Government to govern the city effectively was a strong argument in favor of passing the job on to the SPD, even if one did not entirely agree with the party's policies. But more important, as the election returns show, the SPD was able to pick up sufficient strength from nonlabor groups to compensate for whatever support it may have lost from labor.[44] The nearly 38,000 votes cast for the USPD in January 1919 could easily be discounted by a party that had polled 280,000 votes in the same election.

The situation was very much different for the Free Unions. First of all, contrary to all hopes, animosity toward the ADGB leadership did not lessen as the months wore on. Indeed, under the encouragement of the USPD leaders, it thrived and flourished. Throughout November, December, and January, Trade Union

Hall was a frequent target for leftist demonstrations. On one occasion, the building was completely occupied by demonstrators, the union officials expelled, and the treasury of the unions seized and put under lock and key.[45]

Most of the various demonstrations against the Free Unions originated in the harbor, among the metalworkers and others in the large mass industries.[46] The origins of their leadership are less clear. On at least one occasion, the so-called "Revolutionary Shop Stewards" acted as the spokesmen for the demonstrators, but it is not certain that they were responsible for the demonstration itself.[47] During these early stages, the demonstrations were, for the most part, against the wartime domestic policies of the unions and their continuation by the November Agreement.[48] In this connection, it should be pointed out that during the war workers in critical industries (such as shipbuilding) were exempted from military service. It was frequently charged that the employers used the threat of "the trenches" to exact poorly paid overtime from workers so exempted.[49]

The most disturbing aspect of the opposition, as far as the unions were concerned, was the manner in which dissatisfaction with some specific union policy was often accompanied by political opposition to the SPD. On January 9, 1919, for example, there was a great strike and demonstration led by the harbor workers in opposition to the use of the piecework system in a number of plants. Before the war, "*Akkord ist Mord*" (piecework is murder) had been a slogan of the Free Unions in Hamburg, and most trades no longer worked under the system.[50] The ADGB leaders, however, in agreement with the SPD, blithely informed the workers that the requirements of rebuilding Hamburg's economy made it impossible to fulfill their demands.[51] Dr. Laufenberg, who not only opposed the SPD but worked against the unions in a variety of ways, supported the harbor workers. The result was the demonstration against the unions and the SPD, and for Laufenberg and his antiunion policies.[52]

The unions, unlike the SPD, could not turn to the middle-class groups for support. Victory for the common cause in a parliamentary election was little help to harried union leaders attempting to control a rebellious membership. There was one very important difference between the SPD's situation and that of the Free Unions. The SPD's opposition came from without, mostly from the USPD. The unions, on the other hand, were attempting to deal with an opposition that came from within. During this period thousands of workers in the industrial trades were flocking into the Free Unions, bringing with them a vigorous opposition to the policies of the established union leaders. The result was a widespread movement to overthrow the union leaders and replace them with new men, more agreeable to the wishes of the left opposition.[53]

In Hamburg, the most striking example of the development of the left opposition took place in the German Metalworkers' Union (DMV).[54] This union, one of the largest in the city, was a leader of the opposition within the ADGB.[55] Before the war, the Hamburg DMV had played a leading role in the national movement to decentralize unions. The metalworkers' opposition to its union leadership had increased during the war (chiefly as a result of the piecework issue), and by 1918 was at a very high pitch. It was widely believed that the leader of the Hamburg DMV, Koch, had informed the military administration during the war about the activities and whereabouts of Heinrich Laufenberg, Hamburg's future revolutionary and leader of the SPD left wing.[56]

The opposition continued to gain strength in the Hamburg DMV until, in March 1919, it was able to win a majority in an election of the local leadership; a new "Local Administration" (Ortsverwaltung) consisting of 13 USPD and seven SPD members was formed.[57] The result was complete chaos. The Majority Socialist metalworkers stayed away from meetings in protest, and even elected their own representatives to national conventions.[58] "More than ever," reports the Hamburg DMV's official publication, "party positions determined trade-union matters."[59] Ultimately, the USPD-dominated administration resigned in the face of the solid opposition, but not before the union had been irreparably split into two warring factions.[60]

Throughout Germany, the left opposition, which had grown up primarily in response to trade-union matters, soon found itself involved in political controversies. Thus the unions, much to their leaders' distress, were transformed into the battlegrounds upon which many of the major issues of the day were fought.

### THE COUNCIL MOVEMENT

In the earlier discussion of the role of the SPD in the Hamburg revolution, it was pointed out that the "council idea" was in many ways at the center of the disagreements between the SPD and the Independents. This idea was far more than a plan of political organization: in practice, it would have meant vast changes in the labor movement and all its organizations. During the early days of the revolution, it was believed by some, especially in the left wing of the USPD, that it would be possible to govern Germany by council from November 1918 on.[61] But Dr. Laufenberg in Hamburg and his colleagues in Berlin very soon discovered the impracticability of this idea—at least for the immediate future. Thereafter, the issue was taken over by the labor movement, and the controversy that followed seemed to embody every one of the major disputes then current among the working classes. The proponents of the councils tended to view them as an infallible nostrum for all the ills of the working classes.

The councils, which were to be organized by plant, were to eliminate the craft concept from the labor movement. The basis of the movement was to be the industry, and no distinction would be made between skilled, semiskilled, and unskilled workers. Democracy would be restored in the movement because the plant organizations would directly elect delegates to represent them in the district, and hence in the national economic council, where general economic and social policies would be negotiated with industry and government. In individual plants employment practices, work rules, and so on would be decided by "codetermination," that is, consultation between the council and management, with the council having a power of veto. It was felt that this system would counteract the undesirable effects of the increasing size and centralization of the unions, and that it would give to labor, through the "right of codetermination," its first real voice in industrial policy. And most important of all, perhaps, was the feeling that the council system would reunite the labor movement. Since the councils would serve both the economic and the political interests of labor, labor political parties would have no more reason to exist.[62]

It does not require an especially astute observer to see that such a system, if instituted, would have also meant the virtual end of trade unions. To be sure, the council advocates in the USPD protested the contrary: the institution of the council system would only "alter" the unions, not dissolve them.[63] But the actual "institution" of councils was neither the major nor the most immediate threat posed by the council system. As far as the unions were concerned there was much more danger in the way the council dispute served to unify and consolidate the various fragments of opposition to the unions, and to interpret this opposition in clearly political terms. Indeed, it was this aspect of the council idea that accounted for the most important and lasting effects of the Laufenberg Government.

As was mentioned earlier, the most significant exercise of governmental power by the Laufenberg Government after November 18, 1918, was through the new Labor Office. The activities of this office were extremely distressing to the trade-union leaders in Hamburg, for Laufenberg used it primarily to stimulate the formation of works councils throughout the large-scale industries of the city.[64] For one thing, these councils completely excluded the unions from negotiations with employers. In a number of instances, Laufenberg arranged for direct negotiations between council and management to establish hours and wages, and to settle other labor disputes.[65] These inroads, however, were fairly temporary and came to an end when the Council Government was dissolved.

But the implications of Laufenberg's encouragement of the councils went much further. In effect, what he had done was to introduce a new element of political and plant organization precisely among those groups where the organizational techniques of the unions and the SPD had been least effective, where opposition to the unions was strongest, and where the level of political participation had been lowest (see Chapter 8). For the first time, there was an organizational nucleus around which all those who had long held grievances against the SPD and the trade unions might gather. On the one hand, the councils provided the bases of USPD support, and on the other, the means by which the dissatisfied industrial workers might gain control of the old unions and remake them according to their own design. Although Laufenberg did not succeed in building a basis of support sufficiently strong to keep him in office, the seeds he planted during that time grew very rapidly and flourished. The council movement spread quickly throughout Hamburg's large-scale industries.[66]

Under the circumstances, it is scarcely surprising that the leaders of the Free Unions took a dim view of this development. The basic trade-union position in regard to the councils is well illustrated in this statement by Carl Legien, chairman of the executive of the ADGB in Berlin:

> The council system would not be a feasible kind of organization.... There is no purpose whatever to be served by a council system; and an incorporation of the councils into the present system of labor organizations would be unthinkable.[67]

But in spite of the unions' hostility and the SPD's marked lack of interest, the council system engendered a wave of enthusiasm that could not be entirely ignored.[68] Almost certainly as an attempt to placate the labor movement and to demonstrate their willingness to compromise with the left, the leaders of the SPD and the ADGB finally approved the inclusion of the council system in the Weimar Constitution, albeit in a highly modified form.[69]

As early as May 1919, well before the acceptance of the Weimar

Constitution, a draft of a proposed law establishing the works councils was published. With minor alterations, it became the law of the land on February 4, 1920.[70] To the dismay of the council advocates, however, the law gave the councils only a token "right of codetermination" (their power was merely advisory), and set them up in a way that virtually guaranteed their subordination to the existing trade unions.[71] If a plant was already controlled by the ADGB, the council was simply integrated into the union organization. The elections to the councils were conducted by the unions, candidates had to be union members, and so on.[72] Moreover, the councils could only negotiate within the scope of the collective agreement made by the unions.

On the basis of what we have observed about the nature of the council movement, it is obvious that this plan fell far short of many expectations. The basic form of the labor movement would not in any way be altered. The November Agreement would stand as before, the bureaucratic structure of the trade unions would remain, and the industrial workers would, at best, be only slightly better off than before. In fact, the kind of council envisioned in the draft law would only provide a new unit of trade-union organization in the plant.[73]

The reaction in Hamburg to the new law was immediate and violent. Several works councils got together at once, and sent telegrams to Berlin demanding that the law be changed. Then they proceeded to organize a Committee of Nine to unify the existing councils in opposition to the law.[74] On May 30, representatives from all the Hamburg works councils met and declared their opposition to the draft:

> The . . . meeting . . . unanimously raises the sharpest protest against the . . . draft law concerning the factory councils. This law would take away the last achievements of the revolution and would completely return to the entrepreneurs and the capitalists control over all economic life. This draft flatly contradicts [the wishes of] the organized proletariat, and shows how unlikely the present Reich Government is to accomplish anything significant.[75]

That this was not considered merely a meeting of a handful of flaming radicals from the shipyards is shown by the fact that the newly elected SPD-dominated Workers' Council was very careful in its dealings with the Committee of Nine, and even sent representatives to negotiate with it.[76]

But in Hamburg, as in Berlin and elsewhere, the protests and negotiations had little effect on the law. For, in spite of severe opposition, which included nationwide protest meetings of works councils in July and October of 1919, the law remained essentially unchanged.[77] The Free Unions set about constructing an imposing administrative structure to see that the councils remained firmly under union control.[78] Although their efforts to do so were considerable, they succeeded only in part. The councils continued to serve as the primary focus of opposition to the unions throughout the Weimar period.

The publication of the draft law in May 1919, and the opposition it aroused, did have, however, some extremely important results in Hamburg, results that could scarcely have been more at odds with the policies of the Free Unions and the SPD. In the Committee of Nine, the opposition elements in Hamburg had a single representative organ for the first time since the fall of the Laufenberg Government in January.* Moreover, as the above quotation clearly shows, the opposition addressed its protest not to the unions (as it had on previous occasions)[79] but to the Reich Government. To the opposition, it was now obvious that an unholy alliance existed between the employers, who opposed an "effective" council law, and the union leaders, who supported the November Agreement and opposed reform proposals, and the politicians of the SPD, who were largely responsible for the draft law.[80]

The consolidation of the opposition within the labor movement in Hamburg could not have come at a more inopportune time. For, when a serious crisis, the *Sülze* Riots, broke out in June, the Committee of Nine was still in existence. It then became the Com-

* Divided on the issue, the USPD leadership did not serve as the unifying force. Compare USPD, *Handbuch für die Wähler der USPD, Reichstagswahl 1920,* Heft 3, pp. 232–34; and *Hamburger Volks-Zeitung* (June 13, 1919), "Beilage."

mittee of Twelve, and, as may be recalled, assumed the leadership of the "proletarian" military forces in Hamburg.[81]

The significance of this development for the politics of labor in Hamburg can scarcely be overestimated. The transition of the Committee of Nine, formed to oppose the Council Law, to the Committee of Twelve was accomplished by the addition of three representatives from the Volkswehr.[82] Opposition to the social and economic policies of the SPD, to the unions, and to the military was thus united in a single body in response to a single issue. In this case, of course, it was summarily dealt with by the forces of General von Lettow-Vorbeck.

The spring of 1919 very decidedly marks the end of a period in the development of the left opposition in the Hamburg labor movement. Thereafter there were two very important changes that profoundly altered the nature of labor politics. One was in the role played by the Free Unions, and the other in the form of the opposition itself. By June 1919, the extremely destructive effects of the political controversy raging within the trade unions had begun to be acutely felt by the ADGB's national leadership. Events much like those in Hamburg had been occurring all over Germany, with the result that union leaders everywhere were being divided into two warring camps. The extent of the split became painfully apparent at the national congress of the ADGB in June 1919 at Nuremberg. At one point, a full third of the deputies cast their ballots against the union leadership.[83] This congress was an extremely important one from several standpoints. First of all, the centralization of the federation was carried still further by an increase in the number of appointive offices and other changes.[84] But more important, the ADGB significantly altered its political policy. According to the resolution:

> This agreement [Mannheim] had as a presupposition a unified political representation of the German workers. This presupposition is no longer valid. The split of the SPD also endangers the unity and solidarity of the German trade unions. The Congress of Trade Unions, accordingly, finds it necessary to declare the neutrality of the trade unions in regard to the political parties.[85]

As we shall see, the word "neutrality" had a rather special meaning in this context, but there is no doubt concerning the general significance of the statement. The Free Unions were formally dissociating themselves from the policies of the SPD. This, of course, did not mean that the unions would no longer support the SPD, quite the contrary, but it did mean that the policies of unions and party were to be separate. Henceforth the unions were to occupy themselves with the critical job of uniting the working classes.[86] The change in union policy outlined in the Nuremberg proclamation had in fact begun to take place some time before the congress met. With the exception of the stand taken by one group of unions at the time of the Bremen crisis, the unions in Hamburg were conspicuously absent from the military conflicts of the spring of 1919.

Although the new policy had its negative aspects, it also contained certain very important positive features. The position of the leadership of the Free Unions, on the basis of the November Agreement, the Weimar Constitution, and certain union regulations, was very strong. During the latter half of 1919, this strength was used to initiate an intensive campaign to bring the union membership under control. Some unions, making use of the strong centralizing provisions in their constitutions, simply replaced radical local leaders with "more reliable" men.[87] And mass expulsions of leftists from union ranks were apparently also common.[88] The Hamburg ADGB, in spite of a huge influx of new members, reported a slight membership loss between 1920 and 1921 "to some extent because of the policy of expulsion."[89] More indirect methods were also used. In Hamburg, during the summer of 1919, several leftist workers were dismissed from their jobs as a result of the demands of their trade-union "colleagues."[90] On some occasions, this latter technique was apparently accomplished simply by means of a demonstration or strike. But, in at least one case, opportunity for such "disciplinary" action was written into the contract between the union and management. If a worker was expelled from the union, the employer was forced to fire him.[91]

These new aggressive policies of the ADGB, combined with other events in the spring of 1919, considerably altered the conditions under which the left opposition could operate. The threat of losing one's job in Hamburg, at a time when unemployment figures continued to mount, was a serious one.* No doubt many workers preferred to suppress their dissatisfactions rather than run the risk of coming into conflict with their union. Moreover, the Council Law would probably not be changed, and it seemed quite apparent that the ADGB was going to make the most of the provisions guaranteeing its control over the councils. And, in addition, the military occupation of the city seemed to presage a tougher attitude on the part of the state.

The SPD's handling of the Committee of Twelve gives us some idea of the difficulties confronting the left opposition at this time. The very prominent role played by the Committee in Hamburg's "June days," had caused considerable concern among the members of the SPD-controlled Workers' Council. The latter, after all, claimed to represent the council movement in Hamburg, and was not favorably disposed toward competition. Accordingly, the Workers' Council took steps to bring the Committee under control. Three representatives were sent from the Council to serve permanently on the Committee of Twelve, and it was officially declared an organ of the Council.[92]

Some time after the rather confused national congress of works councils in Halle in July 1919 (to which the Committee sent deputies), the Committee of Twelve came together to elect deputies for the next national congress, to be held the following month.[93] On this occasion, some representatives of the right wing of the USPD, in alliance with the SPD representatives from the Workers' Council, were apparently able to gain control of the Committee. They immediately passed a resolution calling for the merging of the Committee with the Hamburg ADGB.[94] This was followed

* See the compilation of unemployment statistics in ADGB-Hamburg, *Bericht 1922*, p. 11. In August 1919, there were 66,000 unemployed in Hamburg. For comparison, in August of the following year the figure was 26,000.

by another resolution, put forward by an SPD member, pointing out that the work of the Committee was accordingly finished, that "in spite of all the trouble and confusion it has caused," it had not fulfilled its objectives, and that it should be considered dissolved.[95]

But the works-council movement in Hamburg was not so easily disposed of. In September, a full assembly of the works councils of the city was convened to consider these resolutions. The SPD representative who attempted to present the motion calling for the end of the Committee of Twelve was scarcely able to make himself heard over the outcries of protest. The meeting was thereupon forcibly dissolved (Hamburg remained under martial law through December 1919) amid considerable disorder, and it was ordered that no new committee be formed.[96]

Events such as these must have made the leaders of the left opposition wonder whether they could ever fulfill any of their objectives without coming sharply into conflict either with the mobilized power of the trade-union organization or with the entire political system of the Weimar Republic. The oft-encountered "dilemma of democratic socialism" confronted the far left in a new and critical form.[97] How would it be possible to support the Republic, from which labor had derived such gains and in which, basically, most USPD leaders believed, and still fulfill the objectives of the radical left? How could one, in other words, work for social democracy (according to the USPD definition) without opposing the political democracy already in existence?

This dilemma led a number of USPD leaders to reconsider their policies in several respects, especially those concerning the trade unions. In Hamburg a "right wing" of the USPD, led by Bergmann, a member of the local executive of the USPD and the Committee of Twelve, had begun to form early in 1919.[98] At the same time, a similar development was taking place throughout Germany.[99] To this "right wing" of the USPD it seemed apparent that "the first phase of the revolution . . . had come to an end," and that "the changed situation demanded a changed tactic on the part of the USPD." For one thing, "the trade unions had once again become the principal bearers of the economic movement of the working classes."[100] Ultimately, these leaders came to the conclusion that they must work through and with the trade unions for the attainment of socialism.[101] There was, of course, also a "left wing" of the USPD (representing the majority of the party, as it turned out), which continued its adherence to the council idea and its opposition to the unions. This was one of the divisions which split the USPD convention in Leipzig late in 1919, and which contributed to the final breakup of the party in Halle in October 1920.[102]

In Hamburg the division among USPD leaders was clearly reflected in the party's highly ambivalent attitude toward the Committee of Twelve. The Committee was by no means an organ of the party, and while some USPD leaders, such as Bergmann, did belong, others equally prominent did not.[103] Indeed, if the USPD leadership had been unified in its policies concerning the council system in May there would have been no need for the representatives of the works councils to create the Committee of Twelve in the first place. In the end Bergmann was probably among those who supported the dissolution of the Committee in September 1919.*

In addition to the two wings of the USPD, there were also several factions that comprised a small but growing Communist movement. In Hamburg the Communists were for a time led by Laufenberg.[104] Apparently largely in protest of certain provisions of the Versailles Treaty, Laufenberg wanted to mount a crusade against the Entente, a crusade led by the German proletariat in alliance with the Soviet Union and perhaps with the German Army. This policy was sometimes referred to as "National Bolshevism."† Condemned by Lenin, "National Bolshevism" soon lost favor, and

* Bergmann appears on the Vorstand of the Hamburg SPD after the unification of the parties in 1922. See SPD-Hamburg, *Jahresbericht 1921–24,* pp. 46–47.

† Ruth Fischer, *Stalin and German Communism* (Cambridge, 1948), pp. 90–96; Schüddekopf, *Linke Leute von Rechts* (Stuttgart, 1960), pp. 107–20. Laufenberg's colleague, Fritz Wolffheim, was not involved in the Hamburg KPD, but in that of the neighboring Prussian city of Altona.

Laufenberg became associated with a segment of the Communist movement known as the Communist Workers' Party of Germany (KAPD). For our purposes, the importance of the KAPD lies particularly in its totally negative attitude toward the Republic and trade unions. This "left wing" of the Communists believed that participation in elections and membership in trade unions was a violation of the true revolutionary spirit. In its refusal to deal with the bureaucracies of union or party, this movement was perhaps closest to the council movement of earlier days. But it also included a kind of syndicalist or anarchist emphasis on "direct action"—sabotage, bomb-throwing, and the like.[105]

Reliable evidence on the strength of Communist movements in Hamburg is lacking, but none of the accounts of the events of 1919 indicate that the Communists played a very prominent role.* On the basis of what we have observed about the origins of the left opposition, it seems extremely unlikely that any movement with such a policy toward the unions could, in any case, have had much continuing success.

As might be imagined, the confusion that reigned among the leaders of the left opposition over the tactics to be used under the new conditions was scarcely conducive to effective action. At the time of the Kapp Putsch, for example, the effects of the successful general strike of March 13–17, 1920, were almost totally negated by a hodge-podge of proclamations and demands by the various leftist

* The development of the KPD is treated in detail in Chapter 6. Before 1920, it is extremely doubtful whether anything one could call a "Communist Party" really existed in Hamburg. There are occasional mentions of "Communists" in the newspapers and in the reports of the Arbeiterrat (e.g., p. 59 in *Jahresbericht 1919–20*). However, a check on a number of these references reveals that "Communist" was a very loose term which was used to describe any of a multitude of varieties of left radicals. It is likely that Laufenberg had a number of followers and that they called themselves "Communists," but they were important because of their connection with the *Betriebsräte* movement, not because of their organization into a party. The Communists, therefore, have been included here under the general heading of "left opposition." In addition, of course, the KPD was illegal until shortly before the election of 1920. See Rettig's unpub. diss., "Die Gewerkschaftsarbeit der KPD" (Hamburg, 1954), pp. 20–23; compare Schüddekopf, *Linke Leute von Rechts* (Stuttgart, 1960), p. 108.

groups. The USPD wanted to continue the strike until the workers were allowed to keep the weapons they had been issued.[106] They made two attempts to do so: on one occasion, they were supported by a meeting of the works councils, on the other, only by some representatives of the DMV.[107] The SPD and the Free Unions, of course, took the position that if the workers wanted to be armed, they could join the Einwohnerwehr.[108] Their proclamation called upon the workers of Hamburg to return to their jobs.[109] The strikes continued for a while in a few shipyards, but eventually most of the strikers did return to work.[110] One or two shipyard owners used the occasion as an excuse to eliminate the strikers permanently from their payrolls.[111]

The Kapp Putsch showed how deceptive was the apparent strength of the labor movement. No segment of the labor movement really succeeded in accomplishing its objectives. The ADGB, of course, fell far short of the ambitious demands put forth by its national leadership.[112] And as the *Echo* wryly pointed out in the weeks following, the joint ADGB-SPD demands of "punishment of all treasonable people" and "democratization of the administration" were not very fully complied with by the Government in Berlin.[113] Moreover, those Hamburg workers who had so firmly displayed their loyalty to the Republic were paid for their efforts in layoffs and new overtime requirements.[114] The Workers' Council could not even persuade the employers to pay the wages the workers had lost while striking in support of the Republic.[115]

There was a new bitterness in the air after the Kapp Putsch. Left and right faced one another more squarely than before. From the standpoint of the left opposition, the show of strength by the right radicals provided a stimulus for new action. In March 1920, however, the left opposition was in no condition for action. That growing current of dissatisfaction that had been channeled into an impressive political force by the USPD was now diffused among any number of would-be leaders, each with his own idea of the direction to be followed.

A little less than a month after the Kapp Putsch, a new kind of left opposition began to take shape in Hamburg. On April 1, 1920, the USPD ordered all but two of its Bürgerschaft deputies to withdraw from that chamber because of their ideological shortcomings. One of those remaining was Ernst Thälmann, soon to become a prominent leader in the Communist Party (KPD), both in Hamburg and Berlin.[116] The aims and methods of the Communist organization opened up a new phase in the development of the politics of labor in Hamburg. The aggressiveness and vitality of the Communist movement, together with the unscrupulousness of many of its leaders, posed an extremely dangerous threat both to organized labor and to democratic labor politics. In Hamburg, as in many other parts of the world, the Communist movement was to put liberal democracy to a severe and costly test of strength.

*Chapter 6*

# The Decline of the Hamburg Labor Movement

In 1920 it was still possible for the Hamburg labor movement to unite, if only briefly, to help turn back the enemies of the Republic. The official publication of the Free Unions in Berlin could then proudly proclaim: "We are more aware than ever that the destiny of the Republic depends upon the strength of the working classes, and we have accepted the responsibility of protecting the Fatherland against reaction."[1] Four years later, it was all the unions could do to protect themselves. The story of the decline of the labor movement in Hamburg, and elsewhere in Germany, contains two basic elements: the rise of the Communist Party and the Great Inflation of 1923. Together these forces reduced the proud old Hamburg labor movement to a weakened state from which it never fully recovered during the Weimar period.

Certainly, the Communists did not create the divisions in the labor movement. These had existed well before the First World War, and during the revolutionary period they had formed the basis of an important political force, the USPD. But the KPD, more than any other party, was able to capitalize on the dissatisfaction within the labor movement. How this was done and how the rest of the labor movement responded, or failed to respond, to the KPD threat provides the unifying theme in the development of Hamburg labor politics between 1920 and 1924.

In Hamburg, as elsewhere, the history of the Communist movement is involved and confusing. Splits and countersplits, heated controversy over this or that point of doctrine, and a variety of tactical shifts followed one another in rapid succession. But from the standpoint of the labor movement, one aspect of Communist policy remained constant throughout the period. The leaders of the Hamburg KPD, more than any of their predecessors or competitors, recognized the necessity of tying a leftist political program to a program of labor reform. They drew the conclusion that the struggle for labor's political loyalties would have to be fought out in the plant, and they fought it there.

The Communist approach to winning political support from labor was formulated in a secret conference held by the illegal KPD in August 1919. At that time, the Spartakist policy of nonparticipation in elections and trade unions was replaced by a policy that called for the use of all political means (which included votes, trade unions, and works councils) to achieve the party's goals.[2] Thereafter, the party engaged in a number of heated battles over the so-called trade-union question. In the first of these battles Laufenberg and Wolffheim were expelled from the party, largely because of their desire to use sabotage and other "direct" means of action.[3] From time to time, others followed them. For a brief period after 1924, the Communists experimented with forming their own unions, in Hamburg, at least, with scant success.[4] Throughout this period the basic policy of the Communists was the same, although it was sometimes called "United Front," and sometimes "To the Masses!"[5] The KPD waged an aggressive and unrelenting campaign to win the loyalties of the worker in the plant, with the hope of bringing him ultimately into the voting booth, and occasionally out onto the streets.

The maneuverings by which the United Communist Party (VKPD)* established itself in Hamburg are obscure. It is clear that the "purge" of the USPD Bürgerschaft fraction on April 1, 1920, was the first important step. Almost all of those who re-

* This title was sometimes used to refer to the KPD after the merger with the KAPD in December 1920. Ossip K. Flechtheim *Die Kommunistische Partei Deutschlands in der Weimar Republic* (Offenbach, 1848), pp. 71–72.

mained in the reorganized fraction were to reappear as Communist deputies after 1921. On the other hand, many of those who were expelled from the USPD fraction could be found among the SPD leadership by 1922.[6] By the end of 1920 Ernst Thälmann and Hugo Urbahns had emerged as the two principal leaders of Hamburg Communism.[7]

The dialogue in Hamburg between Urbahns and Thälmann reflects on a small scale the basic division in German Communism that lasted at least until 1926.[8] The constant shifting of doctrinal standpoints in response to events makes it impossible to neatly categorize groups of Communist leaders. But, in general, the schoolteacher Urbahns may be thought of as belonging to the group of intellectual Communists that centered around Paul Levi, Karl Radek, and Heinrich Brandler. As a rule this group tended to favor a kind of pressure-group role for the party; they felt that KPD participation in the trade unions and the works councils would ultimately force the labor movement to integrate both Communists and Communist doctrines.[9] Thälmann, on the other hand, was an ex-sailor and dockworker, apparently rather inarticulate, but still a very effective "proletarian" leader because of his dramatic, dynamic manner. Often while making an impassioned speech, he would rip off his shirt collar, as if losing patience with the constrictions of conventional society.[10] From the start, Thälmann represented a more "bolshevist" point of view. He believed that vigorous revolutionary action, not cooperation with groups further to the right, would be the means by which the masses were to be won over to Communism.[11] What Ruth Fischer calls the "unquenchable antagonism" between these two leaders was a factor of very great importance in the development of the KPD in Hamburg.[12]

Although the Hamburg Communist leadership could frequently disagree on how the party should operate, there was very little disagreement in those early years about where it should operate. As the national party newspaper once observed, "Elections to works councils are more important than elections to the Reichstag.

The destiny of the working classes does not depend upon any parliamentary election, but upon this struggle [in the plant]."[13] The basic Communist organization was, therefore, the "plant fraction." All Communist workers in any given plant were automatically members of the fraction, which met at least once every week to agree upon tactics, hear new policies, and so on.[14] When a union or works-council meeting was to take place, the Communist fraction met shortly before it began and decided its position, in order to present a united front. Workers who failed to attend such sessions were frequently sought out at their homes and urged to come along.[15] An "action committee" was formed from the most active Communists in each fraction to serve as the basic unit of control and agitation. The leaders of these committees dealt directly with the local controlling body, the Hamburg Executive Committee (Vorstand).[16]

One result of the organizational form adopted by the Communists was that the annual works-council elections soon evolved into heated partisan contests. Several lists of candidates were usually submitted for election; each list had to be endorsed by three eligible plant employees.[17] At first the Communist fraction in the plant simply submitted a "Communist list," which all Communist workers were supposed to support.[18] The advantages inherent in this technique are obvious. While the votes of the non-Communist workers might be scattered among a dozen or so lists, the Communist votes went as a bloc. Since the list that won a simple plurality of all votes cast won the election, a Communist minority might well be in a position to rule the plant council.[19] Later, because of countermeasures from the trade unions, the Communists took to submitting lists identified only as "trade-union lists," but the effect was the same as before.[20]

Works-council elections gave the Communists an opportunity to identify disagreements within a union or a plant with a political standpoint. In a very adept way, the Communists merged national political issues with specific plant problems, and presented the amalgam as the platform of the "Communist List." An attack on a national economic or social policy of the SPD, for example, might appear side by side with a demand for increased wages.[21] Moreover, the Communists waged vigorous and extended pre-election campaigns in order to bring the Communist message home to as many workers as possible.[22]

Having once won control, or perhaps merely a strong position, in a works council, the Communists used their authority in a manner calculated to appeal to workers in the large industries. They very quickly became the champions of the movement for industrial unionism. In several instances, the Communist-controlled works councils in a number of plants in the same industry attempted to form an industry-wide "Group Council," which in practice would have functioned as a local industrial union.[23] The Communists also strongly advocated the formation of a giant dockworkers' union, and were apparently instrumental in bringing about at least one merger of two large industrial unions in 1922.[24]

The response of the Free Unions to the Communist threat was very similar to their response to trade-union opposition in 1919. During the summer of 1920, when the first plant-council elections were being held under the new law, the national ADGB announced its policy on the works councils: all members must belong to a trade union, and no member could run for election on an opposition list. The ADGB also established a complex organizational pattern designed to ensure union control over the elections.[25] Several unions adopted strict regulations aimed at limiting Communist activity. A worker might be expelled, for example, for cooperating with a Communist fraction, for having his name on a Communist election list, or for attending any conference of the KPD.[26]

During the early years of Communist activity in Hamburg, the SPD, in a striking departure from previous policy, entered plant politics. Perhaps in imitation of the Communists, the Hamburg Social Democrats began to establish fractions in local plants. And, like the Communist organizations, the SPD fractions also elected action committees to distribute party propaganda and to campaign for works-council elections.[27] At first these SPD plant units seem to have caused some consternation among ADGB leaders, but generally there was a great deal of cooperation between the two organizations.[28]

Perhaps as much in response to this cooperation with the SPD as in response to the Communist threat, the Hamburg ADGB came very close to stepping over the line drawn by the national congress concerning political activity. A few weeks before the Bürgerschaft election in February 1921, the Hamburg Free Unions sent out to each party a list of nine points constituting the policy wishes of the trade unions.[29] Two days before the election, the Hamburg ADGB distributed 100,000 copies of a handbill listing both the nine points and the response of each party to them. As it turned out, only the SPD and USPD were in full agreement with every point. "No votes," urged the handbill, "to any party that does not recognize just trade-union demands and that will not stand up for them."[30] The policy of the SPD in the election, similarly, was that "we must with the same sharpness guard against attack from the left as well as the right."[31]

In spite of the considerable efforts of the Free Unions and the SPD, Communist strength was clearly on the increase early in 1921. The first proof of that fact was the 59,000 votes won by the KPD in the Bürgerschaft election. The second proof came a month later, at the time of the so-called "March Action."

## THE "MARCH ACTION"

At first glance, Hamburg in early 1921 would not appear to be a particularly favorable spot for a revolutionary attempt. For the first time since the end of the war, unemployment figures were down, and wages were on the rise.[32] But it was precisely these conditions that seem to have brought about a wave of strikes, many of which were called against the wishes of the ADGB. Early in March, the machinists, dockworkers, transportation workers, and others had conducted such strikes, largely to obtain higher wages.[33] This wave of strikes, coupled with the success of the Hamburg

KPD in the Bürgerschaft elections the preceding month, was apparently enough to make a number of Hamburg Communists feel more optimistic about the growing strength of the party.

On March 23, 1921, the Communist newspaper in Hamburg proclaimed a general strike in support of a strike in Mansfeld where armed Communists, led by the romantic Max Hölz, were engaged in a small but bloody civil war. The Hamburg Communists called upon the workers to take up their weapons and occupy the factories.[34] The first response to the strike call was a mass meeting of unemployed workers at the Heiligengeistfeld, a large field at the edge of town. Then the demonstrators marched to the harbor and forced their way into one of the largest dockyards, Blohm and Voss.[35] There they demanded jobs, and ordered the employees to join them in a general strike. The second demand set off a battle between the workers who wished to comply and those who did not; it ended in the departure of the latter. The strikers then took over the plant, sounded the siren to proclaim the strike, and hoisted a red flag over the administration building of Blohm and Voss. Similar scenes took place in several other dockyards. Later in the day, another mass meeting was called, but this time the demonstrators encountered a formidable array of Ordnungspolizei drawn up to prevent just such a meeting. Inevitably, shooting broke out, and violence spread to other parts of the city. By the time darkness had fallen and order had been restored, nineteen had been killed and forty-two wounded.[36]

In general, the March Action hurt the Hamburg labor movement. A number of important dockyards used the demonstrations as an excuse to close down entirely, refusing to reopen until the workers had made certain concessions. The works councils were thenceforth to be considered merely "negotiating committees"; they could not even advise unless requested to do so. "Disciplinary action" was taken against several hundred workers: they were simply not rehired. Apparently, SPD as well as Communist workers were so "disciplined," and the SPD report claims that the dock owners had taken advantage of the occasion to remove troublesome union representatives along with the "irresponsible agitators."[37] The March Action led to a perceptible hardening of attitude toward the labor movement among the police, the Senate, and the city's businessmen.[38]

As far as the Communists themselves were concerned, the attempted insurrection in Hamburg (and the one in Central Germany) showed quite clearly that the party had still a long way to go before it could take power by such means. Accordingly, the balance in the party tilted somewhat in the direction of the more moderate wing (in Hamburg represented by Urbahns); as a result, an even greater value was placed upon effective work in the plants.[39]

In the months following the March Action, the Hamburg Communists made strenuous efforts to regain their former position among labor, apparently with considerable success. By early 1922 the Communists had gained control of a number of important works councils in the transportation and textile industries, and were making broad gains everywhere in the harbor.[40] In November 1921 an election of delegates to an international dockworkers' conference was held, and of the six delegates chosen, three were KPD, two SPD, and one USPD.[41] A survey of twelve important industries in Hamburg, most of which were located in the harbor, showed that the KPD could claim ninety-two of 148 works-council members, while the USPD and SPD together accounted for only fifty-three.[42]

In spite of the rising strength of the Communist movement in Hamburg, the climate in the spring of 1922 was unusually favorable for increased cooperation among the city's various labor organizations. For one thing, the Communists had learned a lesson from the failure of the March Action. As a result, the moderate wing in the party was for a time in a stronger position than it had been before. This shift was made evident at the seventh congress of the KPD (Jena, August 1921) by the adoption of the policy known as the United Front.[43]

It is difficult to define the term "united front" as it was used in

Hamburg in 1921. Part of the confusion arises from the fact that it was interpreted by the two wings of the KPD in very different ways. To the Urbahns wing of the Hamburg KPD, the United Front was somewhat like the USPD's 1919 policy. They interpreted it to mean cooperation with the SPD and the Free Unions in order, first, to save the Republic from the right radicals, and, second, to make themselves strong enough to be able to force the non-Communist labor organizations to recognize their legitimacy as a labor party.[44]

To the left wing of the party (Thälmann), however, the "United Front" was seen more as a tactical diversion, a feigned cooperation by means of which the leaders of the Free Unions and the SPD might be discredited. At the same time, it was hoped that through such cooperation the Communists might be able to enter at least the provincial governments. Once there, the Communists would be able to use governmental powers to strengthen the party, obtain arms, and so on. During 1922 and 1923, dispute over this policy dominated the German Communist Party.[45]

In the spring of 1922, however, Urbahns was still in control of the Hamburg party organization, and the United Front was carried out in the form of offers to run joint lists with the SPD in works-council elections, to cooperate in wage demands, and so on.[46] At about the same time the United Front was developing in the KPD, a somewhat similar movement was taking place in the ADGB. For the first time, the leaders of the Free Unions expressed a certain willingness to compromise with the opposition, quite in contrast to the "hard line" taken in 1919 and 1920. In Hamburg, and probably elsewhere, the unions' experiences in the March Action made them realize the futility of trying to wage a two-front war. Attacked first by the Communists, the unions helped to put down the rising, only to be attacked by the employers in return. The report of the Hamburg ADGB for 1922 reflects a rising bitterness toward their erstwhile allies to the right and an awareness of the very great dangers that confronted the labor movement.[47]

At its national convention in 1922, the ADGB showed a more conciliatory attitude toward the far left by virtually abandoning the November Agreement, which had been such a sore point, and by promising a vigorous campaign for the organization of new industrial unions.[48] In Hamburg the ADGB leadership spoke out in favor of the unity of all labor representatives in the Workers' Council, asked for a unified May Day demonstration in 1921, and appeared much more interested in the well-being of all workers, regardless of their political orientation, than it had been in the previous two years.[49] The catalyst for these very tentative attempts to close the gap between the left and the right wings of the Hamburg labor movement was an outburst of radical-nationalist violence in the spring of 1922. This wave of violence, which had been sweeping over Germany since the summer of 1921, first hit Hamburg in May 1922. A series of bomb explosions shook the city; among the targets were the "Monument of the Revolution of 1918," the office of the Communist newspaper, and the home of Ernst Thälmann. The perpetrators, some of whom were apprehended, proved to be members of a rightist terror group called "Organisation Consul."[50]

The response of the KPD was surprising. Instead of a call to arms, Urbahns quietly issued a proposal to the SPD to hold a massive joint demonstration in protest of the rightist attacks.[51] The Social Democrats, perhaps distrustful of the KPD's motives, delayed giving an answer time and again. To the dismay of the "bolshevist" element in the Hamburg KPD, Urbahns continued to negotiate, and refrained from unilateral action.[52] The matter was settled finally on June 24 by the murder of German Foreign Minister Walter Rathenau by members of "Organisation Consul."[53] The response of the labor movement was immediate. The ADGB, from its national congress in Leipzig, issued a call for a one-day general strike "in defense of the Republic."[54] The leaders of all the German labor organizations, including the Communists', formed a national strike committee, and on June 27 shops and factories throughout Germany remained closed.[55] Once more, as at the time of the Kapp Putsch, the labor movement formed solid ranks in defense of the Republic.

In Hamburg, labor's impressive protest of June 27, 1922, had an ironic and tragic end. The day of the general strike was marked by a huge mass meeting at the Heiligengeistfeld, called by a joint proclamation of all the labor organizations in Hamburg.[56] At the end of the meeting thousands of workers filled the surrounding streets, which were lined with Ordnungspolizei. A group of policemen, finding themselves unable to control the direction of the mass of men in accordance with their instructions, apparently panicked and opened fire. One worker was killed, and four seriously wounded.*

The events of June 27 were repeated in other parts of Germany, and the national KPD leadership interpreted them as proof of the fundamental antagonism between the Republic and the proletariat. Consequently they decided against further cooperation with the unions and the SPD. A demonstration was held on July 4 without the participation of the Communists.[57] In Hamburg the followers of Thälmann now had a strong talking point in arguing against any further attempts at that sort of united front.[58] There were no further unified demonstrations in Hamburg throughout the Weimar period.

The outcome of the demonstration of June 27 in Hamburg is a dramatic illustration of what one is tempted to call the "irreversibility" of the events of this period. Many among the working classes, remembering all too well the events of the spring of 1919, harbored a deep hostility toward the police. It was perhaps inevitable that contact between crowds of workers and police units should lead to conflict. And in the end, this antagonism between workers and police, both of whom presumably considered themselves the defenders of the Republic, operated very much against the Republic's interests.

* A Bürgerschaft committee, formed to investigate the matter, found the police at fault and recommended changes in the techniques of handling crowds. Lothar Danner, *Ordnungspolizei Hamburg* (Hamburg, 1958), pp. 55–62.

## THE GERMAN OCTOBER

By the time most of the excitement generated by the murder of Walter Rathenau had subsided, traces of a much greater crisis to come were already visible in Hamburg. In September 1922, there were 28,000 unemployed in the city, the highest number for that month since 1919.[59] And prices had already begun that dizzying upward spiral which was to reach such incredible heights by the end of 1923.[60] The occupation of the Ruhr by French and Belgian forces in January 1923 ushered in one of the most fateful years in Germany's history. The fantastic inflation, the catastrophic policy of "passive resistance," violent separatist movements in the Rhineland and Bavaria, and Hitler's "Beer-hall Putsch" in November—these were the major milestones in that troubled year. Strikes, demonstrations, and wild outbursts of violence came to be commonplace occurrences as wages became valueless in the face of rising prices. The actual extent of unemployment in Hamburg during the inflation is uncertain, but it is clear that it was the greatest the city had ever known.[61] The general situation in Hamburg is aptly described in this *Echo* editorial written at the peak of the inflation:

> The terrible price rises . . . have evoked widespread fear among the population. It is extremely difficult for salary and wage earners to procure even the most necessary foodstuffs; pensioners and the unemployed simply face starvation if they do not receive help at once. The price of bread, which triples from day to day, has aroused particularly intense bitterness. . . . The irresponsible [plundering] raids of young hoodlums are frequently supported by [groups of unemployed workers.][62]

Economic distress of such magnitude presented a grave challenge to the organized labor movement. The organizations themselves were directly struck by the inflation. War chests and strike funds simply evaporated overnight, for the unemployed workers could scarcely pay dues.[63] In Hamburg, as in Berlin, union and SPD leaders were at a loss for a feasible policy. They demanded price controls, uniform unemployment compensation from the national government, a modest program of public works, and an agreement from the employers to scale wages to the rising prices.[64] A program to feed the unemployed was established: during the winter of 1923 to 1924, the Free Unions distributed more than 500,000 hot meals from fourteen locations in the city.[65] This effort was hotly criticized by the Communists, who called for a massive daily distribution of milk, sugar, meat, potatoes, flour, and coal. Long on demands, the Communists were also short on solutions to the problem of how these goods were to be obtained and paid for.[66]

The most acute problem faced by the labor organizations was that of retaining some sort of control over the great mass of unemployed workers. Having no connection with a shop, these workers soon drifted out of reach of the union organization. At any moment of crisis great numbers of these men appeared on the streets, ready to be led in almost any direction. The Communists, of course, made some efforts to win control over the unemployed; they undoubtedly had a certain amount of success, exactly how much is not known. But it is highly unlikely that the Communists were ever able to channel the resentment of the unemployed for the accomplishment of political goals.

In March 1923, for example, a gathering of unemployed workers elected a "Committee of the Unemployed," which was to represent their interests whenever and wherever necessary. As might be expected, the Free Unions objected strenuously to such an organization, and emphasized that "representation of the unemployed can only be practical and successful when [it] is in close connection with the trade unions."[67] The leaders of the ADGB, with the full support of the Workers' Council, attempted to take over the Committee in much the same way they had won control of the Committee of Twelve in 1919. The Workers' Council announced that a formal election was to be held for the Committee of the Unemployed, and that all candidates had to have been trade-union members for at least two years.[68] The already existing

Committee objected strongly to this and other conditions, and submitted a list of candidates in opposition to those put forward by the Free Unions. In the result the Free Union list received only 1,906 votes, while the Committee of the Unemployed received 6,800.[69] As on some other occasions, the Free Unions took their defeat badly. Promptly declaring void the election they themselves had managed, the union leaders announced that henceforth they would deal only with the small minority that had supported the union list.[70]

Although one might suspect that the tactics of the union leaders operated very much in favor of the Communists, there is no evidence to show that the KPD was involved in the election at any stage. The Workers' Council yearbook does not even mention the Communists in connection with these events.[71] The Communist leadership was, in fact, ineffective throughout most of 1923. The KPD did not even take advantage of the opportunities provided by the severe disturbances in Hamburg in mid-August. These disturbances were apparently related to what on the national level was called the "Cuno strike," a strike that culminated in the fall of the Cuno Government and its replacement by one headed by Gustav Stresemann. This was the first government since 1921 to include Social Democratic ministers.[72]

In Hamburg the Cuno strike was touched off on August 11 by the closing, first, of Blohm and Voss and then of all the major dockyards in the city in response to a wage demand.[73] The immediate result was a rash of riots. Food stores were plundered, and groups of workers clashed with police at a number of points throughout the city. Two days later when the dockyards reopened (the Cuno Government had resigned the day before), violence exploded once again. The harbor workers refused to return to work until wages were scaled up to meet a new price rise; they also demanded daily payment of wages.[74] The strike spread rapidly to other industries, and until at least August 15, much of Hamburg's industry was at a standstill. Again, armed clashes between workers and police cost several lives.[75]

Once the strike had broken out, of course, the Hamburg KPD was quick to support it, but it is very unlikely that the Communists had much to do with the initial outbreak. At all events, they were unsuccessful in their attempt to prolong the strike once it had lost its momentum.[76] On one occasion during the strike, the members of several SPD action committees met and emphatically proclaimed that the strike was from "purely economic causes," and had nothing to do with the KPD. This was at a time when the official position of the Hamburg SPD was "back to work."[77] Moreover, none of the accounts of the strike, even those in the *Echo*, describes the outburst as Communist inspired.[78] The failure of the KPD to take "decisive action" in such disturbances led to a virtual revolt of the party's left wing, and to a mounting clamor for a change in party policy.[79] Ruth Fischer and Arkadi Maslow in Berlin and Thälmann in Hamburg became increasingly convinced that the period of retrenchment was over, and that the time had come for the great Communist rising in Germany.

To the leftists, the August strike was proof that the masses were ready to move. The KPD had only to supply the leadership. In Hamburg the Thälmann group gained control over the organization, and passed a resolution urging the central committee in Berlin to prepare for an immediate armed rising.[80]

Perhaps in response to the excited demands of the left wing in the KPD, the Politburo in Moscow summoned Karl Brandler, chairman of the KPD, to Moscow to discuss the situation in Germany with Zinoviev, Trotsky, and other Soviet leaders.[81] On September 1, 1923, a group representing various German left wing organizations also arrived in Moscow, and an agonizing reappraisal of KPD policy ensued.[82] The details of the decision finally reached in Moscow early in September are obscure. Apparently it was agreed in principle that the time for a rising was near, but that the final decision should be left in the hands of Brandler, a spokesman of the more moderate group.[83] It is certain, however, that it was decided that the KPD should enter provincial governments in alliance with the SPD. "United Front" governments were formed shortly afterward in Saxony and Thuringia.[84]

Toward the end of September the crisis of 1923 came to a head. On September 26 Stresemann, under pressure to do something about the economic and political chaos on all sides, declared the policy of "passive resistance" at an end. At the same time he proclaimed a state of national emergency and placed the country under martial law.[85] Civil war threatened in the form of a conflict between the right-wing government led by von Kahr in Bavaria and the new popular-front governments in Saxony and Thuringia. Early in October the latter were sternly warned to stop the steady flow of violent revolutionary propaganda that was stirring up the Bavarians. When the warning was not heeded, the two governments were forcibly deposed by Reichswehr forces on October 21.[86]

Berlin's response to the activities of the united-front governments in Saxony and Thuringia generated considerable excitement in Hamburg. On October 21, before the news of the entry of Reichswehr troops into Saxony had become generally known, a conference of Hamburg dockworkers, who were already out on strike, declared their intention to proclaim a general strike if the Reich moved against Saxony. At various points throughout the city, there were demonstrations and street-corner gatherings in support of the united-front governments. That same afternoon the Hamburg KPD sent Urbahns and two workers to Chemnitz to meet with other Communist leaders and coordinate plans.[87]

The following day, October 22, the feverish tension in Hamburg mounted. The morning papers carried the news of Stresemann's decision to move against Saxony, and military units were moving through Hamburg, apparently on their way to Saxony.[88] That afternoon the Hamburg ADGB called a conference of delegates from all working-class organizations in the city, evidently in an attempt to turn the mounting tide of unrest away from destructive channels. The trade-union proposal was that all organizations should avoid local or isolated actions. Instead, each organization should send a telegram to its national headquarters, urging the unity of all working-class organizations in a concerted general strike throughout Germany. The Communist representatives to the conference opposed this resolution, promising to present their formal position the following day after consultation with the local leadership. By the time the document setting forth their position was delivered the following morning it was no longer necessary. Armed Communist bands had launched their attacks some hours before.[89]

The events of the following two days, October 24 and 25, were subsequently described by Zinoviev as "the brightest spot in the workers' movement in Europe in 1923, and perhaps in the last few years."[90] This could be read as an ironic commentary on the state of world communism in the 'twenties. To the historian the Hamburg rising presents a grim spectacle indeed—a tragic blend of deceit and misinformation that led to useless violence, death, and destruction.

The basic plan for the rising does not seem unrealistic. Shortly before dawn Communist "hundreds" launched simultaneous attacks on the police stations that circled the city center. These attacks had several purposes. It was hoped that a major part of the revolutionary force could be armed with weapons captured from the police arsenals. It was also hoped that these attacks would at least delay the mounting of organized resistance against the rising. Moreover, the Communists hoped that a number of successful attacks might undermine police morale, weakening the will to resist.[91] In most instances, the police were taken totally by surprise, and were, as a consequence, rather easily routed from their strongholds. Seventeen of the twenty-six stations attacked were in Communist hands after the first few hours of the rising. In many cases the rebels withdrew from the stations at once, deploying themselves on surrounding rooftops, from which they could command the important thoroughfares. Barricades and tank traps were constructed to pin down police reinforcements within range of the cross fire from above. The major rail line into Hamburg from the south was blocked to delay the arrival of military reinforcements.[92]

The chief purpose of this military action was not to overthrow the government of the city-state, but to provide the impetus for a mass rising. The Communists felt that if they could delay effective armed resistance for a short time, the immediate fear of police retaliation would be removed, and the masses would then rise in rebellion behind the Communist leaders. Therefore, a major part of the revolutionary force was assigned to "agitation" in the streets, while the rest fought off the police from the rooftops.[93] It is only in the context of this plan that one can appreciate the true pathos of the Hamburg rising. The military part of the plan was, for the most part, efficiently and successfully executed. And then—nothing happened! There was no mass rising, no demonstration, no general strike. The soldiers of the "Red hundreds," who had in many cases fought well and bravely, were isolated on their rooftops and behind their barricades. By noon on the twenty-third, the Ordnungspolizei had begun to recover from the shock of the attack, and their overwhelming superiority in men and weapons began to make itself felt in one part of the city after another. From then on it was just a matter of time. The armored cars, backed up by police machine guns and hand grenades, cleared the streets. The rebels vanished from the rooftops. By nightfall of the twenty-fourth, only a few isolated pockets of resistance remained. What was to have been the "German October" was over after thirty-six hours, at the cost of seventeen policemen killed and twenty-six wounded, with probably somewhat higher casualties among the Communists.[94]

What had gone wrong? There is little doubt that the Hamburg leaders expected their action to be just one part of a great revolution that would sweep over all Germany on October 23.[95] This expectation was the major element in their belief that the masses would quickly line up behind the "hundreds." But the rest of Germany remained quiet. The Communists were certainly aware of the fact that even in the early hours of the rising, when there was little news concerning events in the rest of Germany, the Hamburg working classes were remarkably indifferent and even hostile to the movement.[96] On the day of the rising most went to their jobs as usual, paying no heed to the proclamations of general strike. Throughout the two days, the Communist cadre fought in almost total isolation. The dockworkers, to be sure, were out on strike, but they had left the plants several days before the rising.[97] And their strike continued for several days after the Communists had admitted defeat and called off the general strike.[98] The two actions appear to have been unrelated. Surely this is one of the most interesting aspects of the rising. Although the Communists clearly enjoyed substantial support in a number of industries in Hamburg, and were to win some 114,000 votes seven months later in the Reichstag election, they could muster only a very small degree of support for the armed rising. Obviously, a certain amount of care must be used in evaluating the criteria of Communist strength. It is also interesting to note that both the Communists and the police cited insufficient contact with the workers as the major cause of their respective failures.[99] Unfortunately, it was rather late in the day for all concerned to discover the extent to which they had allowed a large element of the working classes to go their own way in such times of hardship.

For the Hamburg KPD, the unsuccessful rising marked a turning point. Thereafter, this organization (and its national counterpart in Berlin) rested firmly in the hands of the radical wing. Thälmann himself replaced Brandler as chairman of the KPD in Berlin, and his followers remained in control in Hamburg.[100] This sort of odd twist was perhaps possible only in Communist circles. For Urbahns, it turned out, had had almost nothing to do with the rising. At the very moment the Communist bands were advancing on police stations in Hamburg, Urbahns slept peacefully in his bed, apparently quite unaware of the impending action.[101] And he took little part in the fighting of the following days. So little, in fact, that he was expelled from the Hamburg leadership in February 1924 for "cowardice before the enemy."[102] On the other hand, if any one individual could be held responsible for the catastrophic Hamburg rising it was Ernst Thälmann.[103] And he was raised not only to the leadership of the party but to the ranks of the great in Communist mythology.[104]

Because of the overriding effects of the Great Inflation, it is difficult to evaluate the effects of the October rising on the Hamburg labor movement. But certainly the days of violence left a legacy of deep bitterness that served to emphasize the very important alteration in labor's position after 1923. For Hamburg labor the period of "stabilization" that began in 1924 meant an "almost complete loss... of the gains won since the war."[105] On January 1, 1924, a new "Labor Regulation" was published by the Reich Labor Office. To the shock and dismay of the labor movement, the eight-hour day, considered one of the chief gains of the 1918 revolution, was qualified almost out of existence. In addition, the new regulation contained a provision that allowed the government to enforce arbitration decisions under certain circumstances. To the unions, this represented a serious infringement of their "right" of collective bargaining.[106] In Hamburg the new regulation was followed by an immediate extension of working hours. A survey taken in 1924, for example, shows that well over half of all workers in the harbor were working more than fifty-one hours per week.[107] Several unions reported, in February 1924, that their members were working fifty-four hours and earning less than they had previously earned for forty-eight.[108]

Much more important than the loss of the eight-hour day was the use of new offensive techniques by the employers. The employer associations developed the use of "black lists" to prevent workers from changing jobs in search of better wages, and to make sure that "radicals" or troublesome union men who were fired from one plant could not get work in another.[109] In Hamburg the employer associations also established a new policy in regard to lockouts, and levied heavy fines against employers who failed to cooperate.[110] The clearest evidence of the shift of balance in labor relations is provided by a comparison of the figures on strikes and lockouts in 1922 and 1924. In 1922, 465,000 man-days were lost from strikes, and 67,000 from lockouts. In 1924, by contrast, only 436,000 man-days were lost from strikes, while lockouts cost 1,280,000.[111]

These measures were so successful because the unions were in no position to fight back. For one thing, the unions still had to fight strong Communist pressure in the plants. Indeed, in the course of the year 1924, more "Communist-oriented" trade-union members were expelled from the ADGB than in all previous years together.[112] But these huge membership losses gravely damaged the unions' bargaining power in the shop. As one Hamburg union reported at the end of 1924, "we were no longer even in a position to represent the interests of those who stayed in the union."[113] Attacked from every side, the unions adopted a careful, almost timid, policy, and membership dropped still more. The Hamburg ADGB declared, a little foolishly, that the employers were trying to use the issue of the eight-hour day to draw the unions into a struggle. This, the unions would avoid. Realizing that progress for the workers could come only from the reconstruction of German industry, the Free Unions would discourage the use of the strike weapon, and would "react instantly to every disturbance of production."[114] The ADGB's earlier interest in the formation of industrial unions was now almost totally forgotten.[115]

The very conservative tactics of the ADGB after 1923 naturally emphasized the existing divisions in the labor movement. The political effects of this split were demonstrated in the two elections of 1924. In the campaign for the new Reichstag in May, the Free Unions entirely abandoned their policy of "neutrality," and came out unequivocally in support of the SPD.[116] Symbolically, the SPD ticket in Hamburg was headed by Peter Grossman, an ADGB leader from Berlin.* The Communist vote was larger than it had ever been before, while the SPD suffered a substantial defeat.

In the election for the Bürgerschaft, some five months later, the SPD regained some support, but it was soon quite obvious that the party had lost its controlling position in the government of Hamburg. The Social Democrats no longer commanded a majority in

* *Echo* (May 28, 1924). Symbolically, too, the DNVP ticket was led by the strongly anti-labor director of Blohm and Voss.

the Bürgerschaft, even when allied with the Democratic party. The Communists immediately suggested the formation of a "workers' government," an alliance of SPD and KPD deputies.[117] This offer the SPD rejected out of hand, and formed instead a "Great Coalition" with the Democrats and the Peoples' Party. These events may be taken as indicators of the underlying situation. The SPD and the ADGB, now firmly allied on every level, had in effect renounced all hope of achieving labor unity. The constant threat of attack from the left tended to encourage the liberal, moderate positions held by many labor leaders to harden into rigid, organization-oriented stands. As we have seen, the leaders of the SPD and ADGB had a tendency to view all opposition, from whatever quarter, with fear and suspicion, and to deal with it in tough, uncompromising ways. Perhaps such policies were necessary if these organizations were to retain the support they had, but there can be little doubt that they made the divisions in the labor movement deeper and wider. As these divisions became more pronounced, faith in the democratic political system was undermined among radicals and moderates alike.

The disputes within the labor movement destroyed the effectiveness of organized labor as a political force. The once imposing "fortress of socialism," seemingly impregnable to attack from without, was easily dismantled from within. Constantly engaged in a futile internecine combat, neither of the two wings of the Hamburg labor movement could command much political strength after 1923, a fact that was to be frequently demonstrated throughout the remaining Weimar years and with finality early in 1933.

*Chapter 7*

# The Sociology of Hamburg Labor Politics: The Leaders and the Led

The rapid decline of the Hamburg labor movement as an effective economic and political force raises some very important questions concerning the nature of the labor movement as a political force. The most obvious conclusion one can draw from the Hamburg events is that the attempt to develop democratic institutions and practices among the working classes shattered against the rocks of hard times, low wages, inflation, and unemployment. This conclusion, however, depends upon the assumption that the groups which suffered most from the postwar economic conditions were also the groups most attracted to anti-republican, left-wing movements. But even if this assumption is correct, are we then forced to conclude that, given the difficult economic and political conditions of the early Weimar years, widespread disenchantment with the Republic and the growth of a large Communist movement were in some sense inevitable? This question cannot be answered directly. But we can ask, and answer, the question whether every effort was made, in spheres other than the economic, to counteract the "natural" centrifugal tendencies of these years, and to integrate the working classes into the political life of the Republic. In other words, was the democratic political system really given a fair chance among the working classes of Hamburg?

To deal with such questions effectively, we must first of all understand that during the period covered by this study, large portions of the working classes were what may be called politically "emergent." As we have seen, social and economic developments shortly before and during the World War were responsible for a rapid increase in the number of workers employed in the large-scale, or "mass," industries. Largely semiskilled or unskilled, these workers were not very well integrated into the established labor movement. And although they could legally do so, only a relatively small proportion of these workers exercised their suffrage in Wilhelmian Germany. In local elections, of course, they were for the most part prevented by law from taking active part in political life.

All of this suddenly changed after 1918. The Weimar Republic, by extending full civil privileges to all, made the votes of this numerically important group of critical significance. For the Social Democrats, it was essential that these votes be cast in their favor, and consequently in favor of the Republic. But how were these votes to be won? It is frequently maintained that such emergent working-class groups tend to be more interested in concrete economic problems than in abstract political ones. "Consequently," Seymour Martin Lipset concludes, "it may be suggested that satisfaction or dissatisfaction with rights in the economic order is more important for workers than access to the political order."[1] The Social Democratic solution, of course, was to point out that concrete economic objectives could best be won through the development of the democratic political system. The major shortcoming of such a program is that it demands a willingness to sacrifice present concrete gains for the sake of a future abstract victory. The voter is called upon to retain a considerable faith in the long-range dependability and consistency of the party leaders.

The Social Democrats were somewhat hindered in their advocacy of this program by their own traditional practices and political language. As a "class party," they had considered and spoken of their political opponents as "class enemies," not to be compromised with or trusted. In close alliance with the trade unions, they had fought hard for immediate economic gains, and had used their successes in this area as the measure of their success as an organization. More or less forceful techniques, such as strikes or demonstrations, had been the normal weapons by which such gains were won. After 1917, all this changed. The Majority Socialists, almost to a man, now firmly believed that they must cooperate with liberal middle-class groups in defense of the Republic. Specific economic gains had to be sacrificed to the development of a strong economy, and the old political weapons of strike and demonstration replaced by techniques of negotiation and compromise.

Convincing the working classes of the wisdom of such an approach would certainly have required a major educational effort. Since time was short, this job would have had to have been done quickly and efficiently. The time-honored Social Democratic technique of performing such educational tasks was, of course, organization. The worker who became a member of an ADGB union or a Social Democratic group of one sort or another could generally be depended upon, if not to become a party member, at least to accept the party's promises and support it at the polls. Union gains operated in the direction of increasing SPD votes, and the two organizations worked hand-in-glove for common objectives.

How well suited, then, were the organizational structures of the SPD and the ADGB to the task of assimilating the "new" working-class groups into the political life of the nation? This question may be answered, to considerable extent, through an analysis of the social composition of the leadership and membership of the various significant working-class organizations. Comparison of the findings from this analysis with the social composition of the voters who supported the major working-class parties will provide some clear indications of the reasons for the failure of the SPD.

In Hamburg, where neither the Christian Center Party nor the Christian Trade Unions played a major role, the SPD, USPD, KPD, and Free Unions constituted, for all practical purposes, the organized labor movement. It is extremely unlikely that any other political party had a significant number of workers in its membership (at least until the rise of the National Socialist movement in the late 'twenties). From time to time, opposition unions were formed, but they were usually integral parts of the KPD, and were in any case short-lived. Anything like complete or accurate membership data for the USPD or the KPD is unavailable, and may remain so, as Werner Sombart wrote in 1924, "for all time."[2] Therefore, we are limited to a consideration of what kind of workers were, or were not, organized into the SPD and the ADGB. However by comparing the composition of the SPD and the ADGB with the overall composition of the Hamburg labor force, we will be able to form a general picture of those who were—and those who were not—closely integrated into labor organizations that supported the Weimar Republic.

Turning to the leadership of the SPD, one notices first of all that most leaders of the Hamburg party were experienced men. Examining the list of SPD Bürgerschaft members between 1919 and 1925, we find that of 104 members, 55 (or 53 per cent) were over fifty years of age in 1925, 21 were over sixty, four were over seventy, and the oldest was a venerable seventy-six.[3] The median age for SPD Bürgerschaft members during this period was about fifty-four years.

We may compare these figures to those for the USPD and KPD members. The median age for USPD members of the Bürgerschaft was forty-eight years, with only 30 per cent older than fifty.[4] Communist leaders were younger still. Their median age was thirty-five years. No Communist member of the twenty-one for whom birth dates are available was older than fifty in 1925, only one was older than forty-five, and 18 were thirty-five or younger.[5]

A comparison of the occupations of these same Bürgerschaft members also yields some interesting, though not surprising, information. First, let us consider the leaders from the standpoint of their life work, rather than from the standpoint of the specific job they held when elected to the Bürgerschaft. About a third of the SPD members had worked primarily as teachers, white-collar workers, or professional men. Another third had worked in the building trades or in printing, and the remainder were scattered among various trades, for the most part the more traditional ones.

All but a very few could be classified as belonging to what is generally known as the "labor aristocracy."[6] Little change can be observed in the occupational character of the SPD members throughout the period, and there was little turnover in personnel.

The USPD leaders present a rather heterogeneous picture, being about equally divided among white-collar intellectuals, skilled craft workers, skilled industrial workers, and semiskilled industrial workers.[7] The Communists, again, carry the process one step further. The building trades and other skilled crafts were virtually unrepresented in the Communist leadership; their Bürgerschaft seats were largely divided between a group of rather hard-to-define intellectuals and a group of semiskilled and unskilled workers in the industrial trades.[8]

In passing, it is interesting to note that except for the white-collar and professional groups, almost every one of the SPD and USPD members had spent several years "wandering."[9] In Germany before the First World War, it was still customary for a "journeyman" craftsman to journey about for three or four years to gain experience in his craft. One can easily imagine that this tradition must have played a very large role in the development of the socialist movement. "Wandering" (sometimes all over Europe) undoubtedly facilitated the exchange of ideas and information, and probably played a major role in the formation of conceptions of class and nationality.

Returning to our group of Bürgerschaft members, there is still one important observation to be made. By noting the occupation that each member listed at the time of his election to the Bürgerschaft, we can make some approximation of the means by which one normally achieved a leadership position in each of the three groups studied. The most frequent "way up" for the working-class SPD members was clearly through the bureaucracy of the trade unions (34 per cent), the cooperatives (13 per cent), or one of the other miscellaneous labor organizations (12 per cent). The party bureaucracy itself was the means to the top for only about 5 per cent of the leaders. Most of the white-collar and professional members entered the Bürgerschaft directly from their jobs.[10] The various nonparty labor bureaucracies, which together accounted for 59 per cent of the SPD members, accounted for a much smaller percentage of USPD leaders (25 per cent); here, the party was a much greater source. No official of a trade union or cooperative served as a Communist member in the Bürgerschaft between 1921 and 1925. Nearly half of all Communist members had come up through the party or the party press.[11]

In general, then, one can say that the leadership of the Hamburg SPD was predominantly an amalgam of middle-class white-collar and professional people and skilled craft workers who had worked their way up through one or another of the labor bureaucracies. This latter group might best be described as belonging to the "labor-based middle class."[12] Compared to the composition of the work force of the city as a whole, these leaders were drawn from a rather narrow segment. The age of many of these leaders and the extent of their experience in labor organizations might very well lead us to conclude, as Robert Michels does, that they would have formed a very close attachment to labor organizations as such, and would be somewhat less than zealous in their support of any actions that might tend to jeopardize the form and nature of those organizations.[13] The bulk of these leaders, moreover, probably did not view the World War from the unfavorable vantage point of a front-line trench.[14] These generalizations become less valid as we move toward the left. The USPD leaders were younger and had had far less experience in labor organizations than the SPD leaders. The Communists were younger and more inexperienced still.

Some of the implications of these statistical findings can be understood through a closer study of the Hamburg KPD's leaders. Fortunately, a considerable quantity of detailed autobiographical information is available on fourteen of Hamburg's leading Communists. These men, called to trial for their part in the rising of October 1923, talked at some length about their lives, including their reasons for joining the Communist Party. Taking into account the fact that these statements were made at least in part with an eye toward winning the sympathy of the court, we can still find much of interest in them.[15] Most striking about the lives of these Communist leaders is the pattern of failure, frustration, and hostility. Unlike the leaders of the SPD, most were not clearly associated with one particular trade. Several of the leaders had worked in a number of semiskilled trades, but none was working in the trade for which he had been originally trained. Unsuccessful in their trades, these men did not attain any significant measure of success in branches of the labor movement other than the USPD or the Communist Party. Although almost all had been at one time members of the SPD, there were no trade-union or cooperative officials in the group.

The majority of the leaders for whom information is available participated in the war as front-line soldiers. Several had been arrested for "breach of military discipline," an event that seems to have served as a confirmation of their opposition views. None, it appears, held important leadership positions in the military. Disappointment in career expectations figures importantly in almost all of the statements.[16] Some of these men were apparently ne'er-do-wells, moving from job to job without particular interests or abilities. One man frankly admits that he lost several jobs "because I made too many mistakes."[17] Most of the others, however, refer to one particular "bad break" that forced them out of their chosen field. One man recounts that he passed all the examinations for his ship-pilot's license, only to be refused because of faulty eyesight. He then drifted from one job to another, finally gravitating, as is usual in Hamburg, to unskilled labor in the harbor.[18] Others attribute their position to layoffs or hard times.[19] A considerable number date their difficulties from wounds received in the war. A typesetter stated that he had to give up his work in 1919 because he suffered from "headaches and weakened mental processes as a result of a war wound.[20] An electrician came out of the war with "stiff elbows," a steelworker with a damaged back, and so on.[21]

With the exception of perhaps only one or two of the youngest men, all of these leaders harbored a deep resentment against the society in which they had encountered so many difficulties. One man dates this antipathy from the Anti-Socialist Law, as a result of which, his father, a Social Democrat, was expelled from the country, to return years later with an incurable disease.[22] Another tells about the time when his teacher forbade him and his friends to wear the traditional students' cap "so that the distinction between us and the boys at the private school across the street could be made clear."[23] Most, however, refer to the war as the source of their rejection of "bourgeois" society. The testimony of one leader consists almost entirely of descriptions of his war experiences, his dislike for the military, and his resentment of the distinctions made between officers and men. He recalls that, even at the front, one knew about the hardships endured by the civilian population during the "turnip winter." "This," he remarks, "made us feel somewhat disenchanted with the war."[24]

Without even attempting to pass judgment on the extent to which their troubles and hostility stemmed from themselves or from the society in which they lived, we may observe that, with possibly one exception, there was no doubt in the minds of these men. Society was at fault. Certainly, this feeling is easy to understand. But it is curious to notice the extent to which they emphasized personal hardships in explaining their earlier social behavior and their ultimate attraction to Communism:

In the evenings we all pulled off our lice, and because I was the youngest, I always had the most.[25]

When I was five years old my father was killed in an accident at work. Naturally, this had an effect on my later life.[26]

During the war I was alone with my mother. My father was in the army. There were many children.... Times were very hard then, and I became embittered. It was for this reason that I joined the Communist movement.[27]

What is interesting about these statements is that almost all of these men, and several were among the leading figures in the Hamburg KPD, spoke only about their grievances against society. None had much to say about what he was for, how society was to be improved, or the lot of the workingman bettered. One or two referred vaguely to their belief in "council democracy," but apparently just belonging to the Communist Party was enough of a statement for most of these men.* This apparent lack of concern with party ideology would seem to bear out Gabriel Almond's conclusion that interest in such matters does not usually extend much beyond the top echelons of party leadership, and that most members found in the party, among other things, a means of protesting against personal circumstances in association with others similarly aggrieved.[28]

Comparing the Communist and USPD leaders with those of the SPD, several important differences stand out. The most obvious one, of course, is the difference in age. Since they were younger, Communist and USPD leaders were more likely to have had first-hand experience of the war, and were almost certainly influenced by it in a different way than were older men. The very great excitement generated among leftist circles by the military problem in the spring of 1919 is one example of the political importance of this difference.[29] But perhaps the most important difference between the SPD and Communist leaders was in their relationships to the labor movement as a whole. The large majority of the SPD leaders as we have seen, were also labor leaders. Whatever criticisms might be made about their ages or bureaucratic inclinations, it must be recognized that these men had worked their way to prominent positions through years of work on behalf of the labor movement. Successful men in their own right, most of the SPD leaders had important personal followings in the unions, cooperatives, and other branches of the labor movement. To this extent, at least, they may be considered as "representative" of a certain segment of the labor movement.

The Communist leaders, on the other hand, owed their positions

* Unfortunately, the record of Hugo Urbahns's statement is incomplete. Leader at that time of the Hamburg KPD, Urbahns would doubtless have been more explicit regarding Communist policy. Two other KPD members, Köppen (who admits to a reputation as a "*gewaltätiger Mensch*") and Rühl, are obviously familiar with the vocabulary of the labor movement, but neither is very articulate about aims and purposes. (Sources for these statements are cited in note 3, p. 204.)

solely to the party; for the most part, they had shown no such continuing interest in the development of the labor movement. It is striking to notice how much these leaders resembled what has come to be called the "alienated" man. Without exception, they had not formed a lasting identification with a specific trade, a particular plant or firm, or with any part of the organized labor movement. Traveling about from place to place and from job to job, these men formed no permanent social ties. They performed an anonymous kind of labor under very anonymous circumstances. The Communist movement offered them alienation from society on the one hand and unity with their fellow workers on the other, a mixture these men were bound to find appealing. And the Communist ideology, of course, provided an appropriate rationale, one that permitted them to identify with an abstract international ideal rather than with the German nation.

This difference in the nature of the leadership of the SPD and the KPD might well have been expected to have important political effects. The fact that the Communist leaders were more independent than other labor leaders made them in a sense more free, more "irresponsible" in the formation of policy. Not having to suit their tactics to the wishes of any certain group over a long period, the Communists could more readily keep an eye on the main chance and switch policy to pursue it. It is difficult to imagine, on the other hand, the policy of the SPD contradicting to any great extent the wishes of the leaders of the Free Unions. The leaders of the two organizations were, of course, largely the same persons. Moreover, the trade unionist, secure in his status in the labor movement, was in a position to offer determined and effective resistance to policies with which he did not agree, without having to be seriously concerned about the threat of party sanctions.

The interrelationship between the Free Unions and the SPD becomes even clearer when one examines the development of the memberships of the two organizations. For this purpose, we have selected the years 1914, 1921, and 1924 as significant dates: the first is the last peacetime year, the second is the year that most clearly reflects the postwar growth, and the third shows membership conditions after the inflation of 1923.

The Hamburg organizations of the SPD and ADGB reported a significant growth in membership in 1921. The Hamburg SPD, with a total membership of 72,246, showed an increase of 6.5 per cent over 1914 figures—a considerably higher percentage gain than that recorded by the national organization.[30] The Hamburg ADGB, with a total membership of 243,971, registered a 105 per cent increase over 1914.[31] Again, in a way very similar to the national organizations, both groups suffered severe losses in the 1924 count. The SPD membership had decreased 41.4 per cent from 1921, and the ADGB, 46 per cent.[32] Within these larger trends, the development of the SPD membership was largely what we would expect on the basis of other evidence. More and more white-collar workers and lower civil servants were joining the party. At the same time, industrial-worker membership steadily decreased, and the proportion of skilled craftsmen became larger.

The party membership of 1914 presents a picture of a highly diversified and representative organization. The participation of the building trades was quite high, as one might expect from a study of the leadership, but the unskilled trades were still well represented. Virtually every important trade was represented in a number seemingly related to its importance in the city.[33]

Although the SPD suffered badly during the war, its membership began a steep upward climb in 1918, and by 1921 showed a substantial gain over 1914. The major portion of this gain, as the party report neglects to point out, came from the ranks of women workers, who entered the labor market in great numbers during the war.[34] The total gain over 1914 was 4,384, of which 3,227 were women. Although the number of women in the party (and the labor force) decreased in succeeding years, the percentage of women in the party membership remained substantially higher than it had been before the war.

The decrease in party membership reflected in the figures for 1924 was rather evenly spread over all occupations. Numerically, of course, the larger unskilled trades accounted for the major portion of the membership losses. But on a percentage basis, these unskilled workers did not leave the party on a much larger scale than any other group. Compared to both 1914 and 1921, the party in 1924 was composed of a larger proportion of white-collar and civil-service workers (13.78 per cent in 1924 as compared to 5.68 per cent in 1914), a larger proportion of women and of workers in the highly skilled trades, and a smaller percentage of workers in the large industrial trades.[35] In addition, it was a much smaller party in 1924, with only 42,363 members as compared to 67,942 in 1914.[36] Never again during the Weimar Republic was the Hamburg SPD to regain its prewar membership, let alone its all-time high of 1921.

The significance of these statistics can only be appreciated by considering them in relation to trade-union statistics of the same period. Although every one of the fifty or so trade unions affiliated with the Hamburg ADGB shared to considerable extent in the membership growth at the end of the war, by far the major proportion of the new union members came from the new white-collar organizations, and (as was not the case with the SPD) from the four most important industrial unions: the Metalworkers, Factory Workers, Transportation Workers, and Textile Workers. These four unions alone accounted for over 52 per cent of the total membership increase. Whereas women made up nearly 75 per cent of the SPD's membership gain, they accounted for only 33 per cent of the ADGB's.[37] These gains represented a substantial expansion of trade unionism in Hamburg into important new areas. Some 70,000 workers in large-scale industries joined unions for the first time between 1919 and 1921.[38] But many did not stay long. These large industrial unions, which had grown so rapidly at the end of the war, suffered the greatest losses after the events of 1920–21, and again after 1923. They lost about 45 per cent of their members, while the craft unions lost only about 15 per cent.[39]

The overall results of these violent fluctuations in membership were somewhat different for the ADGB than for the SPD. The drop in trade-union membership indicated in the 1924 figures, though more drastic than the SPD's when compared to the 1921 membership, was much less so when compared to the 1914 figures. The ADGB, in other words, had a significantly larger membership in 1924 than it had in 1914, while the SPD was smaller by nearly a third.

The participation of the industrial trades in the SPD and the ADGB is compared in the following tabulation. The percentages indicate the proportion of total membership derived from these trades.[40] A constant percentage would indicate that industrial workers joined or left the organization at the same rate as members from other trades:

| *Year* | *SPD* | *ADGB* |
|---|---|---|
| 1914 | 31.0% | 39.4% |
| 1921 | 27.7 | 43.6 |
| 1924 | 27.2 | 43.2 |
| 1925 | 27.1 | 41.5 |

Several important developments are reflected in this table. It is clear, first of all, that even while the relative size of the major industrial unions was increasing, workers from these unions formed an ever-smaller proportion of the SPD membership. Within the union federation itself, these unions were strongest in 1921, when membership was at its peak. But thereafter they decreased at a faster rate than the others. By 1924, the four major industrial unions were only slightly larger in relation to the total union membership than they had been in 1914.

It is quite obvious from this material that both the SPD and the ADGB were failing to keep pace with the industrialization of Hamburg. As we have seen, the most pronounced growth in the labor force during the prewar and war years was in the large-scale or mass industries. These new members of the labor force were largely semiskilled or unskilled workers. And yet, looking at the percentage figures for 1914 and 1924, one can see that the growth in this quarter of the work force was not reflected by a similar growth in the SPD and ADGB membership rolls. The figure below indicates the very small proportion of the *total* working-class population of the city involved as members of the two organizations.[41] Reviewing all the material collected here concerning the membership and leadership of the various organizations of the labor movement, we can make several interesting observations concerning the development of the movement and its role in politics.

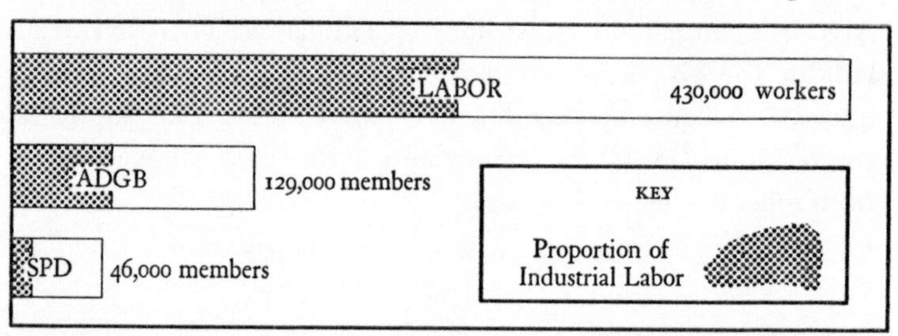


FIGURE 2 Labor and the Membership of the SPD and the ADGB in Hamburg, 1924

An examination of the SPD leaves one with an overwhelming impression of stagnation. The party's leadership did not alter significantly during the period under study: it remained dominated by a stable group of aging trade-union leaders and labor-movement organization men. There is no evidence of an influx of young men, or of men representing the newly important industrial trades. This impression is borne out by the breakdown of party membership. Although there was an increase in membership shortly after the war, the bulk of this increase was accounted for by women who had probably entered the labor market when the men went to the front, and left it as soon as they came back. In relative terms, of course, the growth in SPD membership fell far behind the actual growth of the labor force during the same period, and the party won very few members among the workers in the industrial trades. By 1924, the party's total membership was smaller than it had been in 1914; the party found itself more than ever composed of a core of craft-union workers and a much smaller group of white-collar workers.

Taking into consideration the new political conditions of Weimar Germany, it is not surprising that the SPD developed in this direction. One could argue that the party was changing from a membership party to a "mass party," one that would form the base for a large group of nonmembers who associated with the party only at election. The basic work of integrating the emergent working-class groups into the social life of the community could then have been left to the trade unions. The role of the party, in this formulation, would be to generalize in national, democratic terms the specific class interests of various segments of the working classes, and to mobilize the voters at election time. The unions, in close alliance with the party, would serve as a link between the individual worker and the larger community, helping him to achieve a satisfactory role in the community, and, at the same time, informing him of the requisites of that role.

To be sure, such a picture of the respective tasks of party and union was never formulated by the leaders of the Hamburg labor movement, but the political objectives of the SPD implied such a division of function. Only by effectively freeing itself from identification with specific working-class interests, could the SPD hope to form the broad coalition of support it needed. And yet, the large groups of new workers in the industrial trades needed and wanted leadership and a means of expressing their specific needs. The trade unions would appear to have been the appropriate institutions to perform this task, for in the early years of the Republic especially, they had direct access to a far greater proportion of the working classes than any other working-class institution. In 1914, for example, the SPD membership was 57 per cent of that of the Free Unions; in 1921 it was only 29 per cent, and by 1924 it had stabilized at about 35 per cent.[42] In terms of the total effectiveness of the two organizations, even these figures overstate the SPD's importance because they do not take into account the many white-collar members in the party.

The significance of these figures becomes clearer when we compare the relative effectiveness of the two organizations among industrial workers. For example, while the ADGB could boast 35,000 new members in the huge Transport Workers' Union in 1921, the SPD lost more than 200 of these workers. The ADGB could also report that the German Metalworkers' Union, the second largest union in Hamburg, increased its 1914 membership by some 18,000. The SPD claimed 76 new metalworkers in 1921.[43]

Our study of the history of the Hamburg labor movement suggests that the unions failed to take advantage of the favorable position they enjoyed after the revolution. Although the ADGB was enormously successful in winning new members from the industrial trades during and shortly after the war, it was markedly unsuccessful in holding them. The struggle within the union movement concerning the council idea and industrial unionism was reflected in the organizational structure of the ADGB. As the issues and difficulties of the Weimar years developed, the ADGB, like the SPD, tended to depend more and more on the traditional union cadres of craft workers for both members and leaders. As a result, the Free Unions in Hamburg cut themselves off—in some cases deliberately—from a large and extremely important segment of the working classes.

It is, of course, by no means certain that the Free Unions could have won more extensive support among industrial labor under any circumstances. But it is clear that they made no great effort to do so. The union organization refused to compromise on the council issue, to undertake organizational reform, or to take effective steps to integrate the new labor leadership into the union hierarchy. The membership figures of the Hamburg ADGB show that by 1924 the Free Unions were representing only a rather narrow segment of the working classes, and were, as a result, in a poor position to control the labor movement, or to enlist labor sentiment in support of the Republic. On the contrary, the history of the Hamburg labor movement suggests very strongly that the activities of the trade-union leadership may have operated to undermine the SPD's attempt to win support among industrial workers.

This conclusion is reinforced by the fact that the SPD leadership was to a considerable extent derived from union ranks throughout the period 1919 to 1924. For example, in the Bürgerschaft elected in 1919, thirty-four of the eighty-two SPD deputies were either trade-union officials or had been so until a short time before taking office.[44] In addition, there were three trade-union officials serving for the USPD, and probably a few others scattered throughout the various parties. Eight of the twelve members of the executive committee of the Hamburg ADGB were serving in the Bürgerschaft in 1920.[45] Altogether, probably well over half of all Socialist deputies were at least members of trade unions.[46]

From these facts, we must conclude that the established unions were well represented in the Bürgerschaft. Indeed, it seems likely that the voices of union leaders were very often dominant in party councils, although how often and on what issues it is very difficult to say. In any case, it is reasonable to assume that the industrial workers' hostile feelings toward established unions and union leaders did not change when the union leaders assumed their party roles. This hostility undoubtedly played an important part in the SPD's inability to gain the confidence of these industrial workers or to win their support at the polls.

*Chapter 8*

# The Sociology of Hamburg Labor Politics: How Labor Voted

The social history of Hamburg labor in the early years of the Weimar Republic provides some striking indications of the depth and complexity of the differences that divided the labor movement. We have remarked several times upon the very destructive effects these differences had on both the labor movement and the republican political system. We have focused primarily on the manner in which these differences contributed to the inability of the Social Democrats or any other pro-republican organization to integrate the bulk of the working classes into some orderly movement favoring the continuation of the Republic. The growth, by 1924, of a large and important Communist movement in Hamburg is one indication of organized labor's failure to convince the workingman of the advantages of the existing political system.

In the preceding chapter, we saw how the ideological differences in the labor movement were reflected in the form and structure of the major labor organizations. In this chapter we will try to relate the social history of the labor movement to the behavior of the workingman at the polls. By using some of the techniques of electoral sociology, we will be able to form a fairly exact picture of the larger movements of political opinion in Hamburg, and to evaluate their significance for the political life of the labor movement.[1]

From 1919 to 1924, Hamburg voting trends more or less followed national voting patterns. In both cases the parties of the extreme left and right grew steadily at the expense of the republican parties. These organizations showed great temporary gains immediately after the economic crisis of 1923, and then grew steadily again until the depression years. The tables in Appendix II, however, point up certain important electoral variations in Hamburg. Table 2, comparing the percentages of the total vote won by the major parties in Hamburg and the Reich in the four Reichstag elections of the period, indicates first of all the relative unimportance of the Center Party in Hamburg. Probably because of this fact, the Peoples' Party, the Democratic Party, and the SPD were all proportionately stronger in Hamburg than in Germany as a whole. Both of the extreme parties, the German National People's Party (DNVP) and the Communist Party, had in the beginning relatively less support in Hamburg than they had on the national level. Very soon, however, the Communists' electoral strength became proportionately larger in Hamburg, and remained so throughout the Weimar period. The Hamburg DNVP, though matching the national average in the election of May 1924, was rather less successful than the national party.

Although the far right was in general less successful at the polls in Hamburg than in the rest of Germany, it was probably somewhat stronger than the election returns indicate. A number of nationalist organizations had their headquarters in the city, and it was frequently a center of rightist terror activity.* Probably a number of Hamburg businessmen (especially in shipping circles) contributed heavily to the war chests of the militant rightist organizations.[2] The relative weakness of the right-wing parties at the Hamburg polls may be chiefly attributed to the absence of a large peasant population, which elsewhere accounted for a major portion of the vote of such parties.[3] In very general terms, the Nation-

* The Deutschvölkischen Schutz- und Trutzbund, the Deutsche Bund, and a number of youth organizations had their headquarters in Hamburg. See Helga Anschütz, "Die NSDAP in Hamburg," unpub. dissertation (Hamburg, 1956), p. 26; and *Pressestelle* I, L. 1.19, "Faschistenbestrebungen, Putschpläne, Skagerfeiern." (Hamburg State Archives.)

alists in Hamburg stood somewhat to the right, and the People's Party somewhat to the left, of their respective national organizations. There was very little cooperation between the two parties in Hamburg.[4]

After the war Hamburg's local politics were, for the first time, shaped by political developments on the national level. Most of the old local parties had disappeared by 1919; they were replaced by clearly defined "fractions" of national parties, which functioned continuously in the Bürgerschaft, demanding and usually getting "party discipline" on important matters. Most often, the local organizations presented programs at election time only after consultation with national leaders. In the case of the SPD, for example, the party program in a national election was usually reprinted from *Vorwärts,* the party's national newspaper.[5]

The Weimar Constitution had preempted some of the state's former functions, such as the income tax, the school system, regulation of transportation facilities, and so on.[6] And there was an ever-increasing tendency to carry really vital issues to Berlin rather than attempt to deal with them on the local level.[7] In general, the proceedings of the Bürgerschaft throughout the period reveal that it was far more of an administrative than a legislative body; the Bürgerschaft also served as a forum for the presentation of the various parties' positions on national issues.[8] Campaigns for Bürgerschaft elections, therefore, became increasingly concerned with national issues, or, in a few cases, with local applications of national policies.[9] As a result, the Bürgerschaft elections reflected public opinion in much the same way the national elections did, and the results may be safely compared. It is necessary only to keep in mind that Bürgerschaft elections generally engendered much less political excitement than those on the national level, and fewer voters participated in them (see Figures 3 and 4). Moreover, the extreme parties generally did less well in Bürgerschaft than in national elections (see Table 5).

Table 1 shows the proportion of seats held by the major parties in the Reichstag and the Bürgerschaft. With certain variances due

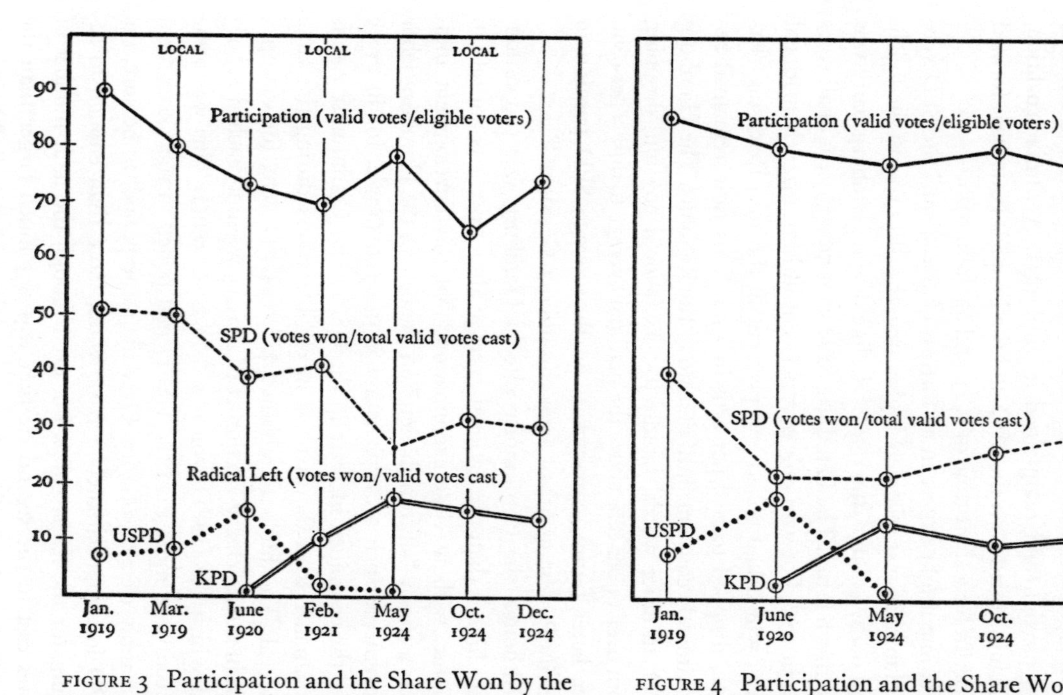


FIGURE 3 Participation and the Share Won by the Parties of the Left in Hamburg in Seven Local and National Elections, 1919–24

FIGURE 4 Participation and the Share Won by the Parties of the Left in Germany in Five National Elections, 1919–24

to vagaries in the representational system and the different timing of local and national elections, this table reflects much the same situation as Table 2. Lacking the support of a Center Party, the Hamburg Social Democrats formed the Great Coalition after the 1924 election and maintained it until 1931. A similar coalition, which included both the SPD and the People's Party, was formed in Berlin for a short time in 1923, and again in 1928.

As one might expect in a "fortress of Socialism," the SPD vote in Hamburg was relatively higher than the SPD vote in the Reich. And oddly enough, the rate of decline of the Hamburg party was also much faster. The Hamburg SPD won 51.3 per cent of all votes cast in 1919, but won only 27.5 per cent in May 1924; the national party, which had polled 37.9 per cent in the 1919 Reichstag elections, dropped to 20.5 per cent in 1924. This ratio remained approximately constant until the end of the Republic. The Hamburg SPD, in other words, rapidly lost its favored position, dropping from over 13 per cent above the national average to only 7 per cent. The latter figure represents about the average SPD position in heavily Protestant urban areas throughout Germany.[10]

Although the Communist vote in Hamburg was proportionately higher than the national average after 1920, it is not safe to assume, without close examination, that this development indicates a steady "shift to the left" on the part of the Hamburg labor movement. Such an explanation is just too simple, for in every case the combined increase in the USPD and Communist vote is far smaller than the increase in eligible voters during the same interval. The highest combined USPD-KPD vote, for example, was in the Reichstag election of May 1924, when it reached 113,983 (of which the USPD won less than 2 per cent). This was some 76,000 votes more than the USPD had polled in the Constituent Assembly election of 1919. Over the same period, to be sure, the SPD lost approximately 126,000 votes, more than enough to account for the leftist gains. But even though the total number of votes cast in the second election was not much larger than the number cast in the first, there were 139,000 voters eligible in 1924 who were not on the lists in 1919. In other words, it is also conceivable that the Communist-USPD gain could have been derived entirely from the newly eligible voters. As will become clear, neither of these explanations for the origins of the radical vote in 1924 is completely satisfactory, but the example serves to show that the factor of participation must be taken carefully into account, especially during a period in which both electoral participation and political loyalties fluctuated very widely (see Figures 3 and 4).

The extensive fluctuation in the degree of participation in elections is one of the more interesting and difficult problems that confront the student of Weimar politics.[11] As Figures 3 and 4 show, both Hamburg and Germany as a whole reported a very high turnout for the Constituent Assembly election of 1919.* Indeed, on the national level, this rate of participation would not be equaled again until 1932. It is certainly not difficult to find an explanation for Hamburg's unusually high participation rate in the election of 1919. Cities generally show an above-average participation rate, and Hamburg, with its highly developed and well-organized labor movement, might well have been expected to show an unusually great interest in elections, especially at a time when it was under the rule of the minority Council Government. But when we look at the figures for the election of 1920, we find that Hamburg's participation rate fell that year to a point well below the national average. Hamburg never again regained its 1919 participation rate (90.4 per cent), and remained below the national average throughout the Weimar period.

Unfortunately, there is no simple explanation for the low rate of participation in Hamburg. Numerous election studies have shown that labor in general—and unskilled labor in particular—participates less in elections than other groups in society.[12] On this basis, the relatively large number of unskilled dock workers in Hamburg could account for the low participation rate. And, to be

* Even though the rate of participation fluctuated widely in Weimar Germany, it was still quite high by U.S. standards.

sure, the parties of the left did win an ever-smaller proportion of the votes cast in Hamburg (see Table 5). But in none of the elections studied, can we find a significant correlation between the proportion of workers living in a particular district and that district's rate of participation. Indeed, such comparisons seem to indicate quite clearly that there was no significant relationship between these phenomena.* This is not to say, of course, that there was no decline in working-class participation during the period. On the contrary, increasingly larger groups of labor voters did not make use of their franchise after 1919. But there is no evidence to show that working-class participation at the polls declined at a rate greater than the one established for the city as a whole (see Table 4). Taking the process one step further, there is no evidence of a particularly low participation rate among all semiskilled and unskilled workers taken together, or among unskilled workers alone.† However, by comparing certain important working-class districts that had a low participation rate with similar districts that had a higher rate, it is possible to pick out certain consistencies.‡

In general, among districts having a large proportion of working-class inhabitants, a low participation rate was associated with a high proportion of workers (skilled and unskilled alike) in the metalworking trades, in transportation, in the harbor, and in the warehouses. Workers employed as "loaders" and such by commercial firms are also included in this category. Again, among working-class districts, a relatively high participation rate was

* For example, in the election to the Constituent Assembly in 1919, the two variables correlate to the extent of .03; for the Reichstag election of May 1924, the figure is .16. Correlations for other elections are similar. The method by which these correlations were obtained is discussed in Appendix I (pp. 175–78). For additional material on correlations, see Appendix notes, p. 207.

† These correlations were consistently slightly higher than those for labor in general, but still well below the level of significance. Compare Juan Linz, "The Social Bases of West German Politics," dissertation, Columbia, 1958 (Univ. Micr., 59–4075).

‡ As a rule, I have considered a district an "important working-class district" when it had a working-class population of at least 40 per cent. However, this figure was not the only criterion; I also consulted occupational data and Hamburgers who knew the old city well.

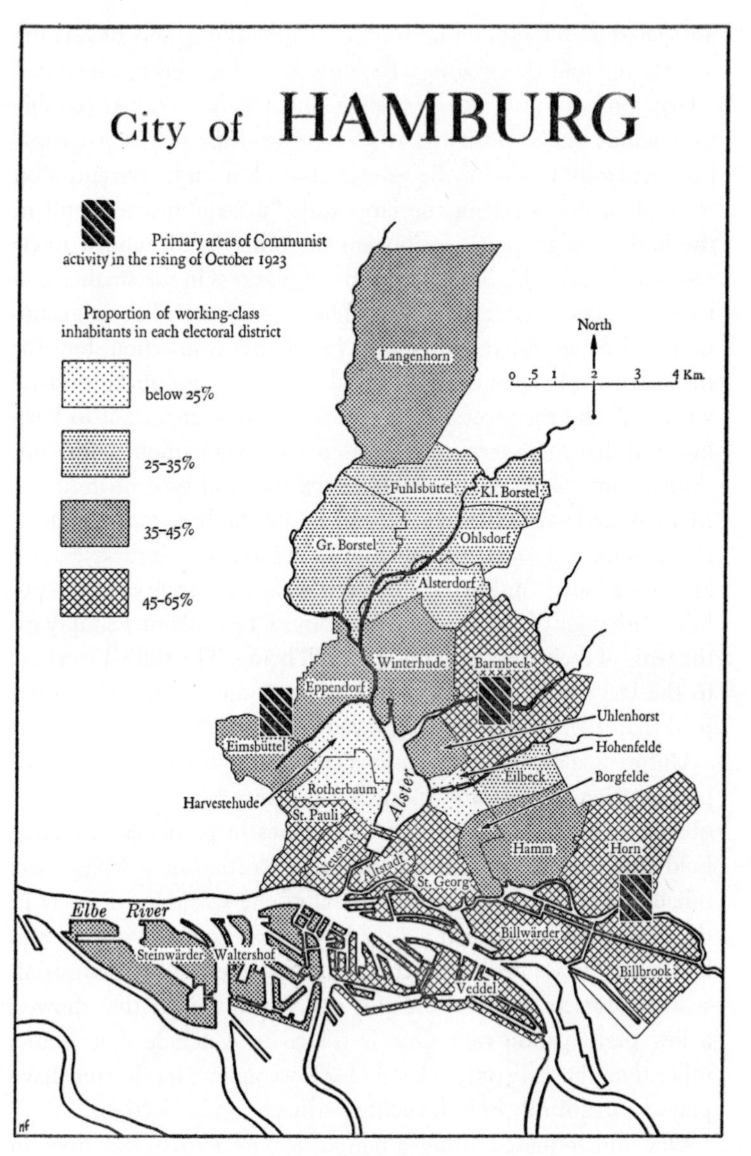


Hamburg, October 1923

associated with the building trades, woodworking, and such crafts as tailoring and shoemaking. Because these seven groups included a large proportion of the total labor force of the city, it is possible to conclude that in primarily working-class districts, low participation generally tended to be associated with a high concentration of workers employed in the large-scale "mass industries" and in the harbor; high participation, on the other hand, tended to be associated with a high concentration of workers in the smaller and more traditional craft industries. The significance of these groupings will be considered elsewhere in another connection, but, for the moment, it is convenient to label the first group "industrial workers," and the second "craft workers." It is important to keep in mind that these terms are by no means synonymous with "unskilled" and "skilled," but refer to the size and type of industry. Many skilled workers, such as metalsmiths, machine-tool operators, electricians, and so on, were employed in large-scale industries, and are here labeled "industrial." Therefore, any differences in the political behavior of these two groups cannot be explained simply on the basis of their relative economic well-being. The skilled workers in the large-scale industries were as well, and frequently better, paid than their colleagues employed elsewhere.[13]

Unfortunately, our observations concerning the relative rates of participation of craft and industrial workers fall far short of adequately explaining the various differences in participation. They hold true only in districts where the proportion of working-class inhabitants is relatively high. Several of the wealthier districts in the city, which contained a very low proportion of workers, also had a very low rate of participation.[14] In other words, industrial-worker districts were not the only districts in the city that showed a low participation rate. One is forced to conclude that factors other than those directly related to socioeconomic levels must have played a major role in influencing participation in elections.

One much-quoted study attempts to cut across class lines in explaining the participation rate by attributing the decline in participation to a lack of interest among young voters.[15] There is a certain amount of rather indirect evidence to support this conclusion as applied to the working classes alone. The "industrial" trades had a high proportion of young workers.[16] There was also a relatively high percentage of young apprentices in these trades.[17] However, when we compare by districts the proportion of residents who were between twenty and twenty-five years of age with the 1925 electoral participation rate, we can find nothing to account for the fluctuations we have noted.[18]

Perhaps the most intelligent explanation of these differences in the rate of electoral participation is that those groups, working-class or other, which had the longest tradition of political action tended to exercise their franchise at every opportunity, while those groups that were relatively new to political life tended to vote only in times of excitement or crisis. Young people, lower-echelon civil servants (*Beamten*), and industrial workers were all newcomers to political life; none of these groups played an active part in political life before 1914. In fact, a comparison of the proportionate increase in votes per district in 1919 with the relative stability of the rate of participation in each district bears out this explanation. Those districts that had the largest influx of new voters in 1919 tended to be the most unstable in terms of participation thereafter.

This tendency of the new voter not to participate regularly had far-reaching implications for the SPD. To begin to understand these implications we must take a close look at the position of the party in 1919, with reference to its situation before the war. Although the SPD in Hamburg was able to win a majority (51 per cent of all valid votes cast) in the election to the National Assembly in January 1919, the acute observer might have seen that the party's future was not necessarily a bright one. In the Reichstag election of 1912, the last election in Hamburg before the war, the SPD had won over 61 per cent of all valid votes cast.[19] How is this change to be explained?

The central fact, of course, is that the new political system and the revolution had operated to nearly double the number of participating voters. These new voters came, for the most part, from the following groups: women, who voted for the first time in Germany in 1919; industrial workers, who as a group tended to participate very little before the war; and a large and important group of lower-middle-class civil servants and white-collar workers, who were undoubtedly shocked into political action by the exciting and frightening events of the revolutionary days.

The obvious conclusion to be drawn here is that the SPD failed to attract enough of these new voters. But in fact the opposite appears to have been the case. A comparison of the statistics of the 1912 and 1919 elections indicates that the SPD won its greatest gains in those districts in which the proportion of new voters was largest.* In other words, it would appear that the SPD actually won a disproportionately large share of the votes cast by new voters in 1919.†

The election results from January 1919 present a rather complex picture. Apparently, along with the increase in participation, there was a major shift in middle-class sympathies from the SPD to parties further to the right. At the same time, of course, the USPD appeared on the ballot in competition with the SPD, and undoubtedly attracted a number of traditionally socialist voters. It would seem that the SPD actually lost a large number of its traditional supporters to parties on both the left and right, while gaining just enough among the newly activated voters to win a majority. This conclusion seems quite plausible in the light of the other information we have concerning the development of the SPD.

Before 1914 the SPD was the only party that had a full-time

* Districts that had a high percentage of industrial workers and lower-middle-class white-collar workers and civil servants showed the highest proportionate increase in new voters in 1919.

† This was probably at least partly due to the fact that women were voting for the first time; women who had taken jobs in shops and factories during the war were likely to vote Social Democratic. It is unlikely, however, that the Social Democratic share of the feminine vote was *proportionately* very much larger than that won by other parties. The Hamburg SPD organization, in fact, came to feel that it was doing less well than other parties in winning the sympathies of women voters. (See SPD-Hamburg, *Bericht 1919–21*, pp. 96–100.) The results of the Bürgerschaft election of October 1924, in which the ballots were marked according to sex, confirmed these fears. (See SPD-Hamburg, *Bericht 1924–25*, pp. 51–53.) A very good recent study of the political role of women in post-Weimar Germany is Gabriele Bremme, *Die Politische Rolle der Frau in Deutschland* (Göttingen, 1956).

organizational apparatus in Hamburg, and it was also the most outstanding critic of the political and social policies of Wilhelmian Germany. As we have seen, the centralizing tendencies of Imperial Germany were extremely unpopular in Hamburg. It seems likely that the SPD won considerable support from non-working-class groups because of its hostility to Bismarck, and its "liberal" position on political and social reform. At the same time, of course, the SPD was the *only* labor party in Hamburg.

By 1919 the situation had changed. The SPD was no longer the only labor party in the city, and it was no longer the outspoken critic of an unpopular central government. Most citizens had accepted the idea of national unity. Therefore, the People's Party and the Democrats were no doubt able to attract some of the middle-class elements away from the Socialists, especially those who had gotten something of a fright during the revolution. And as we have seen, some supporters were drawn away to the left. The appeal of the Social Democrats remained powerful, of course, because they seemed to be in control and seemed to know what they were doing at a time when few other groups did. But as subsequent elections showed, the foundation of votes on which the Hamburg SPD's control rested was a shifting one. How was the SPD to establish a relatively permanent and expanding base for the "social-democratization" of Hamburg?

The intention of the party leaders, of course, was to expand the appeal of Social Democracy to voters of both the left and right. As the SPD changed from a "class" to a "mass" party, specific socioeconomic interests would play a smaller role in party policies, and the Social Democrats would be able to gather in a broader spectrum of support under the aegis of "democracy." This aspiration on the part of SPD leaders to broaden the base of the movement was to some extent a reflection of German society's increasing acceptance of the ideas and the social classes represented by the SPD. The internal stresses of the war years had considerably accelerated the process of integrating the SPD and the labor movement as a whole into the political, social, and economic life of the nation. During the war years, the Hamburg SPD had proven itself a useful ally to the ruling groups by helping to suppress labor disputes, by postponing action on political reforms, and by assisting in the distribution and control of food and fuel supplies. As a result, the SPD won a degree of acceptance its leaders would, at one time, have scarcely believed possible.[20] And as we have seen, the Social Democrats found it relatively easy to cooperate with commercial and industrial leaders in the fight against "Bolshevism" during the initial stages of the revolution.

As a result of its increased "respectability," and its reassuring opposition to "Bolshevism," the postwar SPD was far from being a purely labor party. As nearly as it can be calculated, about twenty-five to thirty per cent of the SPD vote in January 1919 was derived from non-working-class voters, largely white-collar workers and officials.* Another interesting indication of the nature of the SPD vote in 1919 is provided by comparing the number of votes with the number of members in the party. In 1912 one SPD vote in three was probably cast by a party member, but in 1919 no more than one vote in five could have been cast by a card-carrying Social Democrat.[21]

Bringing together all the data collected here, we can make several important generalizations about the Hamburg SPD's electoral situation in 1919. It seems quite clear that the SPD was brought into power by a very loose coalition of old established party members and a large number of new voters, many of them women. To stay in power, then, the party would have to work much harder than it had before the war to retain its electoral support, let alone expand it. The party was on trial, not as a representative of narrow working-class interests, but as an instrument of government. To maintain or broaden its base, the SPD would have to demonstrate

* This is a most conservative estimate, based on the assumption that the tendency to participate in elections was the same for the working-class voter as for other voters. Clearly, this assumption tends to weight the figure in the direction of understating the proportion of SPD votes cast by non-working-class voters. Compare R. Blank in *Archiv für Sozial Wissenschaft* (1905) as cited in Sigmund Neumann, *Die Deutschen Parteien* (Berlin, 1932), p. 29.

that it could provide effective leadership on both national and local levels.

This analysis of the SPD's situation in 1919 also sheds some light on the circumstances surrounding the party's decline thereafter. The SPD's loss of support at the polls actually occurred in two different stages. The first was between 1919 and 1920, when the SPD vote dropped from 51.3 per cent of the total vote to 38.7 per cent. This loss was in conjunction with a huge drop in participation, from 90.4 per cent of those eligible in 1919, to 74.5 per cent in 1920. The second stage was from 1920 to 1924. Again, the SPD lost substantially, this time dropping to 27.5 per cent of all votes cast. But participation this time increased to 75.9 per cent.

In the Reichstag election of June 1920, the primary issue was the Weimar Republic itself. The Hamburg SPD quite plainly called upon the electorate to demonstrate its adherence to the Republic and its disapproval of the Kapp Putsch by voting Social Democratic.[22] Moreover, the SPD was prepared to accept responsibility for the actions of the national and Hamburg governments, including the military occupation of Hamburg.[23] In other words, both the Republic and the SPD's ability to govern it were on trial. The verdict was not very reassuring: the SPD's percentage of the total vote dropped 12.6 per cent from 1919 (see Table 5). Careful study of the returns from the election of June 1920 provides some interesting insights into the development of the parties of the left. Comparing the results of this election with the previous one, we find: (1) There were some 97,000 new voters on the lists in 1920. (2) There were nearly 30,000 fewer votes cast. (3) Both the Nationalists and the Independent Socialists made very large gains, together winning nearly 100,000 votes. (4) The SPD and the Democrats were the big losers, together losing over 135,000 votes.

One's first impulse is to conclude that there was a clear "swing to the extremes" on the part of labor and nonlabor voters alike. But this does not appear to have been the case. A rather large number of SPD and Democratic voters did indeed "swing to the right," and vote DVP and DNVP. Developments on the left, however, were rather more complicated. It is fairly clear that the USPD gains were not predominantly at the expense of the SPD.* On the other hand, there is a very close correlation between the number of new voters on the list in a given working-class district and the gains of the USPD. In 1920, therefore, the SPD was the victim of a large-scale electoral desertion, some voters shifting to the right, some to the left, and many simply not voting. These losses appeared to have occurred among working-class voters and other voters more or less equally. At the same time, the USPD was very successful in attracting support among the groups of working-class voters who appeared on the lists for the first time in 1920.

A look at the Bürgerschaft election held on March 1919 (only two months after the election to the National Assembly, and before the occupation of the city or the Kapp Putsch) helps to clarify the nature of the shift in votes during this period. The rate of participation was lower in this election, as was usual in local contests, but already the SPD had begun to lose ground in relation to the other parties, dropping from 51.3 per cent of the total vote in January to 50.8 per cent in March. This was a reversal of the usual pattern, which generally showed the SPD as doing rather better (relative to the other parties) in local elections than in national. While the USPD gained slightly in the city in general—and in many of the most important working-class districts in particular—it, too, slipped back somewhat from its earlier percentage (see Table 5). The SPD loss was by no means reflected everywhere in a USPD gain.

The big difference in 1920, of course, was made by the very large number of new voters on the lists. It is impossible to find out just who these new voters were, but most likely they were recently demobilized soldiers.[24] In every case, a relatively large increase in eligible voters was associated, in working-class districts, with a large increase in the USPD vote. From the socioeconomic standpoint, it is also clear that the major portion of the USPD vote was derived from workers in the "mass industries."

* The correlation between SPD losses and USPD gains was found to be only .51; that between SPD losses and percentage of working-class voters, .55.

We can derive two very important conclusions from this analysis of the 1920 election. First, the SPD proved unable to retain the support it had won in 1919. It lost votes to both left and right. In addition, it was badly hurt by the tendency of many of its supporters not to vote. Second, it seems clear that the USPD had managed to develop a new basis of support for itself among industrial workers and returned soldiers, most of whom were young and new to political life.

The significance of these developments becomes clear when we turn to the Reichstag elections of May 1924. This election was held under very different circumstances from the previous national election in 1920. Since then, there had been two serious economic crises—a "recession" or deflationary crisis in 1920–21 and a serious inflation in 1923. Both had given rise to unemployment and economic distress of unprecedented magnitude. At the same time, political differences had sharpened dangerously during the period. Rightist terrorists had made themselves conspicuous through a series of brutal political murders. And the Communists had given considerable evidence of their increasing strength and mounting bitterness. Throughout 1922 and 1923, acts of political force and violence had become commonplace—in Bavaria, the Ruhr, Saxony, and, as late as October 1923, in Hamburg itself. By the time of the elections in May 1924, the situation had improved somewhat. The currency was stabilized, civil peace was more or less restored, recovery from the worst of the financial difficulties seemed imminent, and unemployment had begun to decline.[25] But political feelings still ran high, as the extensive gains won by the extremes of left and right showed. And there seems to be little question, on the basis of the campaign materials, that the most important issues in the election were those relating to the inflation.[26]

The proportion of the total vote won by the SPD again dropped sharply, this time to 27.7 per cent. Again, it is reasonable to assume that the SPD lost some of its middle-class supporters to right-wing parties, but this time the factor of nonvoting did not contribute to the SPD decline (see Table 4). The SPD (as well as the USPD) lost heavily among the industrial workers, many of whom defected to the Communist Party.* The significance of this shift for the future development of Hamburg's political system was very great. The SPD was never again to win a significant segment of the labor groups that voted Communist in 1924. The decline in Communist vote until 1928 was closely related to the decline in participation in the districts in question, and shows little relation to SPD gains.[27] In other words, by 1924 a large portion of the working classes had rejected the Republic, never again to be enrolled in the ranks of its supporters.

It is, of course, far easier to observe shifts in voting behavior than to explain them, but reference to our earlier examination of the organizational development of the various labor organizations makes this task somewhat easier. Focusing on the development of the USPD, we can conclude with some certainty that the party was almost completely dependent on workers employed in large-scale "industrial" enterprises. As was pointed out earlier, the USPD did win the major share of its votes in the industrial-worker districts. And although complete membership data for the USPD is not available, it is certain that the party in fact did have its most important following in the Metalworkers' and Transport Workers' Unions, and that it recruited most of its membership from the large-scale industries. Of the three USPD leaders in the Bürgerschaft who were also trade-union officials, two were from the Metalworkers' and one was from the Transport Workers' Union. It may be recalled that these were the unions primarily responsible for the rapid expansion of ADGB membership between 1919 and 1921, and that the SPD won very few new members in this sector of the working classes. It would seem that the Free Unions and the USPD between them had managed to activate a large and previously passive segment of the electorate.

Turning to the second major political event mentioned above, the movement of industrial labor to support of the Communist

* The correlation between the proportion of these workers and the Communist vote was .93; SPD loss with Communist gain was .75.

Party between 1921 and 1924, we can observe a similar parallel. The great gains of the Communists among the industrial workers were reflected in the unions by a mass exodus of this same type of worker. Indeed, the number of workers who left just the four great industrial unions between 1921 and 1924 (most never to return) was great enough to have accounted for over half of the total Communist vote in 1924. And the SPD, of course, although it had never had a very large segment of industrial workers as members, lost many of those who had joined the party.

These observations make one realize that the trade unions, whether they wished to be or not, were very much involved in the political activity of the working classes. Indeed, it seems clear that the policies and actions of the trade-union leaders frequently had quite direct political repercussions. In 1920, for example, the USPD managed to attract and hold the loyalties of many who later voted Communist. The USPD at this time had basically republican leanings, and varied from the SPD in only a few particulars, most important, perhaps, in its demand for reform of the trade unions.[28] But during 1920 the pseudo-council-system became law, and the ADGB clearly demonstrated its resistance to reform and its intransigence in the face of opposition. The following year there was a Bürgerschaft election in Hamburg, and the new Communist Party won over ten per cent of the vote, leaving the USPD with only the barest remnant of its earlier force. At the same time, there was a mass exodus from the industrial unions of the ADGB.

The role that unemployment and economic hardship played in the development of the Communist movement was probably more supplemental than decisive. The industrial workers, the group in which the left opposition had consistently found its primary bases of support, were by no means the hardest hit by the effects of the inflation.[29] But no doubt these workers' growing dissatisfaction with the Republic was reinforced by the widespread poverty and misery. The crisis, of course, provided numerous occasions for the focusing of existing dissatisfactions, and operated as a very strong stimulus to action of one sort or another.

There may be one very important exception to this evaluation of the effects of the unemployment. In both of the great unemployment periods (1920–21 and 1923–24), apprentices and young assistants were apparently the first to be laid off and the last to be rehired. The several unions for which information is available reported that their loss of younger members after 1923 was proportionately much higher than their overall membership loss.[30] This could explain the young workers' alienation from republican labor organizations. And, as we have seen, the Communist Party had a relatively young following in any case. It is possible, then, that after 1924 the KPD was able to gain more support from young workers, regardless of their union affiliation.

The single most interesting conclusion to be drawn from this brief foray into electoral sociology is that the extent of the voter's previous political experience appears to have been the major determinant of his political behavior during the years covered by this study. Social Democratic control in 1919 rested on a very weak base of new voters who lacked traditions of political action. In the face of adversity, these voters were quick to switch to other parties or simply retire from the scene. The great importance of the USPD was that it managed to attract and stimulate into political action that vast new political force, the industrial worker. Again, these workers were quick to desert the USPD in favor of the KPD, or in relatively quiet times to stay away from the polls altogether.

The major characteristic which distinguished the various elements that composed this very large group of uncommitted voters was their relative "alienation" from the society. To a considerable extent, these citizens had not yet become full members of their community. The Social Democrats' failure to integrate these voters into political life was to have tragic consequences, both for the SPD and for the German Republic.

*Chapter 9*

# Conclusion

The dismantling of the "fortress of Socialism" did not take very long—only five years. Through a series of misfortunes, mistakes, and crises of the severest sort, the unions and labor parties ultimately lost much of their political strength, the respect and confidence of other portions of society, and their favorable bargaining position in the plant. In some respects, these results may have been avoidable, in others, perhaps not.

One must, of course, sympathize with the leaders of the SPD in their efforts to transcend class lines and build a broad republican coalition. But in attempting to maneuver between left and right during the revolutionary period, the SPD was following an extremely dangerous course. Even without the particular crises that forced the party to take a clear stand, the SPD probably had little chance for success. It would seem, first of all, that the heads of the SPD leaders were somewhat turned by the acceptance accorded the party by conservative circles at the war's end. As a result, the Social Democrats were perhaps a little too eager to avoid policies that might have jeopardized their new-won respectability.

At the same time, the SPD did not have a completely free hand to develop policies that might have appealed to the left wing of the labor movement. The relation of the Hamburg SPD to the national party in Berlin ruled out the possibility of approaching the left on the military issue. And the very close relationship between the SPD and the Free Unions precluded any real concessions on the works councils and other important matters concerning the nature and organization of industrial relations.

The role played by the Free Unions in Hamburg labor politics varied from time to time, but there can be no question of its real importance. Not only were the unions the primary source of the SPD's leadership and membership and its connecting link with the plant, but they were frequently in a position to exert a direct pressure on the course of events. This relationship between the party and the trade unions immensely complicated an already very difficult situation. The SPD almost certainly paid in votes for the union leaders' uncompromising handling of their own internal disputes. Unable to break away from its close trade-union connections, the SPD failed to gain the support it needed, either among the middle classes or among the anti-ADGB industrial workers. As a result, Germany's most important republican political party became, like its trade-union allies, very dependent upon a rather narrow group of skilled craft workers.

Indeed, it could well be argued that the outcome of the SPD's unifying efforts was actually decided at union headquarters. The leaders of the Free Unions appear not to have made much effort to understand or appreciate the very real problems that lay behind the opposition in their ranks. Rather than adjust to the new situation created by the growth of large-scale industry, the conservative union leaders chose to fight it through expulsions and other forceful techniques. In general, union policies operated to heighten, rather than minimize, the divisions in the labor movement. No really substantial concessions were ever granted to the leftists in the unions; for example, industrial unionism was not officially approved of until 1922, and even then nothing was done to increase the role of such unions in the federation. The desire of the union leaders to hold the federation together at any cost is understandable. But it seems very likely that the opposition might have been brought under control at an early stage by the granting of concessions that would have demonstrated the unions' concern with some of the very real needs of their members.

The failure of the unions to deal adequately with the problems posed by industrial unionism had extensive political repercussions. There can be little doubt that the opposition of many workers to trade-union policies was a major factor in the formation of the council movement and in the growth of the USPD. And this left opposition, in turn, politically activated large groups of industrial workers who had been relatively untouched by the trade-union and SPD organizations. In a sense, the council movement served as the catalyst in the creation of a new political force.

The USPD, as we have seen, very quickly found itself unable to provide the leadership for this new force. The "hardening" of the political situation in 1919 led to a division in the party leadership which in essence revolved around the question of acceptance or rejection of the Republic. Those USPD leaders who attempted to persuade their followers to renounce the "council idea," and the reforms it represented, for the sake of the Republic were unsuccessful. The USPD had been able to capitalize on the currents of dissatisfaction in the labor movement as long as its political goals were in harmony with them, but the party was not able to run counter to those currents and continue to hold its followers.

In this respect, the Communists picked up where the USPD left off. But they, like the Independents, were plagued by the difficulties inherent in translating a series of deep social and economic dissatisfactions into a concrete political program. The constituency they hoped to marshal presented frustrating problems for their would-be political organizers. Unaccustomed to political activity of any kind, the great numbers of industrial workers had a tendency, in relatively quiet times, to express their dissatisfaction by staying away from the polls. It was really only in response to considerable immediate pressure, in the form of inflation, unemployment, or some major act of government, that they constituted a viable political force. As a consequence, the Communists were actually much less successful in this period than one might have expected. It is rather surprising, in fact, that they were not able to achieve more. The Communists were consistently able to amass substantial support in matters limited to the labor movement, such as council elections in the plants, but their success at the polls was uneven, to say the least, and they failed to win significant support for any of their various "actions." It seems clear that there was very little consensus concerning political aims among either the leadership or the membership of the KPD. And the unexpected fluctuations in the strength of the party's support was reflected in violent fluctuations in party policy and leadership as Moscow and Berlin tried to harness the political power that seemed always just out of reach.

During the period we have studied here, the KPD seems to have served primarily as a vehicle of protest for the otherwise nearly powerless industrial worker. In Hamburg, at least, the Weimar Republic did not really do much to alleviate the worker's fundamental alienation from the society in which he lived and worked. Even the labor movement, it seemed, denied him his rightful place and influence. From the "politics of reform," represented by the USPD, the industrial worker moved increasingly toward "the politics of despair," which included occasional support of the Communist Party. And the political potential of that large group of citizens was dissipated in hopeless risings, such as that of October 1923, and vain protests of one sort or another. Convenient as it might be, it is dishonest to blame "Moscow" alone for the frequently very destructive political techniques of the KPD. To considerable extent, those techniques were little more than "improvements" on practices widely used in labor politics. The extensive use made by all parties on the left of mass meetings and demagogic propaganda seems ill-suited to the requisites of democratic politics. Moreover, the Free Unions, through their close connections with the SPD and their various efforts to ensure political uniformity in their membership, set the pattern for the intensive conduct of party politics at the plant level.

All considered, the labor movement was not a very adequate

"school for democracy." At the same time that the workers were being asked to forgo immediate economic rewards for the sake of abstract democratic goals, they were treated to the spectacle of manifestly undemocratic behavior on the part of those leaders, in party and union, with whom they were in closest contact. And these same leaders, captives perhaps of their own heritage, seemed unable to forgo the use of the traditional symbolism of "class warfare," which was doubtless taken seriously by many and which was clearly unsuited to the purposes of the pro-republican labor movement. On the basis of our study of the politics of labor in Hamburg, it is not surprising that the very large group of industrial workers who became politically active for the first time in late 1918 did not display a high degree of commitment to democratic political techniques. At the same time, of course, the high pitch of partisan activity in the plants served to weaken the efforts of the labor movement there. In the years after 1924, this conflict at the plant level did not diminish; if anything, it was intensified by a much stronger emphasis on forceful techniques. Strike actions in the late 'twenties frequently led to conflicts between the SPD paramilitary organization, the "Reichsbanner-Black-Red-Gold," and the KPD's "Red Front Fighters."

This picture of the Hamburg labor movement, deeply divided along socioeconomic and party lines, fighting in the workshops and on the streets, is a picture that we shall see again in German history. Party organizations in the plant and armed political bands were not new to Germany in 1933. They were only associated with a new party, the National Socialists. In Hamburg, the divisions within the labor movement that we have studied here were to play an important role in bringing that new party to power.

# Appendixes

*Appendix I*

# Statistical Methods Used in Chapter 8

Statistical materials are potentially among the richest sources available to the historian. This is perhaps particularly true for the student of German history. One has only to spend a few hours browsing in the *Statistik des deutschen Reiches* to become impressed with the thoroughness and industry of German statisticians, and with the amazing quantity of important information modestly presented in the neat rows of figures. The statistical materials compiled by the various *Land* governments are only slightly less comprehensive.

For the most part, historians have made little use of these materials, leaving them instead to the sociologist and the political scientist, who are often better equipped to handle them. This is not an entirely satisfactory arrangement. Scholars from other disciplines employ data in ways which are not always very useful for the historian, and which often leave something to be desired in terms of the historian's ideas about documentation. At the same time, historical literature is frequently full of rather careless and inexact statements concerning political and social developments. These statements are often based upon an inspection of the raw data, and while they may be useful and valid as far as they go, their inexactness precludes the possibility of careful comparative study.

The material in Chapter 8 demonstrates one technique by which the non-mathematically-educated historian can use available statistical data in a simple but rewarding way. For this purpose, the Spearman rank-order correlation is perhaps the most appropriate basic tool. This method of correlation has certain drawbacks, but has the overriding advantage of being very simple to use, requiring no more complicated apparatus than a desk-top computer and a slide rule. In the Spearman correlation, one arranges the quantitative statements of the two variables to be compared in rank-order—let us say, from the smallest to the largest—assigning a value to each position on the scale and observing the extent to which the two rankings are related. This is done according to the following formula:[1]

$$r_s = 1 - \frac{6(\Sigma d^2)}{N(N+1)(N-1)}$$

in which: $r_s$ = the coefficient of correlation;
$\Sigma d^2$ = the sum of the squares of the differences in rank; and
$N$ = the number of cases (here the 25 city districts of Hamburg).

The coefficient of correlation will always be a value between −1.00 and 1.00. If, for example, we are interested in the relationship between the proportion of working-class inhabitants in a district and the proportion of the total vote won by the SPD in that district, we would rank the districts from one to 25, first by proportion of workers and then by proportion of votes won by the SPD. The rank number in one column is then subtracted from the rank number having the same position in the other column, giving us the value for d (difference). Each difference is then squared, and the sum of all the differences applied to the formula. If $r_s$ should equal 1.00, we could say that for every increase in workers, there was a corresponding and proportional increase in SPD votes; if $r_s$ should equal −1.00, we could say that for every increase in workers, there was a corresponding and proportional decrease in SPD vote. If $r_s$ should be equal to 0.00, we could say that there was no relationship between the proportion of workers living in a district and the vote won by the SPD.

To determine whether any given correlation is a significant one, it is necessary to compare it to a computed "standard error of the coefficient of correlation." This figure will represent the "degree of correlation which might have occurred by chance."[2] It is closely related to the number of cases involved. The more cases, the smaller the standard error and the greater the dependability of the correlations. Here, where only 25 cases were used, the standard error is relatively large, and it is sometimes difficult to form a clear idea of the significance of borderline results. Only correlations greater than twice the coefficient of error have been considered significant in this study.* The correlations found in this study would of course have a much greater significance if they could be compared with the results of similar studies conducted for other parts of Germany.

The most important shortcoming of the Spearman correlation in a

* With 25 cases, a correlation of .40 would be twice the standard-error coefficient. In fact, all of the important correlations in Chapter 8 are greater than .60.

study of this kind is that it allows the comparison of only two variables at a time. In the study of participation, for example, the obvious approach would have been to compare a number of factors (age, social class, income, previous participation rates, etc.) to the participation rate, while controlling for one or more variables. Such comparisons are indeed possible through the use of multiple correlations, but are so complex that one needs electronic computers. Neither the time nor the funds necessary for such techniques were available for this study.

As was mentioned in the chapter itself, considerable care must be used in the application of correlations; their significance can easily be exaggerated.[3] They are perhaps best considered in the same light one considers any other isolated piece of historical evidence: they may be either confirmed or discredited by other evidence.

Certainly the most troublesome, time-consuming, and important methodological aspect of the analysis in Chapter 8 was determining the social composition of the various city districts, a problem that has long hindered the thorough exploration of the development of social classes and political parties in Germany. The author cannot claim to have solved this problem completely, but it seems likely that the technique used here, refined and improved perhaps, could very well be used for further studies of this kind.

The basic data was collected from the Occupational Census of 1925 and is presented in *Statistik des deutschen Reiches, Statistik des hamburgischen Staates, Statistische Mitteilungen des hamburgischen Staates* and *Hamburger statistische Monatsberichte.** Similar information, incidentally, is available for 1907 and 1933. The material collected by the *Land* government, which is considerably more detailed than the material in *Statistik des deutschen Reiches* (the latter does not include a breakdown by districts), was absolutely essential for the study.

Readily available in the statistical sources are figures for the percentages of self-employed (*Selbstständige*), white-collar (*Angestellten und Beamten*), workers (*Arbeiter*) and domestic servants in Hamburg as a whole and in each of the 25 districts.[4] These categories, in spite of the extensive use made of them in other studies, were not satisfactory when I attempted to associate them with political behavior. The problem, then, was to devise a means of breaking them down into more meaningful categories.

The occupational census (fortunately reported on the same basis as the election returns) provides data on the number of people in each district employed in each of 160 different economic groupings (*Wirtschaftszweige*), which in turn are subsumed under 27 larger headings.[5]

* See p. 179 for the precise locations of the most important data.

The narrower classifications were used here only in special cases because of the difficulty of processing large quantities of data by hand.

The number of persons employed in each of the 27 groupings in each district was first converted into a percentage of the total persons living in each district. These percentages were multiplied by the figures showing the city-wide average of the percentage of persons employed as workers in a given grouping to provide an estimate of what percentage of each district's population worked in each of the groupings.

The census also included a further breakdown into: "c-1, *Arbeiter in charakteristische Berufe*; c-2, *Betriebshandwerker und wichtige Hilfsberufe*; c-3, *Übrige Arbeiter*." These correspond quite well to the usual terminology of "skilled," "semiskilled" and "unskilled."

The process used to obtain the percentage of workers in each grouping in each district was then repeated to obtain percentages of "skilled" and so on in each grouping in each district. It was then possible to say, for example, that 9.1 per cent of the total population of St. Pauli were workers in Group XXII (transportation), and 4.8 per cent of the total population were unskilled workers in that field, and so on.

The figures thus obtained were found to vary in a regular way from figures that showed what proportion of the total population of each district were workers, and were accordingly corrected.[6] A number of checks were applied to these figures, and all indications point to the conclusion that the approximations thus obtained were reasonably accurate (probably within two to three per cent), and therefore usable for the purposes of this analysis. Parenthetically, it should be pointed out that the figures, which were computed with such difficulty, at one time existed on printed tally sheets. These were destroyed in Hamburg during the war, but it is possible that they could be found in other *Länder*. These sheets are available in Hamburg for the 1907 census.

The potential usefulness of the data prepared in this way was by no means exhausted in Chapter 8. Indeed, the surface has hardly been scratched. Oddly enough, a comparable study for all of Germany would in many respects be easier to carry out. One would have far less difficulty in comparing the data obtained from various sources. The only difficulty would be the physical quantity of data, but this could be negated through the use of modern data-processing equipment.

On the basis of the experience gained in handling the Hamburg data, I can see no difficulty serious enough to prevent a really comprehensive study of social class and political behavior in all Germany. The possibilities for gaining new insights into the origins of the National Socialist Party, to take just one example, would make such an effort very worthwhile.

*Appendix II*

# Statistical Supplement to Chapter 8

The charts and tables in this section were compiled from the following sources. *Statistik des deutschen Reiches,* Bd. 406 (Berlin, 1929), pp. 408–24; Bd. 408 (Berlin, 1929), pp. 180–89. *Statistik des hamburgischen Staates,* Bd. 33 (Hamburg, 1927), pp. 43–44, 79, 373–95. *Statistische Mitteilungen über den hamburgischen Staat,* Nr. 21 (Hamburg, 1927), pp. 62–74; Nr. 29 (Hamburg, 1932), p. 41. Meinrad Hagmann, *Der Weg ins Verhängnis* (München, 1946), pp. 9–11. Arthur Dix, *Die deutsche Reichstagswahlen 1871–1930 und die Wandlung der Volksgliederung* (Tübingen, 1930), p. 9. Heinrich Striefler, *Deutsche Wahlen in Bildern und Zahlen* (Düsseldorf, 1946), "Anhang, Tabelle I."

The following abbreviations are used in the column heads of the Tables in this Appendix: NA for National Assembly, R for Reichstag, and B for Bürgerschaft. The dates given are dates of election.

TABLE I

*Proportion of Seats Held by Major Parties in the Bürgerschaft and Reichstag, 1919–24*

| Parties | NA Jan. 1919 | B March 1919 | R June 1920 | B Feb. 1921 | R May 1924 | B Oct. 1924 | R Dec. 1924 |
|---|---|---|---|---|---|---|---|
| DNVP | 10.5% | 2.5% | 15.5% | 11.3% | 21.0% | 17.5% | 23.0% |
| DVP | 4.5 | 8.1 | 14.1 | 14.8 | 9.5 | 14.8 | 10.3 |
| Center | 21.4 | 1.3 | 14.0 | 1.3 | 13.8 | 1.3 | 14.0 |
| DDP | 17.5 | 21.0 | 8.5 | 14.8 | 5.9 | 13.1 | 6.5 |
| SPD | 39.0 | 50.5 | 26.0 | 42.0 | 21.2 | 33.1 | 26.8 |
| USPD | 5.2 | 8.1 | 18.3 | 1.3 | — | — | — |
| KPD | — | — | .9 | 10.6 | 13.3 | 15.0 | 9.1 |

TABLE 2

*Percentage of Total Vote Won by Seven Major Parties in Four National Elections, 1919–24 (Hamburg and Germany)*

| | Jan. 19, 1919 | | June 6, 1920 | | May 4, 1924 | | Dec. 7, 1924 | |
|---|---|---|---|---|---|---|---|---|
| Parties | *Hamburg* | *Germany* | *Hamburg* | *Germany* | *Hamburg* | *Germany* | *Hamburg* | *Germany* |
| DNVP | 2.7 | 10.3 | 12.4 | 14.9 | 19.5 | 19.5 | 17.0 | 20.5 |
| DVP | 11.7 | 4.4 | 15.1 | 13.9 | 12.2 | 9.2 | 14.0 | 10.1 |
| Center | 1.2 | 19.7 | 1.0 | 13.6 | 1.5 | 13.4 | 1.6 | 13.6 |
| DDP | 23.3 | 18.6 | 17.4 | 8.3 | 13.0 | 5.7 | 13.2 | 6.3 |
| SPD | 51.3 | 37.9 | 38.4 | 21.6 | 27.7 | 20.5 | 32.4 | 26.0 |
| USPD | 6.7 | 7.6 | 15.1 | 17.9 | .51 | — | .3 | — |
| KPD | — | — | .5 | 2.1 | 18.3 | 12.6 | 14.7 | 9.0 |

TABLE 3

*Proportion of Skilled, Semiskilled, and Unskilled Workers to Total Population (by district)*

*(Boldface indicates above Hamburg average)*

| District | Pop. (1925) | % Workers | % Skilled | % Semi-skilled | % Un-skilled |
|---|---|---|---|---|---|
| Altstadt | 19,420 | **51.0** | 18.4 | **5.2** | **27.4** |
| Neustadt | 65,136 | **56.9** | **23.1** | **5.4** | **28.4** |
| St. Georg | 96,411 | **46.6** | 17.5 | 3.3 | **26.1** |
| St. Pauli | 69,220 | **60.0** | **26.7** | **6.7** | **26.6** |
| Eimsbüttel | 129,664 | 44.3 | **21.6** | 2.1 | 20.6 |
| Rotherbaum | 31,252 | 17.3 | 6.3 | 2.5 | 8.5 |
| Harvestehude | 29,460 | 11.4 | 3.9 | 1.5 | 6.0 |
| Eppendorf | 85,948 | 36.0 | 14.7 | 4.4 | 16.9 |
| Gr. Borstel | 3,152 | 33.8 | 13.6 | 4.1 | 16.1 |
| Fuhlsbüttel | 8,884 | 26.7 | 11.4 | **7.0** | 12.3 |
| Langenhorn | 7,708 | 43.1 | 18.0 | 4.0 | 19.1 |
| Kl. Borstel | 2,422 | 26.5 | **23.0** | **8.9** | 12.4 |
| Alsterdorf | 3,116 | 31.8 | 13.5 | 4.2 | 14.1 |
| Winterhude | 47,586 | 44.5 | **19.3** | 4.7 | 20.5 |
| Barmbeck | 150,590 | **52.6** | **24.3** | 4.5 | 23.8 |
| Uhlenhorst | 44,785 | 44.4 | 18.1 | 4.4 | 20.9 |
| Hohenfelde | 33,891 | 24.0 | 9.2 | 3.3 | 11.5 |
| Eilbeck | 60,951 | 32.7 | 13.7 | 3.4 | 15.6 |
| Borgfelde | 33,960 | 42.7 | 17.5 | **5.4** | 19.8 |
| Hamm | 73,628 | 37.2 | 15.1 | 4.5 | 17.6 |
| Horn | 9,258 | **54.7** | **23.2** | 3.9 | **27.6** |
| Billwärder | 52,903 | **63.5** | **26.0** | **7.3** | **30.2** |
| Billbrook | 1,091 | **55.1** | 17.2 | **17.8** | 20.1 |
| Steinwärder | 4,401 | 35.5 | 15.2 | **5.2** | 15.1 |
| Veddel | 5,445 | **55.9** | **21.0** | **10.3** | 24.6 |
| City-state[a] | 1,075,024 | 44.6 | 19.2 | 5.1 | 25.2 |

[a] Includes rural districts not shown.

TABLE 4

*Eligible Voters (in thousands) and Percentage Thereof Casting Valid Votes in Eight National and Local Elections (by district)*

*(Boldface indicates above Hamburg average)*

| | NA, Jan. 1919 | | B, March 1919 | | R, June 1920 | | B, Feb. 1921 | |
|---|---|---|---|---|---|---|---|---|
| Districts | *Voters* | *% Voting* | *Voters* | *% Voting* | *Voters* | *% Voting* | *Voters* | *% Voting* |
| Altstadt | 11.4 | **91.8** | 11.4 | 76.2 | 15.8 | 66.2 | 15.5 | 56.6 |
| Neustadt | 36.9 | 88.9 | 37.1 | 77.3 | 48.8 | 64.2 | 48.9 | 55.4 |
| St. Georg | 58.6 | 88.5 | 58.5 | 78.0 | 71.4 | 69.7 | 69.8 | 66.7 |
| St. Pauli | 42.1 | 89.8 | 42.6 | 76.5 | 54.4 | 60.8 | 53.2 | 56.0 |
| Eimsbüttel | 77.1 | 90.1 | 77.5 | **80.8** | 85.1 | **79.2** | 85.6 | **71.9** |
| Rotherbaum | 19.1 | 88.4 | 18.7 | 74.0 | 23.0 | **77.5** | 23.6 | 68.7 |
| Harvestehude | 17.2 | **91.8** | 17.3 | 79.5 | 20.1 | 71.5 | 20.9 | 70.1 |
| Eppendorf | 52.5 | 90.3 | 52.5 | **80.8** | 56.7 | **78.0** | 57.1 | **73.9** |
| Gr. Borstel | 1.8 | 90.4 | 1.8 | **82.0** | 2.0 | **76.0** | 2.0 | **74.5** |
| Fuhlsbüttel | 3.5 | **90.9** | 3.5 | **81.0** | 3.7 | **82.2** | 4.1 | **75.5** |
| Langenhorn | 1.6 | 90.4 | 1.7 | **81.1** | 2.3 | **74.8** | 2.9 | **73.6** |
| Kl. Borstel | 1.3 | **93.0** | 1.3 | **84.5** | 1.4 | **82.4** | 1.4 | **81.5** |
| Alsterdorf | 1.3 | **92.6** | 1.2 | **83.6** | 1.3 | **76.6** | 1.4 | **77.0** |
| Winterhude | 26.6 | **92.6** | 27.0 | **83.4** | 30.1 | **77.9** | 30.1 | **74.9** |
| Barmbeck | 78.6 | **91.1** | 79.1 | **82.3** | 85.8 | **77.7** | 86.0 | **75.1** |
| Uhlenhorst | 24.7 | **92.0** | 25.0 | **81.1** | 27.9 | **76.7** | 28.9 | **72.6** |
| Hohenfelde | 21.4 | 90.2 | 21.4 | 78.8 | 24.1 | **75.0** | 24.5 | **70.6** |
| Eilbeck | 38.0 | **92.1** | 38.3 | **82.2** | 42.3 | **78.8** | 42.6 | **74.0** |
| Borgfelde | 21.0 | **92.0** | 21.3 | **83.3** | 23.5 | **79.0** | 23.7 | **76.8** |
| Hamm | 41.6 | **92.0** | 42.0 | **84.0** | 46.1 | **81.4** | 56.5 | **77.2** |
| Horn | 5.0 | **92.7** | 5.0 | **87.2** | 5.6 | **81.0** | 5.6 | **79.0** |
| Billwärder | 29.5 | **92.6** | 29.7 | **89.8** | 33.4 | **79.5** | 33.2 | **80.7** |
| Billbrook | .6 | **93.0** | .6 | **85.0** | .6 | **84.1** | .6 | **81.7** |
| Steinwärder | 1.7 | 90.4 | 1.5 | **87.0** | 2.0 | **82.4** | 2.3 | **76.8** |
| Veddel | 4.6 | 84.7 | 4.1 | 78.2 | 4.0 | **81.1** | 3.8 | **77.1** |
| City-state[a] | 659.4 | 90.4 | 661.6 | 80.6 | 756.8 | 74.5 | 759.3 | 70.1 |

[a] Includes rural districts not shown.

| R, May 1924 | | B, Oct. 1924 | | R, Dec. 1924 | | B, Oct. 1927 | |
|---|---|---|---|---|---|---|---|
| *Voters* | % *Voting* | *Voters* | % *Voting* | *Voters* | % *Voting* | *Voters* | % *Voting* |
| 15.3 | 70.4 | 15.3 | 57.2 | 16.1 | 69.6 | 15.1 | 67.2 |
| 49.2 | 68.0 | 50.3 | 54.1 | 52.2 | 62.6 | 54.1 | 67.5 |
| 71.5 | 74.3 | 72.4 | 61.4 | 75.2 | 71.8 | 76.0 | 72.1 |
| 52.5 | 67.6 | 54.0 | 52.2 | 56.7 | 60.5 | 56.0 | 67.4 |
| 90.9 | 72.6 | 91.9 | 65.9 | 93.5 | **76.8** | 96.5 | **77.1** |
| 23.7 | 74.4 | 23.9 | 62.7 | 24.9 | 74.6 | 24.9 | 66.4 |
| 21.3 | 77.8 | 21.7 | 64.5 | 22.5 | **77.5** | 23.0 | 68.8 |
| 60.8 | **79.2** | 61.3 | **68.1** | 62.5 | **79.1** | 65.4 | **75.8** |
| 2.1 | **79.4** | 2.2 | **69.4** | 2.2 | **79.7** | 2.2 | **75.8** |
| 4.3 | **83.1** | 4.4 | **76.5** | 4.4 | **83.1** | 5.5 | **79.1** |
| 4.4 | 73.8 | 4.0 | **78.0** | 4.0 | **82.6** | 4.9 | **82.6** |
| 1.6 | **83.3** | 1.6 | **77.0** | 1.6 | **83.5** | 1.9 | **77.3** |
| 1.8 | 67.7 | 1.5 | **68.4** | 1.6 | **76.8** | 1.7 | **79.3** |
| 31.8 | **81.3** | 32.3 | **69.8** | 32.9 | **81.7** | 35.5 | **77.9** |
| 99.5 | **82.0** | 100.7 | **70.3** | 102.3 | **80.0** | 112.1 | **80.2** |
| 30.6 | **79.4** | 31.1 | **68.0** | 31.6 | **78.8** | 32.0 | **76.4** |
| 25.7 | **78.8** | 25.9 | **67.0** | 26.7 | **79.2** | 26.8 | **77.2** |
| 44.3 | **80.4** | 44.7 | **69.8** | 45.4 | **80.6** | 45.7 | **77.0** |
| 24.6 | **80.8** | 24.8 | **69.5** | 25.4 | **80.7** | 26.3 | **78.2** |
| 50.1 | **81.2** | 50.4 | **72.1** | 51.2 | **81.4** | 56.9 | **77.8** |
| 5.9 | **81.6** | 6.0 | **69.5** | 6.1 | **81.5** | 6.5 | **80.3** |
| 35.2 | **81.6** | 35.8 | **72.4** | 36.4 | **80.4** | 37.8 | **83.5** |
| .7 | **86.0** | .7 | **75.9** | .7 | **84.1** | .8 | **82.4** |
| 3.2 | **81.2** | 3.2 | **73.6** | 3.2 | **79.3** | 3.0 | **80.1** |
| 4.1 | **80.1** | 3.9 | **68.3** | 4.2 | **78.4** | 4.6 | **83.6** |
| 804.0 | 78.4 | 813.4 | 66.1 | 833.5 | 76.2 | 871.7 | 75.2 |

TABLE 5

*Percentage of Total Vote Won by the SPD and the Left Radicals in Eight National and Local Elections (by district)*
*(Boldface indicates above Hamburg average)*

| | SPD | | | | | | | |
|---|---|---|---|---|---|---|---|---|
| District | NA 1/19 | B 3/19 | R 6/20 | B 2/21 | R 5/24 | B 10/24 | R 12/24 | B 10/27 |
| Altstadt | 48.9 | 47.7 | 36.2 | 37.1 | 23.6 | 29.2 | 28.3 | 33.4 |
| Neustadt | 48.7 | **55.5** | **41.5** | **44.4** | 26.8 | 31.8 | **32.3** | 34.7 |
| St. Georg | **58.2** | **56.8** | **43.1** | **47.0** | **29.8** | **36.0** | **35.7** | **41.1** |
| St. Pauli | **54.1** | **54.7** | **39.6** | **43.3** | **28.2** | **34.2** | **34.1** | **38.5** |
| Eimsbüttel | **51.4** | **52.4** | **38.6** | 40.0 | **27.8** | **32.7** | 32.2 | **38.7** |
| Rotherbaum | 26.9 | 24.6 | 22.1 | 22.0 | 16.0 | 18.6 | 18.6 | 24.9 |
| Harvestehude | 24.8 | 19.7 | 15.5 | 15.5 | 12.5 | 12.4 | 13.3 | 17.2 |
| Eppendorf | 42.4 | 42.0 | 32.1 | 26.2 | 23.9 | 28.4 | 28.2 | 33.8 |
| Gr. Borstel | 39.8 | 41.0 | 30.0 | 29.6 | 21.1 | 24.3 | 22.8 | 26.3 |
| Fuhlsbüttel | 38.5 | 40.2 | 32.8 | 34.0 | 21.2 | 23.3 | 23.4 | 27.0 |
| Langenhorn | **59.5** | **61.7** | **50.6** | **54.0** | **43.4** | **48.8** | **47.5** | **54.9** |
| Kl. Borstel | 38.7 | 43.2 | 30.8 | 28.8 | 21.3 | 25.2 | 24.7 | 30.9 |
| Alsterdorf | 39.8 | 40.4 | 30.1 | 31.6 | 21.3 | 26.7 | 24.8 | 28.2 |
| Winterhude | **53.4** | **52.3** | **39.9** | **41.6** | 26.4 | **32.6** | **32.5** | **39.2** |
| Barmbeck | **63.6** | **62.3** | **42.4** | **49.8** | **34.4** | **40.2** | **39.4** | **46.0** |
| Uhlenhorst | **52.7** | 46.8 | 35.9 | 37.6 | 25.0 | 29.1 | 29.1 | 35.1 |
| Hohenfelde | 28.2 | 26.2 | 20.2 | 20.8 | 14.8 | 16.9 | 17.6 | 23.1 |
| Eilbeck | **57.6** | 41.2 | 30.7 | 31.8 | 22.4 | 25.7 | 26.5 | 32.8 |
| Borgfelde | **52.5** | **51.9** | **41.3** | **42.8** | **29.0** | **33.2** | **33.1** | **39.3** |
| Hamm | 48.6 | 47.0 | **40.3** | 37.6 | 26.0 | 30.5 | 29.9 | 36.1 |
| Horn | **60.2** | **59.2** | **44.4** | **45.1** | **31.7** | **37.8** | **37.1** | **42.9** |
| Billwärder | **73.5** | **70.8** | **61.5** | **63.0** | **41.1** | **47.8** | **48.5** | **53.0** |
| Billbrook | **73.2** | **64.8** | **58.5** | **62.3** | **45.5** | **50.5** | **47.2** | **56.5** |
| Steinwärder | **51.6** | 49.7 | **53.3** | **52.3** | **38.9** | **47.3** | **48.2** | **52.9** |
| Veddel | **64.6** | **60.5** | **54.8** | **60.6** | **43.8** | **50.0** | **50.8** | **53.2** |
| City-state | 51.3 | 50.5 | 38.4 | 40.6 | 27.7 | 32.2 | 32.2 | 38.2 |

Left Radicals

| NA[a] 1/19 | B[a] 3/19 | R[b] 6/20 | B(2/21) USPD | B(2/21) KPD | R[c] 5/24 | B[c] 10/24 | R[c] 12/24 | B[c] 10/27 |
|---|---|---|---|---|---|---|---|---|
| 4.9 | 6.5 | **16.4** | 1.4 | **11.1** | **20.5** | **16.4** | **17.4** | **20.6** |
| **9.8** | **13.2** | **21.8** | 1.3 | **16.3** | **28.9** | **23.9** | **23.7** | **32.1** |
| 5.8 | 7.5 | **16.6** | 1.3 | **12.7** | **21.8** | **17.5** | **16.8** | **21.2** |
| **17.1** | **16.6** | **25.4** | **3.0** | **19.4** | **29.4** | **23.8** | **23.7** | **29.6** |
| **8.3** | **9.1** | **16.4** | **2.2** | **12.6** | **19.6** | **15.8** | **15.2** | **17.4** |
| 1.9 | 3.5 | 6.0 | .4 | 3.6 | 4.3 | 4.1 | 4.2 | 5.1 |
| 2.0 | 2.0 | 4.9 | .5 | 2.3 | 4.4 | 3.1 | 3.4 | 4.2 |
| 5.4 | 7.0 | 12.2 | .9 | 8.6 | 13.2 | 10.9 | 10.5 | 12.6 |
| 1.8 | 2.7 | 8.5 | **2.9** | 4.7 | 7.6 | 6.1 | 6.6 | 6.2 |
| 3.4 | 4.4 | 4.5 | .2 | 3.4 | 6.8 | 5.2 | 5.5 | 4.8 |
| 3.2 | .9 | 8.6 | — | **11.8** | 18.5 | **15.2** | **14.8** | 14.5 |
| 3.4 | 3.2 | 3.6 | **2.9** | 5.2 | 5.4 | 5.8 | 6.6 | 6.0 |
| 2.7 | 1.3 | 5.1 | — | 3.6 | 6.8 | 7.7 | 4.6 | 5.0 |
| 6.1 | **10.9** | **16.1** | **1.6** | **12.3** | **19.8** | **16.2** | **15.4** | 15.6 |
| **8.2** | **11.1** | **20.0** | **2.5** | **14.9** | **24.4** | **20.0** | **19.4** | **20.5** |
| 5.4 | 7.2 | **16.0** | .7 | **12.9** | **20.8** | **17.1** | **16.7** | **18.9** |
| 2.6 | 3.2 | 6.2 | .5 | 4.2 | 6.4 | 5.0 | 5.2 | 6.1 |
| 3.9 | 3.4 | 8.3 | 1.2 | 5.9 | 9.5 | 7.4 | 7.3 | 9.0 |
| 3.9 | 5.1 | 11.4 | 1.1 | 8.1 | 9.7 | 12.2 | 11.4 | 13.7 |
| 4.6 | 5.5 | 11.1 | .9 | 8.4 | 14.5 | 12.1 | 11.3 | 12.0 |
| 5.4 | 6.3 | **16.1** | **2.2** | **11.9** | **21.1** | **16.7** | **16.6** | **17.3** |
| 6.7 | 7.9 | **17.9** | .6 | **14.4** | **26.5** | **20.7** | **20.5** | **23.3** |
| 3.4 | 1.8 | 6.1 | — | 3.6 | 10.3 | 7.2 | 5.9 | 8.4 |
| 2.6 | 5.6 | 7.0 | — | 8.2 | 13.1 | 7.4 | 8.1 | 11.4 |
| **9.6** | **12.7** | 13.5 | — | 7.9 | 17.6 | 11.3 | 13.2 | 16.7 |
| 6.7 | 8.1 | 15.5 | 1.4 | 11.0 | 18.8 | 15.0 | 14.5 | 16.9 |

[a] USPD.
[b] USPD, KPD combined; KPD less than 1% of total vote.
[c] USPD, KPD combined; USPD less than 1% of total vote.

# Notes

# Notes

Complete authors' names, titles, and publication data are given in Part I of the Bibliography, pp. 209–19. The bracketed numbers in the Notes are numbers assigned for convenience of citation to various documents in the Hamburg State Archives; the titles of these documents are listed in Part II of the Bibliography, pp. 219–21.

CHAPTER 1

1. For a discussion of the concept of legitimacy, see Lipset, Chapter 3. Some of the social and psychological ramifications of a democratic political system are discussed in Almond and Verba, Chapter 10; and in Sidney Verba, "Comparative Political Culture," in Pye and Verba, especially pp. 526–37.

2. See William Kornhauser, *The Politics of Mass Society* (New York, 1959), especially Part I, "The Theory of Mass Society."

3. See the discussion of the "participation revolution" in Almond and Verba, pp. 4–6.

CHAPTER 2

1. See Kiesel for a revealing description of life in St. Pauli.
2. For a discussion of this concept, see Mönckeberg, p. 11.
3. See the chapter entitled "Von 9–3," in Adolf Goetz, pp. 127–31.
4. Mönckeberg, pp. 16–17.
5. From the report of the collegium quoted in Baasch, Vol. II, p. 13.
6. *Ibid.*, pp. 12–29.
7. For example, see Mönckeberg, pp. 16–17.
8. Baasch, p. 141.
9. Herschel, pp. 72–74.
10. Baasch, p. 144.
11. Article 34 of the Constitution of the North German Confederation cited by Baasch, p. 209.
12. *Ibid.* p. 163.
13. *Ibid.*, p. 150.
14. *Ibid.*, pp. 189–91.
15. *Ibid.*, p. 153.
16. *Ibid.*, pp. 153–54.
17. *Ibid.*, p. 155.
18. In Herschel, p. 1.
19. Herschel, pp. 8–9.
20. *Ibid.*, pp. 26–43.
21. Bünemann, p. 23.

22. Baasch, p. 226.
23. *Ibid.*
24. *Ibid.*, p. 155.
25. *Ibid.*, p. 226.
26. This argument is stated at some length by Baasch, pp. 320–21, 324. His presentation of it is especially valuable because he apparently agrees with it.
27. *Ibid.*, p. 320.
28. The best summary of the governmental system is in Bünemann, pp. 12–18.
29. Bünemann, p. 16.
30. *Ibid.*, p. 17.
31. Baasch, p. 112.
32. Bünemann, p. 18.
33. *Ibid.*, p. 19.
34. Quoted in Baasch, p. 112.
35. *Ibid.*, p. 111.
36. With some alterations, Shils's concept of the "modernizing oligarchy" provides an apt description of the political system in prewar Hamburg. See Edward Shils, *Political Development in the New States* (Gravenhage, Netherlands, 1962), pp. 67–74.
37. This is a central thesis of Leonard Krieger, *The German Idea of Freedom* (Boston, 1957).
38. Compare Shils, pp. 67–74, with Almond and Coleman, pp. 55–58.
39. Georg Stenzel, "Die Industrie," in *Hamburg in seiner politischen, wirtschaftlichen und kulturellen Bedeutung* Hrsg. Deutschen Auslands-Arbeitsgemeinschaft Hamburg (Hamburg, 1921), p. 87.
40. *Ibid.*, pp. 88–91.
41. *Ibid.*, p. 88.
42. See the excellent tables and charts in Syrup, "Appendix."
43. Baasch, p. 156.
44. Schult, p. 20.
45. Baasch, p. 241.
46. *Ibid.*, p. 372.
47. This idea is widespread in Socialist literature. The particular quote is from Bünemann, p. 28.
48. Richard Perner, "Hamburg, Hauptstadt des deutschen Sozialismus," *Hamburger Echo* (May 20, 1950), "Sonderbeilage."
49. See Baasch, pp. 237–42.
50. See Schult.
51. Baasch, pp. 242; 244.
52. Hasselmann, p. 19.
53. Rieger, Mendel, and Postelt, pp. 30–67.
54. *Ibid.*, pp. 89–112, 272. See also, Henry Everling, "Hamburg das Zentrum der Genossenschaften," *Hamburger Echo* (May 20, 1950), "Sonderbeilage."
55. Rieger et al., pp. 250–53 (Biographische Anmerkungen).
56. Vieth, p. 152.
57. See, for example, Everling, "Sonderbeilage."

58. The most informative treatment of this relationship is in Schorske, pp. 88–115.

59. ADGB (Ortsausschuss Gross-Hamburg), *Bericht 1924,* p. 145.

60. SPD-Hamburg, *Jahresbericht Landesorganisation 1913–14.*

61. For the early history of the Hamburg labor movement, see Laufenberg, *Geschichte,* Vol. II.

62. Franz Spliedt, "Hamburgs gewerkschaftliche Pionerstellung," *Echo* (May 20, 1950), "Sonderbeilage."

63. Bünemann, p. 28.

64. SPD-Hamburg, *Die Sozialdemokratie,* pp. 105–6.

65. Berlau, pp. 41–44.

66. Sigmund Neumann, p. 29.

67. Anschütz, p. 18.

68. Many of these points are taken up in detail with reference to the nation-wide development of the SPD in Roth.

69. See Baasch, pp. 358–60.

70. *Ibid.,* p. 250.

71. Bünemann, p. 107.

72. *Ibid.*; Mönckeberg, pp. 24–25.

## CHAPTER 3

1. Carl August Schröder, *Aus Hamburgs Blütezeit. Lebenserinnerungen* (Hamburg, 1921), p. 335.

2. *Ibid.,* pp. 104, 335–37.

3. Bünemann, p. 60.

4. [60]. See p. 189 for explanation of bracketed numbers.

5. Bünemann, pp. 55–56.

6. [19]. Emphasis mine.

7. Paul Neumann, p. 89. This is the single most dependable source for the revolution in Hamburg.

8. Compare, e.g., GP, Arbeiterrat Gross-Hamburg, *1919–20,* pp. 65–67.

9. See *Echo* (January 31, 1919).

10. *Arbeitsamt,* Fasc. 26, Nr. 1. (Hamburg State Archives.)

11. See Bünemann, pp. 18–20.

12. Gertrud Bäumer, "Heimatchronik," *Die Hilfe,* Nr. 46 (November 1918), p. 540. Cited in Bünemann, p. 60.

13. Paul Neumann, p. 62.

14. *Ibid.,* p. 3; SPD-Hamburg, *Jahresbericht 1914–19,* p. 10.

15. SPD-Hamburg, *Jahresbericht 1919–20,* p. 10.

16. Paul Neumann, p. 3.

17. *Ibid.,* pp. 3–4.

18. *Ibid.,* p. 4.

19. For Zeller, see Bünemann, p. 75.

20. *Ibid.*, pp. 75–78; Paul Neumann, p. 5.

21. SPD-Hamburg, *Jahresbericht 1914–19,* p. 10; Paul Neumann, pp. 6–7.

22. SPD-Hamburg, *Jahresbericht 1914–19,* p. 10.

23. Baumann, p. 19.

24. SPD-Hamburg, *Jahresbericht 1914–19,* p. 10.

25. Paul Neumann, p. 7.

26. *Ibid.* For a discussion of the significance of the councils and their development throughout Germany, see Tormin; von Oertzen; Kolb; and Schulz, esp. pp. 65–100.

27. Paul Neumann, p. 9; SPD-Hamburg, *Jahresbericht 1914–19,* p. 11.

28. Paul Neumann, p. 9.

29. *Ibid.*

30. *Ibid.*, p. 12.

31. Lamp'l, pp. 12–14.

32. Paul Neumann, p. 12.

33. *Ibid.*

34. Lamp'l, p. 13.

35. Bünemann, p. 89.

36. Carl Schröder describes the working of the system in some detail. *Aus Hamburgs Blütezeit. Lebenserinnerungen* (Hamburg, 1921), p. 345.

37. For example, see *Hamburger Echo* (November 7, 1918).

38. See the maps showing the development of the councils in Tormin, pp. 148–51 ("Anhang").

39. An interesting discussion of the possibilities of the councils may be found in Rosenberg, pp. 20–24. See also von Oertzen, pp. 20–26, 51–68, 109–80.

40. The details of the council system are described in Laufenberg, *Die Hamburger Revolution,* pp. 4–5.

41. See the statement of Hense (SPD) in the negotiations between the representatives of the Senate and those of the Workers' Council on November 16, 1918. "Wörtlicher Auszug aus den stenographischen Protokoll," reprinted in Lamp'l, pp. 95–101.

42. Paul Neumann, p. 16.

43. The Free Unions and the SPD decided on policy together at this time. See Paul Neumann, p. 17.

44. *Ibid.*

45. *Ibid.*, p. 21.

46. SPD-Hamburg, *Jahresbericht 1914–19,* p. 10.

47. Paul Neumann, p. 22.

48. See, e.g., Laufenberg, *Die Hamburger Revolution,* pp. 5–6.

49. SPD-Hamburg, *Jahresbericht 1919–21,* pp. 81–83.

50. Paul Neumann, p. 21.

51. Lamp'l, pp. 14–15.
52. [7]. See also Lamp'l, pp. 95–109.
53. *Arbeiter- und Soldatenrat* 2, "Gemeinschaftliche Sitzung der Fünfer-Kommission des A-S Rats mit Vertretern des Senats am 16-11-18." (Hamburg State Archives.)
54. The proclamation is reprinted in Lamp'l, p. 19.
55. See Paul Neumann, p. 31; Bünemann, pp. 144–45; Laufenberg, p. 6.
56. Ferdinand Vieth, p. 221.
57. Schröder, *Aus Hamburgs Blütezeit,* p. 345.
58. Lamp'l, p. 16.
59. Baumann, p. 50.
60. See Bolland, p. 98.
61. See Laufenberg, *Die Hamburger Revolution,* pp. 8–9, 13–15.
62. Baumann, "Einleitung."
63. *Ibid.*, p. 39.
64. Baumann, p. 47.
65. *Ibid.*, p. 69.
66. Paul Neumann, p. 42.
67. Baumann, p. 63.
68. Bünemann, p. 148.
69. SPD-Hamburg, *Jahresbericht 1914–19,* p. 20.
70. *Ibid.*
71. Paul Neumann, p. 51.
72. Baumann, p. 59. Compare the interpretation in Waldman, pp. 161–91, 211–16.
73. Paul Neumann, pp. 52–54.
74. *Ibid.*, pp. 55–57.
75. *Ibid.*, pp. 59–61.
76. [7], pp. 8–16.
77. Paul Neumann, p. 129.
78. *Ibid.*
79. *Hamburger Volks-Zeitung* (January 21, 1919).
80. Laufenberg, *Die Hamburger Revolution,* p. 19.
81. See Rosenberg, pp. 32, 56–57.
82. See SPD-Hamburg, *Jahresbericht 1914–19,* pp. 26–31.

CHAPTER 4

1. *Stenographischen Berichte über die Sitzungen der Bürgerschaft im Jahre 1919* (March 24, 1919).
2. See the tables in Appendix II, pp. 179–85.
3. Bolland, p. 97. The law is reprinted in full in "Anlage 4," pp. 181–83.
4. Bolland, "Anlage 4," p. 181. Emphasis mine.
5. See the Weimar Constitution, Article 17.
6. The Hamburg Constitution of 1921 is given in full in Bolland, "Anlage 5," pp. 183–91.

7. Weimar Constitution, Article 17. According to the translation in Fisk, p. 150.
8. SPD-Hamburg, *Die Sozialdemokratie,* pp. 9–15.
9. Bolland, p. 98.
10. *Ibid.*
11. *Ibid.*
12. For Diestel, see *Echo* (March 1, 1924), p. 1; and Baumann, pp. 97–98.
13. Schwarz, pp. 3, 58.
14. SPD-Hamburg, *Die Sozialdemokratie,* p. 40.
15. See, for example, *Echo* (March 12, 1921), p. 3.
16. The SPD attitude toward strikes is clearly reflected in *Echo* (January 13, 1920), p. 3.
17. *Echo* (March 12, 1921), p. 3.
18. Bünemann, p. 28.
19. SPD-Hamburg, *Die Sozialdemokratie,* p. 22.
20. GP: Arbeiterrat Gross-Hamburg, *1919–20,* pp. 62–66.
21. *Ibid.,* pp. 122–25. *Hamburger Nachrichten* (March 28, 1919), p. 5.
22. GP: Arbeiterrat Gross-Hamburg *1919–20,* p. 6. Paul Neumann, p. 122.
23. *Echo* (March 21, 1921), "Beilage." ADGB, *Correspondenzblatt der Generalkommission,* 30 Jg., Nr. 37 (September 1920), pp. 495–96.
24. See the Weimar Constitution, Art. 165.
25. See, for example, Tormin, pp. 126–30.
26. Reich, p. 57.
27. The connections between the Senate and one of the old chambers are frequently mentioned in Detaillistenkammer Hamburg.
28. ADGB, *Correspondenzblatt,* 30 Jg., Nr. 7 (September 1920), p. 45.
29. GP: Arbeiterrat Gross-Hamburg, *1919–20,* p. 8.
30. [66].
31. See, for example, [5].
32. Timpke, p. 15.
33. [56], Conv. I, Doc. 51a, "Bericht des Senats betr. Wahlrecht.
34. Baasch, p. 250.
35. Gordon A. Craig, *The Politics of the Prussian Army* (New York, 1956), pp. 351–52.
36. *Allgemeiner Kongress der Arbeiten- und Soldatenräte Deutschlands, Stenographische Berichte,* pp. 61–65, as cited by Craig, p. 352n.
37. *Ibid.*

38. SPD-Hamburg, *Die Sozialdemokratie,* p. 45.
39. See Gustav Noske, *Von Kiel bis Kapp* (Berlin, 1920), pp. 78–84.
40. Paul Neumann, p. 73.
41. *Echo* (January 31, 1919), p. 1.
42. Paul Neumann, p. 90.
43. *Ibid.*
44. *Ibid.,* p. 93.
45. *Ibid.,* p. 97. Bünemann, p. 100.
46. Quoted in Paul Neumann, p. 97.
47. *Ibid.*
48. *Ibid.,* p. 103.
49. *Ibid.,* pp. 98–102.
50. Baumann, pp. 88–90.
51. [17]; and Danner, pp. 11–12.
52. *Echo* (April 16, 1919), p. 1. Germany (*Reichskanzlei*) R431/2268.
53. SPD-Hamburg, *Jahresbericht 1919–21,* p. 8.
54. Danner, p. 13.
55. *Ibid.,* p. 11.
56. *Ibid.,* p. 12.
57. *Ibid.,* p. 13.
58. See [15].
59. Danner, p. 15.
60. [15].
61. *Ibid.*
62. Danner, p. 21.
63. *Ibid.,* p. 17.
64. For the conditions of martial law, see [60].
65. [15].
66. *Ibid.,* p. 20.
67. *Ibid.,* p. 22.
68. Danner, p. 15.
69. GP: Arbeiterrat Gross-Hamburg, *1919–20,* pp. 64–66.
70. Danner, p. 17.
71. *Ibid.,* p. 16.
72. SPD-Hamburg, *Jahresbericht 1919–21,* pp. 15–17.
73. Danner, pp. 18–19. Compare Danner's quotation and the one above to those in Noske, *Von Kiel bis Kapp,* pp. 163–66. Danner's version is almost certainly the correct one. Noske probably quoted from newspaper accounts. The version he gives is very close to the original draft of the letter from the President of the Senate to General von Lettow reproduced in [60]. The Senator, however, corrected his letter before sending it off, and the corrected version is more in harmony with Danner's version. There is no evidence of any document signed "KPD, Ortsgruppe Hamburg," the document that Noske mentions on p. 165 of his book.
74. Danner, pp. 17–18.
75. See Baumann, p. 106.
76. *Ibid.*
77. *Ibid.,* pp. 104–6.
78. [60].
79. See, for example, Germany (*Reichskanzlei*) R431/2118; and *Hamburger Volks-Zeitung* (November 30, 1919), p. 1.
80. Baumann, p. 106.

81. *Ibid.*

82. For the Kapp Putsch, see Waite, Chapter 4.

83. Danner, p. 23.

84. *Ibid.*, p. 24.

85. *Ibid.*, pp. 31–33.

86. *Ibid.*, p. 33.

87. *Ibid.*, pp. 33–34.

88. The role of Hamburg labor in the Kapp Putsch is treated on pp. 106–8 of this book. The events recounted here are from SPD-Hamburg, *Jahresbericht 1919–21*, pp. 20–30; and Danner, pp. 31–45. Also see von Salomon, pp. 160–92.

89. Meyn's curious proclamation to his troops is given in Danner, p. 35.

90. See Danner, pp. 45–48.

91. See Maehl, pp. 301–4 for a summary of the literature on this subject.

92. [15]. See statement preceding "Urteil."

93. See [17]; and Baumann, p. 61. Germany (*Reichskanzlei*), R431/2268.

## CHAPTER 5

1. Weimar Constitution, Article 157. In Fisk, p. 182.

2. Gebhardt, p. 91.

3. Umbreit, p. 195.

4. The November Agreement is given in full in Preller, pp. 53–54.

5. *Ibid.*, p. 53.

6. For the development of the trade unions during the war, see Umbreit; and Reich, pp. 222–24.

7. Reich, p. 224.

8. From the Agreement in Preller, pp. 53–54.

9. See especially Articles 157–65 of the Weimar Constitution.

10. Reich, p. 89.

11. Trade union membership 1913 to 1931 is summarized in Reich, p. 26; and Umbreit, p. 195.

12. Seidel, *Trade Union Movement,* pp. 90–91; and Braunthal, p. 243.

13. Preller, pp. 53–54.

14. The best and most thorough discussion of the problem of industrial versus craft unions in the German labor movement is in Tarnow, pp. 6–11 especially. See also Seidel, *Trade Union,* pp. 35–36; and ADGB, *Correspondenzblatt der Generalkommission,* 29 Jg., Nr. 40 (October 10, 1919), pp. 461–63; 32 Jg., Nr. 24 (June 17, 1922), pp. 335–41.

15. Tarnow, p. 6.

16. See the membership of the executive committee of the ADGB-Hamburg in the "Anhang" to each ADGB *Bericht,* 1920–24.

17. See Michels, *Political Parties,* pp. 142–55; and Schorske, pp. 260–62. See also the autobiographical novel by Willi Bredel, *Maschinenfabrik,* pp. 131–35.

18. Seidel, *Trade Union,* p. 42; and Koller, pp. 44–50.

19. Koller, pp. 49–50.

20. Tarnow, p. 5; Robert Dissmann, "Berufsverbände oder Industrieorganisation," ADGB, *Correspondenzblatt,* 32 Jg., Nr. 24 (June 17, 1922), pp. 335–36.

21. Schorske, pp. 260–62; Dissmann, pp. 339–41; Michels, *Political* Parties, p. 144.

22. "Politische Gewerkschaftszerstörung," ADGB, *Correspondenzblatt,* 29 Jg., Nr. 40 (October 4, 1919), pp. 461–63.

23. This is treated at length in Seidel, *Trade Union,* pp. 32–34; Schorske, pp. 8–16, 36–53; and Hunt, pp. 202–42.

24. Schorske, pp. 108–10.

25. *Ibid.,* pp. 36–58.

26. *Ibid.* S. Prüll, "Industrieverbände," ADGB, *Correspondenzblatt,* 32 Jg., Nr. 24 (June 17, 1922), pp. 337–40.

27. Schorske, pp. 260–61.

28. Bünemann, pp. 53–54. SPD-Hamburg, *Jahresbericht, 1914–19,* p. 9. Snell, pp. 67–68.

29. Rettig, p. 6; SPD-Hamburg, *Jahresbericht 1914–19,* p. 9; [69].

30. Baasch, pp. 245, 250.

31. Rettig, pp. 6, 25.

32. See Giese's novel; and Helwig, pp. 167–74.

33. [69].

34. For example, see Bünemann, pp. 55–56; and [19].

35. Paul Neumann, p. 18. Baumann, p. 19.

36. Paul Neumann, p. 4.

37. *Ibid.*

38. Baumann, p. 15.

39. Varain, pp. 120–21.

40. For example, see Paul Neumann, pp. 2, 19, 48; and SPD-Hamburg, *Jahresbericht, 1914–19,* pp. 10, 21. Unfortunately, the *Bericht* of the ADGB-Hamburg for 1919 is not available.

41. Paul Neumann, p. 2. Compare Chapter 2 of this book.

42. For example, see SPD-Hamburg, *Jahresbericht 1914–19,* p. 19; Paul Neumann, pp. 46, 59–60; and Bünemann, p. 129.

43. Paul Neumann, p. 14–23.

44. Compare pp. 158–61 below.

45. Paul Neumann, p. 52.

46. Compare, SPD-Hamburg, *Jahresbericht 1914–19,* pp. 20–22; and Paul Neumann, pp. 2, 52, 62.

47. Paul Neumann, p. 52.

48. *Ibid.*

49. *Ibid.*

50. *Hamburger Volks-Zeitung* (November 17, 1919), p. 1. See also Seidel, *Die Gewerkschaften,* p. 15.

51. *Hamburger Volks-Zeitung* (October 4, 1919), p. 1.

52. Paul Neumann, pp. 52–54. *Hamburger Volks-Zeitung* (October 4, 1919), p. 1.

53. Rettig, pp. 25, 26.

54. For example, see Rettig, p. 10.

55. For example, see Baasch, p. 239.

56. UP: Deutsche Metallarbeitersverband, *Jahresbericht 1919,* p. 3.

57. *Ibid.,* pp. 6–8.

58. *Ibid.,* p. 7; *Hamburger Volks-Zeitung* (November 6, 1919), "Beilage."

59. UP: Deutsche Metallarbeitersverband, *Jahresbericht 1919,* p. 7.

60. See *Hamburger Volks-Zeitung* (November 25, 1919), "Beilage" and (November 18, 1919), "Beilage"; *Echo* (February 28, 1920), p. 3, (January 5, 1920), p. 3, (January 27, 1920), p. 1; and [24].

61. The group was led by Däumig and R. Müller. See Prager, pp. 191–92. The best history of the council movement is Kolb's. See also Schulz, pp. 65–100; and von Oertzen.

62. See Rettig, pp. 1–11; Prager, pp. 193–94; Baumann, p. 15; and *Protokoll des Parteitages des SPD 1919,* p. 188 as cited in Rettig, p. 11.

63. Varain, p. 161; Prager, pp. 209–11; resolution adopted by the Reichskonferenz der Betriebsräte in Halle, October 24–25, 1919 in *Hamburger Volks-Zeitung* (October 30, 1919), p. 1.

64. See Laufenberg, *Die Hamburger Revolution,* pp. 8–14.

65. *Ibid.*

66. GP: Arbeiterrat Gross-Hamburg, *1919–20,* p. 59.

67. *Correspondenzblatt 1919,* as cited in Varain, p. 146.

68. See Varain, pp. 122–23, 144–45.

69. Weimar Constitution, Article 165.

70. GP: Arbeiterrat Gross-Hamburg, *1919–20,* p. 59; the law is given in full in Guillebaud, pp. 249–72.

71. Seidel, *Trade Union Movement,* p. 105.

72. The ADGB handling of the councils is described in detail in *Echo* (July 5, 1920), "Beilage." Also see ADGB, *Correspondenzblatt,* 30 Jg., Nr. 23 (June 6, 1920), pp. 299–300.

73. The arguments both for and against the draft law are well presented in *Der Grundstein. Organ des deutschen Bauarbeiterverbandes* (Hamburg) (April 12, 1919), p. 1. Also see: DMV, *Der Deutsche Metallarbeitersverband im Jahr 1920*, p. 126; *Hamburger Volks-Zeitung* (July 19, 1919), "Beilage: Zur Frage der Betriebsräte."

74. GP: Arbeiterrat Gross-Hamburg, *1919–20*, p. 59.

75. *Ibid.*, pp. 59–60.

76. *Ibid.*, p. 59.

77. See Rettig, pp. 12–14.

78. See Guillebaud, pp. 45–52.

79. As at the time of the strike supporting Laufenberg on Jan. 9, 1919. See Paul Neumann, pp. 51–54.

80. See Rettig, p. 7; GP: Arbeiterrat Gross-Hamburg, *1919–20*, p. 59.

81. GP: Arbeiterrat Gross-Hamburg, *1919–20*, pp. 60–62, 65–67. See above, Chapter 3.

82. GP: Arbeiterrat Gross-Hamburg, *1919–20*, p. 61.

83. ADGB, *Protokoll der Verhandlungen des 10. Kongresses*, p. 324.

84. Liepart, p. 158.

85. Quoted in Leipart, p. 160.

86. *Ibid.* The ADGB liked to call itself the "Einheitsorganisation."

87. ADGB, *Correspondenzblatt*, Jg. 1921, as cited in Rettig, p. 73.

88. Rettig, p. 77.

89. ADGB (Hamburg), *Bericht 1921*, p. 59.

90. GP: Arbeiterrat Gross-Hamburg, *1919–20*, p. 70.

91. See *Echo* (January 24, 1921), p. 3.

92. GP: Arbeiterrat Gross-Hamburg, *1919–20*, pp. 61–63.

93. *Ibid.*, p. 61.

94. Germany (*Reichskanzlei*) R431/1942.

95. GP: Arbeiterrat Gross-Hamburg, *1919–20*, p. 63.

96. *Ibid.*

97. From the study by Gay.

98. GP: Arbeiterrat Gross-Hamburg, *1919–20*, p. 59.

99. Prager, p. 203.

100. *Ibid.*

101. Leipart, p. 161.

102. Prager, pp. 207–12, 223–29.

103. GP: Arbeiterrat Gross-Hamburg, *1919–20*, p. 62.

104. *Hamburger Volks-Zeitung* (November 21, 1919), p. 3.

105. Fischer, pp. 95, 118–20; *Hamburger Volks-Zeitung* (November 21, 1919), p. 3; (October 27, 1919), p. 1.

106. *Echo* (March 20, 1920), p. 1.

107. *Echo* (March 16, 1920), p. 2.
108. *Echo* (March 20, 1920), p. 1.
109. *Echo* (March 18, 1920), p. 1.
110. SPD-Hamburg, *Jahresbericht 1919–21*, p. 29.
111. ADGB (Hamburg), *Bericht 1920*, p. 9.
112. See Varain, pp. 174–85.
113. *Echo* (March 22, 1920), p. 1; *Echo* (March 23, 1920), p. 1; and succeeding issues.
114. ADGB (Hamburg), *Bericht 1920*, p. 9.
115. *Ibid.*, p. 8.
116. Thälmann will be treated in Chapter 6. The split in the USPD in Hamburg is reported in *Hamburger Volks-Zeitung* (October 27, 1919), p. 3, for the earlier stages; and in *Echo* (April 4, 1920), p. 3; (April 11, 1920), p. 1.

CHAPTER 6

1. *Correspondenzblatt,* Jg. 30, Nr. 16 (April 17, 1920), pp. 194–95.
2. Flechtheim, pp. 59–61; Fischer, pp 118–19.
3. Fischer, p. 118; Schüddekopf, pp. 119–21.
4. Germany *(Reichskanzlei)*, R431/2024; Fischer, p. 395.
5. See Flechtheim, pp. 72, 76.
6. [72].
7. [33], report of May 24, 1921. These Polizeibehörde reports were apparently compiled from information gathered by police spies. The reports for 1921 and 1922 are thoroughly and carefully done, and provide invaluable source material.
8. See Fischer, p. 568; Angress, pp. 254–56.
9. Fischer, pp. 423, 143–47, 171, 225–27; Angress, pp. 40–41, 52–60, 101n.
10. Fischer, p. 423; Angress, pp. 254–55; Bredel, pp. 77–84; interview with Heinrich Brandler.
11. Fischer, p. 405. [33], May 13, 1921, July 24, 1922, and July 31, 1922.
12. Fischer, p. 423.
13. *Rote Fahne,* Vol. 24 (December 1924) cited in Rettig, p. 191.
14. [33], report of June 19, 1922; also see Bredel, *Maschinenfabrik N&K*, pp. 13–17.
15. [33], *ibid.*; Bredel, *ibid.*, pp. 35–42.
16. [33], *ibid.*; interview with Willy Ruhnau.
17. Guillebaud, pp. 273–80.

18. *Echo* (February 18, 1920).
19. Guillebaud, pp. 273–80.
20. [33], March 24, 1922, and August 19, 1922.
21. [33], August 10, 1922.
22. *Ibid.*; UP: Deutscher Metallarbeiter-Verband, *1921,* p. 137.
23. [33], May 30, 1922.
24. [33], March 8, 1922.
25. *Echo* (February 26, 1921), "Beilage."
26. UP: Deutscher Eisenbahners-Verband, *1921,* p. 65; UP: Deutscher Metallarbeiter-Verband, *1920,* p. 8; [33], February 22, 1921.
27. SPD-Hamburg, *Jahresbericht 1919–21,* pp. 67–69.
28. [33], March 14, 1922, and August 10, 1922; *Echo* (February 25, 1921), "Beilage."
29. *Echo* (January 25, 1921).
30. *Echo* (February 18, 1921), "Beilage."
31. *Echo* (January 15, 1921).
32. ADGB (Hamburg), *Bericht 1922,* p. 11.
33. *Hamburger Nachrichten* (March 1, 1921), p. 3 and succeeding issues; [33], report of March 15, 1921.
34. Danner, p. 50; SPD-Hamburg, *Jahresbericht 1919–21,* p. 31.
35. The following account is taken from Danner, pp. 50–51; SPD-Hamburg, *Jahresbericht 1919–21,* pp. 33–34; and *Hamburger Nachrichten* (March 24, 1921).
36. Danner, p. 50.
37. SPD-Hamburg, *1919–21,* pp. 35–37.
38. See, e.g., *Hamburger Nachrichten* (March 26, 1921), p. 1.
39. See Angress, Chapter 6; Borkenau, pp. 221–27; Flechtheim, pp. 75–77.
40. [33], Nov. 28, 1921.
41. *Ibid.*
42. [33], April 27, 1922; cf. UP: Deutscher Metallarbeiter-Verband, *Bericht 1922,* pp. 3–11.
43. See Angress, pp. 223–34; Flechtheim, pp. 76–77.
44. Fischer, p. 227; [33], May 16, 1922; "Vom Leipziger Parteitag bis zum Oktober, 1923," Sonderbeilage zu *Die Internationale,* Heft 10-11 (1924), p. 3.
45. Fischer, p. 227; [33], June 27, 1922, and June 9, 1922.
46. [33], March 8, 1922, May 16, 1922.
47. ADGB (Hamburg), *Bericht 1922,* p. 36.
48. Flechtheim, p. 82; ADGB, *Correspondenzblatt,* Jg. 32, Nr. 26 (July 1, 1922), pp. 369–70.

49. ADGB (Hamburg), *Bericht 1922*, pp. 22–24, 36; *Echo* (July 9, 1921), p. 3; GP: Arbeiterrat Gross-Hamburg, *Bericht 1921*, p. 22.

50. See SPD-Hamburg, *Jahresbericht 1921–24*, p. 7; [34].

51. [33], report of June 9, 1922, and June 20, 1922.

52. *Ibid.*

53. See von Salomon, pp. 304–43; [34]; [44]; and Halperin, pp. 228–35.

54. ADGB, *Protokoll des 11. Kongresses, 1922*, p. 572.

55. SPD-Hamburg, *Jahresbericht 1921–24*, pp. 7–10; ADGB (Hamburg), *Bericht 1922*, pp. 37–43; Flechtheim, p. 83; Angress, pp. 241–44.

56. [34].

57. Braunthal, pp. 58–59.

58. [33], June 27, 1922.

59. ADGB (Hamburg), *Bericht 1922*, p. 11.

60. *Ibid.*

61. Unemployment figures were no longer published after December 1922. Compare ADGB (Hamburg), *Bericht 1923*, p. 128.

62. *Echo* (October 21, 1923).

63. Compare UP: Deutscher Transportarbeiter-Verband, *Bericht 1923–24*, p. 218. The financial report for 1923 is handled with one word "zwecklos."

64. [3]; [48].

65. SPD-Hamburg, *Sozialdemokratische Staats-u. Gemeindepolitik*, p. 78.

66. *Echo* (October 8, 1924).

67. GP: Arbeiterrat Gross-Hamburg, 1923–24, p. 74.

68. *Ibid.*, p. 81.

69. *Ibid.*, pp. 81–82.

70. *Ibid.*

71. See *ibid.*, pp. 74–81.

72. See Anderson, p. 92; Halperin, pp. 241–60.

73. For these events, see [62], especially, "Chef der Ordnungspolizei: Bericht über die Unruhen, 1923."

74. SPD-Hamburg, *Jahresbericht 1921–24*, pp. 21–22.

75. [62].

76. *Ibid.*; *SPD-Hamburg, 1921–24*, p. 24.

77. SPD-Hamburg, *1921–24*, pp. 22–23.

78. In addition to the above, see [48]; and UP: Deutscher Metallarbeiter-Verband, *Bericht 1923–24*, p. 4.

79. See Angress, pp. 314–77; Flechtheim, pp. 81–85; Fischer, pp. 227–30, 255–56; Schürer, p. 59.

80. Habedank, pp. 62–63.

81. Carr, p. 204.

82. *Ibid.*

83. *Ibid.*, p. 206; Angress, pp. 298–99; Fischer, pp. 316–17.

84. *Communist International,* pp. 60–61.

85. *Schultess' Europäischer Geschichtskalender,* Bd. 64, pp. 177–78.

86. *Ibid.*, pp. 180, 183.

87. The major eyewitness accounts of the rising are Danner; Habedank; Reissner; Zeutschel; and Valtin. The most complete, analytical treatment, including a thorough evaluation of sources, may be found in Angress, pp. 426–74.

88. Angress, pp. 448–49.

89. Danner, p. 72.

90. Eudin and Fisher, p. 220.

91. See Valtin, pp. 71–87; Angress, p. 449.

92. Danner, pp. 79–103; Polizeibehörde Hamburg, "Denkschrift über die Unruhen im Oktober 1923," (Zum dienstlichen Gebrauch), pp. 18–20.

93. Habedank, pp. 129–30.

94. Virtually all accounts are in agreement concerning the actual course of the rising as rendered here.

95. Questions concerning the origin of the orders for the rising, and the manner in which they were communicated, have been debated since 1924. The issue is treated by Angress, p. 444n.

96. For example, see *Communist International.*

97. *Echo* (October 21, 1923), p. 3.

98. *Echo* (October 29, 1923), p. 3.

99. See V. Palmberg, "Lessons of the Hamburg Rising," *Communist International,* X, No. 21 (Nov. 1, 1933), pp. 760–66; Danner, p. 79.

100. Fischer, p. 405; *Echo* (April 2, 1924).

101. Danner, p. 73.

102. Polizeibehörde Hamburg, "Denkschrift über die Unruhen . . . ," p. 17.

103. Angress, p. 446n, does not agree with this conclusion, but his evidence (cf. pp. 448–49) would appear to support it.

104. Thälmann's place in party hagiology was assured with the release, in 1953, of the East German Government film, "Ernst Thälmann: Held der Revolution!" The Hamburg Staatsarchiv made it possible for me to see this film, a copy of which is on file at the Polizeibehörde in Hamburg.

105. *Die freie Gewerkschaften* (April 9, 1924), p. 1.

106. ADGB (Hamburg) *Bericht 1924,* p. 72.

107. *Ibid.* p. 39.

108. *Echo* (April 3, 1924).

109. *Die freie Gewerkschaften* (April 2, 1924), p. 3.

110. [52].

111. Statistisches Jahrbuch des hamburgischen staatsgebietes (Hamburg, 1925), p. 274.

112. Rettig, p. 196.

113. UP: Verband der graphischen Hilfsarbeiter, *Bericht 1924*, p. 32.

114. *Die freie Gewerkschaften* (October 8, 1924), p. 1.

115. *Ibid.*

116. *Echo* (May 28, 1924).

117. [39].

## CHAPTER 7

1. "Democracy and the Social System," in Harry Eckstein, ed., *Internal War* (Glencoe, Ill., 1963), p. 287.

2. Quoted in Burks, p. 199.

3. All biographical information concerning Bürgerschaft members was taken from an unpaged manuscript in the Hamburg Staatsarchiv (see [72]). Compare the study of the national SPD leadership by Richard N. Hunt, *German Social Democracy* (New Haven, 1963).

4. [72].

5. *Ibid.* The biographical information on the Communist members is incomplete in many respects.

6. See I. Siemann, "Soziologie der sozialdemokratische Führerschaft 1918–33," phil. dissertation (Göttingen, 1955), pp. 61–67; Hunt, *German Social Democracy*, p. 83.

7. [72]. Compare Hunt, *German Social Democracy*, pp. 225–26.

8. [72].

9. Referred to simply as "Die Wanderung." [72].

10. *Ibid.*

11. *Ibid.* In this respect also, the Communist data is incomplete.

12. Geiger, pp. 72–73; Sigmund Neumann, pp. 28–29. See also Michels, *Political Parties*, Chapter 4, "The Position of the Leaders in Relation to the Masses in Actual Practice."

13. Michels, pp. 185–201.

14. See the age grouping in I. Siemann, "Soziologie der Sozialdemokratische," p. 28.

15. These statements are scattered throughout a series of document folders, sometimes in fragmentary form. My major sources were docu-

ments [9], [10], [11], [12], [13], [14]. Because one man's statements may be recorded in several document folders, reference will be made of the person rather than to the folder or folders in which the statement appears. This archival material was supplemented by interviews with ex-Communists in Hamburg. The most important of these were with Heinz and Willi Ruhnau.

16. The term "career expectations" and some of the categories used here are taken from Almond, *The Appeals of Communism,* especially Chapter 7, "Social Characteristics."

17. Walter Knöpfel.

18. E. Hoffmann.

19. For example, Rühl, Köppen.

20. A. Levy.

21. H. Jensen, E. Hoffman, A. Levy among others.

22. H. Jensen.

23. Köppen.

24. *Ibid.*

25. Rühl.

26. Hermann Esser.

27. Peter Junge.

28. Almond, *The Appeals of Communism,* pp. 127–66.

29. The conflict between generations was of considerable political importance during the Weimar period. Compare Helwig for youth movements in Hamburg, especially pp. 159–61, 177–79.

30. SPD-Hamburg, *Jahresbericht 1914–19,* pp. 78–79; and *Jahresbericht 1919–21,* pp. 136–38.

31. ADGB (Hamburg), *Bericht 1914,* pp. 32–33; *Bericht 1921,* pp. 60–63.

32. SPD (Hamburg), *Jahresbericht 1924–25,* pp. 106–9; ADGB (Hamburg), *Bericht 1924,* pp. 144–45.

33. On the basis of a rough approximation of the occupational composition of the work force derived from GP: Statistisches Landesamt, Bd. 34, p. 37.

34. SPD-Hamburg, *Jahresbericht 1919–21,* p. 138.

35. SPD-Hamburg, *1924–25,* pp. 106–9.

36. *Ibid.*; SPD-Hamburg, *1914–19,* pp. 78–79. But compare SPD-Hamburg, *1913–14,* p. 120.

37. ADGB (Hamburg), *Bericht 1921,* pp. 60–63. See also, ADGB (Hamburg), *Bericht 1925,* p. 131.

38. This is an approximation, not an exact figure. Compare ADGB (Hamburg), *Bericht 1921,* pp. 60–63.

39. ADGB (Hamburg), *Bericht 1924,* pp. 144–45.

40. These figures were derived from the respective yearly publications of the two organizations, as cited above.

41. The graph was constructed on the basis of the data in *Statistisches Reichsamt,* Bd. 406, p. 212; ADGB (Hamburg), *Bericht 1924,* pp. 144–45; SPD-Hamburg, *Jahresbericht 1924–25,* pp. 106–9.

42. These figures were derived from the two organizations' yearly publications, as cited above. For the ratio of union to party membership in twelve important areas in Germany, see Braunthal, p. 135.

43. SPD-Hamburg, *Jahresbericht 1914–19* and *1919–21,* in the places cited; ADGB (Hamburg), *Bericht 1914* and *1921,* in the places cited.

44. [72].

45. ADGB (Hamburg), *Bericht 1920,* p. 22; [72].

46. [72]. Compare Hunt, *German Social Democracy,* p. 229; Braunthal, p. 215.

## CHAPTER 8

1. Probably the best survey of European election studies is in Tingsten; see especially Chapter 3, "Occupation and Social Status in Political Elections." For a more recent summary of the literature, see Lipset, *Political Man*; and Linz, especially pp. 288–412. See also Gosnell, pp. 69–97; Heberle; Lane, pp. 321–34; and the brief summary of some French studies by Goguel and Dupeux.

2. [34]; von Salomon, pp. 304–28.

3. See Heberle, pp. 90–120; Striefler, pp. 55, 57.

4. See, for example, the discussions concerning the formation of a "Bürgerbloc" in 1924 in [38].

5. This development was frequently discussed in right-wing newspapers. See, for example, the clippings in [35]. See also the SPD program for the Reichstag election in 1920 in *Echo* (May 8, 1920), p. 1.

6. See the Weimar Constitution, Articles 10, 8 and 11, and 7 and 88.

7. For example, see Baumann, p. 117.

8. The verbatim accounts of Bürgerschaft sessions are in [16].

9. The nature of the school reform was one such issue. But again, it was most often discussed in terms of the national party policies. See, for example, SPD-Hamburg, *Die Sozialdemokratie,* pp. 55–60; SPD-Hamburg, *Sozialdemokratische Staats- und Gemeindepolitik,* pp. 111–13.

10. Compare Table 2 with Linz, pp. 343–72.

11. See Meyer; Lipset, *Political Man,* pp. 179–219; Tingsten, pp. 135–43; Gosnell, pp. 74–82.

12. See Lipset, p. 183, note 9. Unless otherwise specified, the term "labor" is here used according to the definition presented in connection

with the census of 1925. See GP: Statistisches Reichsamt, Bd. 402, "Einführung in die Berufszählung, 1925."

13. Compare, for example, GP: *Hamburger Statistische Monatsberichte, 1924,* pp. 97, 89, for summaries of the wage situation.

14. For example, Rotherbaum and Harvestehude.

15. See Dix, pp. 32–37.

16. See GP: *Statistiches Landesamt,* Bd. 33, "Altersgliederung der Erwerbstätigen im Staat, 1925," p. 57.

17. GP: Deutscher Metallarbeiter-Verband, *Bericht 1922,* p. 88; GP: Deutscher Transportarbeiter-Verband, *Bericht 1923–24,* p. 24–27.

18. Compare Lipset, *Political Man,* pp. 210–12.

19. The results of the 1912 election are reported in the *Hamburger Nachrichten* (January 13, 1912).

20. See pp. 65–66 above.

21. *Echo* (January 6, 1924).

22. *Echo* (April 8, 1920); (May 8, 1920).

23. SPD-Hamburg, *Bericht 1919–21,* pp. 38–45.

24. See *Echo* (June 7, 1920.)

25. See Halperin, pp. 280–96.

26. See [38].

27. Compare GP: *Statistische Mitteilungen,* Nr. 25, pp. 94–115.

28. *Echo* (May 9, 1920) and (May 10, 1920).

29. See the unemployment and wage data in ADGB-Hamburg, *Bericht 1923,* p. 128; GP: *Statistisches Landesamt,* Bd. 33, pp. 70–71; GP: *Hamburger statistische Monatsberichte,* 1924 (July), p. 129; [51].

30. UP: Deutscher Transportarbeiter-Verband, *Bericht 1924,* pp. 24–27; UP: Deutscher Bauarbeiter-Verband, *Bericht 1925,* p. 24; UP: Deutscher Holzarbeiter-Verband, *Bericht 1925,* p. 5.

## APPENDIX I

1. See Blalock, pp. 317–19.

2. Burks, p. 208.

3. Some of the limitations on the uses of correlations are pointed up in Robinson. See also the answering letter from Herbert Menzel in *American Sociological Review,* XV (1950), p. 674.

4. GP: *Statistisches Landesamt,* Bd. 33, p. 79.

5. For a complete discussion of the methods, terminology and categories of the census, see GP: *Statistisches Reichsamt,* Bd. 402, Teil I, "Einführung in die Berufzählung 1925."

6. GP: *Statistisches Landesamt,* Bd. 33, p. 79.

# Bibliography

Part I of the Bibliography lists books; articles; government, union, and party publications; and documents from the archives of the German Chancellery. Part II lists documents from the Hamburg State Archives.

PART I

Abendroth, Wolfgang. "Aufgaben und Methoden einer deutschen historischen Wahlsoziologie," *Vierteljahreshefte für Zeitgeschichte,* 5 Jg., 3 Heft (July 1957), 300–306.

———. Die Deutschen Gewerkschaften. Heidelberg: Rothe, 1954.

ADGB (Allgemeiner Deutscher Gewerkschaftsbund).

———. Protokoll der Verhandlungen des 10. Kongresses. Berlin: Verlagsgenossenschaft ADGB, 1919.

———. Protokoll der Verhandlungen des 11. Kongresses. Berlin: Verlagsgenossenschaft ADGB, 1922.

——— (Ortsausschuss Gross-Hamburg). Bericht über das Geschäftsjahr, Jg. 1921, 1922, 1923, 1924, 1925, 1926. Hamburg: Auer Verlag, 1922–27.

Almond, Gabriel A. The Appeals of Communism. Princeton: Princeton University Press, 1954.

———, and James S. Coleman. The Politics of the Developing Areas. Princeton: Princeton University Press, 1963.

———, and Sidney Verba. The Civic Culture. Princeton: Princeton University Press, 1963.

Anderson, Evelyn. Hammer or Anvil: The Story of the German Working-Class Movement. London: Gollanz, 1945.

Angress, Werner T. Stillborn Revolution: The Communist Bid for Power in Germany, 1921–1923. Princeton: Princeton University Press, 1963.

Anschütz, Helga. "Die NSDAP in Hamburg: Ihre Anfänge bis zur Reichstagswahl vom 14. Sept., 1930." Unpub. dissertation, Hamburg, 1956.

Baasch, Ernst. Geschichte Hamburgs. Gotha-Stuttgart: Andreas Perthes, 1924. 2 vols.

Baumann, Frederick-Segel. Um den Staat: Ein Beitrag zur Geschichte der Revolution in Hamburg. Hamburg: Alster Verlag, 1924.

Bendix, Reinhard. "Social Stratification and Political Power," *American Political Science Review,* XLVI (1952), 367–73.

Berlau, Joseph. The German Social Democratic Party, 1914–1921. New York: Columbia University Press, 1949.

Blalock, Hubert M., Jr. Social Statistics. New York: McGraw-Hill, 1960.

Bolland, Jürgen. Die hamburgische Bürgerschaft in alter und neuer Zeit. Hamburg, 1959 (private printing).

Borkenau, Franz. World Communism: A History of the Communist International. New York: Norton, 1939.

Bracher, Karl D. Die Auflösung der Weimarer Republik. Stuttgart: Ring Verlag, 1955.

Braunthal, Gerard. "The Politics of the German Free Trade Unions during the Weimar Republic." Unpub. dissertation, Columbia University, 1954 (Univ. Micr., 6584).

Bredel, Willi. Ernst Thälmann: Beitrag zu einem politischen Lebensbild. Berlin: Dietz, 1950.

———. Maschinenfabrik N&K. 2. Ausgabe. Berlin: Dietz, 1960.

Bruck, W. F. Social and Economic History of Germany from William II to Hitler. London: Oxford, 1938.

Buddenburg, Theodor. "Das soziologische Problem der Sozialdemokratie," *Archiv für Sozialwissenschaft und Sozialpolitik,* XLIX (1922), 108–32.

Bünemann, Richard. "Hamburg in der deutschen Revolution von 1918-19." Unpub. dissertation, Hamburg, 1951.

Burks, R. V. The Dynamics of Communism in Eastern Europe. Princeton: Princeton University Press, 1961.

Carr, Edward H. The Interregnum, 1923–24. London: Macmillan, 1954.

Cassau, Theodor. Die Gewerkschaftsbewegung: Ihre Soziologie und ihr Kampf. Halberstadt. H. Meyer, 1925.

———. "Die Gewerkschaften und die Politik," *Gewerkschaftsarchiv,* II (June 1925), 337–43.

Cole, George D. H. Communism and Social Democracy. (Vol. IV of A History of Socialist Thought.) New York: St. Martin's, 1958.

Communist International. Die Lehren der deutschen Ereignisse. Hamburg, 1924.

Coper, Rudolf. Failure of a Revolution. Cambridge: Cambridge University Press, 1955.

Danner, Lothar. Ordnungspolizei Hamburg. Hamburg: Verlag Deutsche Polizei, 1958.

Detaillistenkammer Hamburg. Die Detaillistenkammer Hamburg 1904–29. Hamburg: Druckerei Gesellschaft, 1929.

Deutsche Auslands-Arbeitsgemeinschaft Hamburg, Hrsg. Hamburg in seiner politischen, wirtschaftlichen und kulturellen Bedeutung. Hamburg: L. Friedrichsen, 1921.

Dix, Arthur. Die deutsche Reichstagswahlen 1871–1930 und die Wandlungen der Volksgliederung. (Nr. 77 in Recht und Staat in Geschichte und Gegenwart.) Tübingen: J. C. B. Mohr, 1930.

Eckstein, Harry. A Theory of Stable Democracy. Research Monograph No. 10. Princeton: Center of International Studies, Princeton University, 1961.

Eichhorn, Emil. Partei und Klassen im Spiegel der Reichstagswahlen. Halle: Verlag Produktiv-Genossenschaft, 1925.

Erdmann, Karl D. "Die Geschichte der Weimarer Republik als Problem der Wissenschaft," *Vierteljahreshefte für Zeitgeschichte,* 3 Jg., 1 Heft (January 1955), 1–19.

Eudin, X. J., and Harold H. Fisher, eds. Soviet Russia and the West, 1920–27: A Documentary Survey. Stanford: Stanford University Press, 1957.

Eyck, Erich. Geschichte der Weimarer Republik. Stuttgart: Eugen Rentsch, 1956. 2 vols.

Fischer, Ruth. Stalin and German Communism. Cambridge: Harvard University Press, 1948.

Fisk, Otis H. Germany's Constitutions of 1871 and 1919. Cincinnati: Court Index Press, 1924.

Flechtheim, Ossip K. Die Kommunistische Partei Deutschlands in der Weimarer Republik. Offenbach a. M.: Bollwerk, 1948.

Franz, Günther. Die Entwicklung der politischen Parteien in Niedersachsen im Spiegel der Wahlen. 1867–1949. Bremen: Walter Dorn, 1951.

Friedensburg, Ferdinand. Die Weimarer Republik. Berlin: Habel, 1946.

Gablentz, Otto Heinrich von. Politische Parteien als Ausdruck gesellschaftlicher Kräfte. Berlin: Deutsche Hochschule für Politik, 1952.

Galenson, Walter. "Reflections on the Writing of Labor History," *Industrial and Labor Relations Review,* II (1957), 86–95.

Gay, Peter. The Dilemma of Democratic Socialism. New York: Columbia University Press, 1952.

Gebhardt, Bruno, ed. Handbuch der Deutschen Geschichte. (Bd. 4,

Karl D. Erdmann, Die Zeit der Weltkriege.) Stuttgart: Union Verlag, 1959.

Geiger Theodor. Die soziale Schichtung des Deutschen Volkes. Stuttgart: Ferdinand Enke, 1932.

Germany, Federal Republic. Bundesarchiv, Alte Reichskanzlei.

———. R431/1942. "Akten betr. Arbeiter- und Soldatenräte."

———. R431/2023. "Akten betr. Arbeiterorganisationen und Gewerkschaften."

———. R431/2024. "Akten betr. Arbeiterorganisationen und Gewerkschaften."

———. R431/2118. "Akten betr. Arbeiteraufstände und Streiks allg."

———. R431/2268. "Akten betr. Hansestädte."

———. R431/2696. "Lageberichte des Reichskommissars der öffentlichen Ordnung."

Gerschenkron, Alexander. Bread and Democracy in Germany. Berkeley: University of California Press, 1943.

Geyer, Curt. Der Radikalismus in der Deutschen Arbeiterbewegung. Jena: Thüringer Anstalt, 1923.

Giese, Walter Hans. Die grauen Huller. Hamburg: Hans Köhler, 1933.

Goetz, Adolf. Hamburgischer Püttjerkram. Hamburg: Gebrüder Südeking, 1914.

Goetz, Robert. Les syndicats ouvriers allemands après la guerre. Paris: Loviton, 1934.

Goguel, François, and Georges Dupeux. Sociologie électorale. Paris: Armand Colin, 1951.

Gosnell, Harold F. Why Europe Votes. Chicago: University of Chicago Press, 1930.

GP (Government Publications).

———. Arbeiterrat Gross-Hamburg, Bericht über das Jahr, Jg. 1919–20, 1923–24, 1925, 1926. Hamburg: Verlag des Arbeiterrats, 1920–27.

———. Hamburger Addressbuch (annual city directory).

———. Hamburger Statistische Monatsberichte, Jg. 1922, 1923, 1924, 1925, 1926. Hamburg: Lütke & Wulff, 1923–27.

———. Statistische Mitteilungen über den hamburgischen Staat, Nrs. 7–25. Hamburg: Otto Meissner, 1919–30.

———. Statistisches Landesamt. Statistik des hamburgischen Staates, Bds. 32–34. Hamburg: Otto Meissner, 1925–29.

———. Statistisches Reichsamt. Statistik des deutschen Reiches, Bds. 401–16. Berlin: Reimar Hobbing, 1926–33.

Grzesinski, Albert C. Inside Germany. New York: Dutton, 1939.
Guillebaud, C. W. The Works Council. Cambridge: Cambridge University Press, 1928.
Gulick, Charles A., Roy A. Ockert, and Raymond J. Wallace. History and Theories of Working-Class Movements: A Select Bibliography. Berkeley, Calif.: Bureau of Business and Economic Research and the Institute of Industrial Relations, n.d.
Habedank, Heinz. Zur Geschichte des Hamburger Aufstandes, 1923. Berlin: Dietz Verlag, 1958.
Hagmann, Meinrad. Der Weg ins Verhängnis. Reichstagswahlergebnisse 1919 bis 1933, besonders aus Bayern. München: Beckstein, 1946.
Halperin, S. William. Germany Tried Democracy. New York: Crowell, 1946.
"Hamburg," Encyclopedia Britannica. 11th ed., XII (1911), 871–75.
Hasselmann, Erwin. Die genossenschaftliche Selbsthilfe der Verbraucher. Hamburg: Verlagsgesellschaft deutscher Konsumvereine, 1957.
Heberle, Rudolf. From Democracy to Nazism: A Regional Case Study on Political Parties in Germany. Baton Rouge: Louisiana State University Press, 1945.
Heidegger, Hermann. Die Deutsche Sozialdemokratie und der nationale Staat. 1870–1920. Berlin: Musterschmidt, 1956.
Helwig, Werner. Die Blaue Blume des Wandervogels. Gütersloh: Sigbert Mohn, 1960.
Herschel, Olga. "Die Öffentliche Meinung in Hamburg in ihrer Haltung zu Bismarck, 1864–66." Inaug. dissertation, München, 1915. Printed in Hamburg, 1916.
Heydte, F. A. von der, and K. Sacherl. Soziologie der deutschen Parteien. München: Isar Verlag, 1955.
Hirsch-Weber, Wolfgang. Gewerkschaften in der Politik. Köln: Westdeutscher Verlag, 1959.
Hoebel, Heinrich. "Das organisierte Arbeitgebertum in Hamburg-Altona." Unpub. dissertation, Hamburg, 1923.
Holst, Karl Heinz. "Die Stellung Hamburgs zum inneren Konflikt in Preussen, 1862–66." Inaug. dissertation, Rostock, 1931. Printed in Wismar, 1932.
Horkenbach, Cuno. Das Deutsche Reich von 1918 bis Heute. Berlin: Verlag für Presse, Wirtschaft, und Politik, 1930.
Hunt, Richard N. "The Internal Development of the SPD in the Weimar Republic." Unpub. dissertation, Yale University, 1958.
Kerr, Clark, Frederick H. Harbison, et al. "The Labour Problem

in Economic Development," *International Labour Review,* LXXI (1955), 3–15.

Kiesel, O. E. Wie Schön war unsere Welt. Hamburg: Hammerich & Lesser, 1956.

Kolb, Eberhard. Arbeiterräte in der deutschen Innenpolitik. Düsseldorf: Droste Verlag, 1962.

Koller, Philip. "Das Massen- und Führerproblem in den Freien Gewerkschaften." Ergänzungsheft XVII zu *Archiv für Sozialwissenschaft und Sozialpolitik*. Tübingen: J. C. B. Mohr, 1920.

Krüber, Alf. Der Weg auf dem wir angetreten. Berlin: Wilhelm Limpert, 1938.

Laidler, Harry W. A History of Socialist Thought. London: Constable, 1927.

Lamp'l, Walther. Die Revolution in Gross-Hamburg. Hamburg: W. Gente, 1921.

Lane, Robert E. Political Life. Glencoe, Ill.: The Free Press, 1959.

Laufenberg, Heinrich. Geschichte der Arbeiterbewegung Hamburgs. Hamburg: Leuteritz, 1931. 2 vols.

———. Die Hamburger Revolution. Hamburg: Verlag Willaschek, 1919.

———. Der politische Streik. Stuttgart: Dietz Verlag, 1914.

———. Zwischen der ersten und zweiten Revolution. Hamburg: Verlag Willaschek, 1919.

———, and Fritz Wolffheim. Revolutionäre Volkskrieg oder konterrevolutionäre Bürgerkrieg. Hamburg: Verlag Willaschek, 1919.

Leipart, Theodor. Carl Legien; ein gedenkbuch von Theodor Leipart. Berlin: Verlagsgesellschaft des Allgemeinen deutschen gewerkschaftsbundes, 1929.

Linz (Storch de Gracia), Juan. "The Social Bases of West German Politics." Unpub. dissertation, Columbia University, 1958 (Univ. Micr., 59–4075).

Lipset, Seymour Martin. Political Man: The Social Bases of Politics. New York: Doubleday, 1960.

———. "Party Systems and the Representation of Social Groups," *European Journal of Sociology,* I (1960), 3–38.

———. "Socialism—Left and Right—East and West," *Confluence,* VII (1958), 172–92.

———. "Social Stratification and 'Right-Wing Extremism,'" *British Journal of Sociology,* X (December 1959), 1–38.

Lorwin, Val R. "Working-Class Politics and Economic Development in Western Europe," *American Historical Review,* LXIII (1958), 338–51.

Luther, Arthur, ed. Deutsches Land in deutscher Erzählung. Ein Literarisches Ortslexikon. Leipzig: Karl W. Hiersmann, 1937.

McPherson, William Heston. Works Councils under the German Republic. Chicago: University of Chicago Libraries, 1939.

Maehl, William Harvey. "Recent Literature on the German Socialists," *Journal of Modern History,* XXXIII (1961), 292–306.

Maslowski, Peter. Thälmann. Leipzig: R. Kittler, 1932.

Matthias, Erich. "Zur Geschichte der Weimarer Republik. Ein Literaturbericht," *Neue Gesellschaft,* III (1956), 312–20.

Meyer, Maximilian. "Der Nichtwähler," *Allgemeines statistisches Archiv,* XXI (1931), 495–525.

Michels, Robert. Political Parties. Translated by Eden and Cedar Paul. New York: Dover, 1959.

———. "Beitrag zur Lehre von der Klassenbildung," *Archiv für Sozialwissenschaft und Sozialpolitik,* XLIX (1922), 561–93.

Mönckeberg, Carl. Hamburg vor und nach dem Krieg. Stuttgart: Deutsche Verlagsanstalt, 1917.

Neumann, Paul. Hamburg unter der Regierung des Arbeiter- und Soldatenrats. Hamburg: Verlag Arbeiterrat Gross-Hamburg, 1919.

Neumann, Sigmund. Die deutschen Parteien. Berlin: Junker und Dünnhaupt, 1932.

Oertzen, Peter von. Beitriebsräte in der Novemberrevolution. Düsseldorf: Droste Verlag, 1963.

Okrass, Hermann. Hamburg bleibt Rot. Das Ende einer Parole. Hamburg: Hanseatische Verlagsanstalt, 1935.

Opel, Fritz. Der Deutsche Metallarbeiterverband. Hannover: Norddeutsche Verlagsanstalt, 1957.

Pollock, James Kerr. German Election Administration. New York: Columbia University Press, 1934.

Prager, Eugen. Geschichte der USPD. Berlin: Verlagsgenossenschaft "Freiheit," 1921.

Pratt, Samuel A. "The Social Basis of Nazism and Communism in Urban Germany: A Correlational Study of the July 31, 1932 Reichstag Elections in Germany." Unpub. dissertation, Michigan State College, 1948.

Preller, Ludwig. Sozialpolitik in der Weimarer Republik. Stuttgart: Mittelbach, 1949.

Pye, Lucian W., and Sidney Verba, eds. Political Culture and Political Development. Princeton: Princeton University Press, 1965.

Reich, Nathan. Labor Relations in Republican Germany. New York: Oxford, 1938.

Reissner, Larissa. Hamburg auf den Barrikaden. Berlin: Neuer Deutscher Verlag, 1925.
Rettig, Rudolf. "Die Gewerkschaftsarbeit der KPD von 1918 bis 1925." Unpub. dissertation, Hamburg, 1954.
Rieger, Josef, Max Mendel, and Walter Postelt. Die hamburger Konsumgenossenschaft "Produktion." Hamburg: Verlag Fr. Oetinger, 1949.
Robinson, W. S. "Ecological Correlations and the Behavior of Individuals," *American Sociological Review,* XV (1950), 352–57.
Rosenberg, Arthur. A History of the German Republic. Translated by Ian F. D. Morrow and L. Marie Sieveking. London: Methuen, 1936.
Roth, Günther. The Social Democrats in Imperial Germany. Totawa, New Jersey: The Bedminster Press, 1963.
Salomon, Ernst F. K. von. Die Geächteten. Berlin: Rowohlt, 1935.
Schorske, Carl E. German Social Democracy, 1905–1917: The Development of the Great Schism. Cambridge: Harvard University Press, 1955.
Schüddekopf, Otto Ernst. Linke Leute von Rechts. Stuttgart: W. Kohlhammer Verlag, 1960.
Schürer, Heinz. "Die politische Arbeiterbewegung in der Nachkriegszeit, 1918–23." Inaug. dissertation, Leipzig, 1932. Printed in Leipzig, 1933.
Schult, Johannes. "Die hamburger Arbeiterbewegung als Kulturfaktor." Hamburg: Druckereigesellschaft Weltzien, 1954 (manuscript).
Schultess' Europäischer Geschichtskalender. München: E. H. Beck'scher, 1867.
Schulz, Gerhard. Zewischen Demokratie und Diktator, Bd. I. Berlin: Walter De Gruyter, 1963.
Schwarz, Albert. Die Weimarer Republik. (Sonderdruck aus Brandt-Meyer-Just, Handbuch der Deutschen Geschichte.) Konstanz: Athenaion, 1958.
Seidel, Richard. Die Gewerkschaften in der Revolution. Berlin: Verlagsgenossenschaft "Freiheit," 1920.
———. The Trade Union Movement of Germany. Amsterdam: International Federation of Trade Unions, 1928.
Sellitz, Claire, Marie Jahoda, et al. Research Methods in Social Relations. New York: Holt, 1959 (revised one-volume edition).
Siemann, Joachim. "Der sozialdemokratische Arbeiterführer in der Zeit der Weimarer Republik. Ein Beitrag zur Soziologie der Eliten in der modernen Parteigeschichte." Unpub. dissertation, Göttingen, 1955.

Snell, John L. "Socialist Unions and Socialist Patriotism in Germany, 1914–1918," *American Historical Review* LIX (1953), 61–76.

SPD Hamburg (Sozialdemokratischer Verein für das Hamburgische Staatsgebiet).

———. Jahresbericht der Landesorganisation, Jg. 1914–19, 1919–21, 1921–24, 1925–26. Hamburg: Leuteritz, 1919–27.

———. Die Sozialdemokratie in der verfassungsgebenden Bürgerschaft. Bericht über die Tätigkeit der Bürgerschaftsfraktion, 1919–21. Hamburg: Auer, 1921.

———. Sozialdemokratische Staats- und Gemeindepolitik in Hamburg unter der Verfassung von 1921. Bericht über die Tätigkeit der Bürgerschaftsfraktion, 1921–24. Hamburg: Auer, 1924.

Striefler, Heinrich. Deutsche Wahlen in Bildern und Zahlen. Düsseldorf: Wende, 1946.

Sturmthal, Adolf. The Tragedy of European Labor. New York: Columbia University Press, 1943.

Sulzbach, Walter. Die Grundlagen der politischen Parteibildung. Tübingen: J. C. B. Mohr, 1921.

Syrup, Friederich. Die Arbeiterverteilung in der deutschen Industrie Ende 1921. (Kartenwerk der Reichsarbeitsverwaltung.) Berlin: Verlag des Reichsarbeitsblattes, 1924.

Tarnow, Fritz. Das Organisationsproblem im ADGB. Berlin: Verlagsanstalt des Deutschen Holzarbeiter-Verbandes, 1925.

Tecke, Annelise, ed. Bücherkunde zur Hamburgischen Geschichte. Hamburg: Hans Christians Verlag, 1956.

Timpke, Henning, ed. Dokumente zur Gleichschaltung des Landes Hamburg 1933. Frankfurt a. M.: Europäische Verlagsanstalt, 1964.

Tingsten, Herbert. Political Behavior. London: P. S. King, 1937.

Tormin, Walter. Zwischen Rätediktatur und Sozialer Demokratie. Düsseldorf: Droste Verlag, 1954.

Umbreit, Paul. Die Deutschen Gewerkschaften im Weltkrieg. Berlin: Deutsche Verlagsanstalt, 1928.

Unabhängige Sozialistische Partei Deutschlands. Handbuch für die Wähler der USPD. Reichstagswahl 1920. Berlin: Verlagsgenossenschaft "Freiheit," 1920.

UP (Union Publications). *The following six publications are in the Zentralarchiv der Gewerkschaften of the East German trade-union federation in East Berlin.*

———. Deutscher Bauarbeiter-Verband. Zweigverein Hamburg und Umgegend. Jahresbericht, Jg. 1920–22, 1923, 1924, 1925, 1926. Hamburg 1923–27.

———. Deutscher Holzarbeiter-Verband. Verwaltungsstelle Hamburg. Bericht über die Tätigkeit der Verwaltungsstelle Hamburg im Jahre 1925. Hamburg, 1926.
———. Deutscher Metallarbeiter-Verband. Verwaltungsstelle Hamburg. Jahresbericht, Jg. 1919, 1920, 1921, 1922, 1923, 1924. Hamburg, 1920–25.
———. Deutscher Transportarbeiter-Verband. Verwaltungsstelle Hamburg. Jahresbericht, Jg. 1918, 1919, 1920, 1921, 1922, 1923, 1924, 1925, 1926. Hamburg, 1919–27.
———. Einheitsverband der Eisenbahner Deutschlands. Ortsgruppe Hamburg. Geschäftsbericht, Jg. 1921, 1925, 1926. Hamburg: Verlag E.V.E.D., 1922–27.
———. Verband der graphischen Hilfsarbeiter und Arbeiterinnen Deutschlands. Hamburg-Altona-Wandsbek. Jahresbericht, Jg. 1924. Hamburg, 1925.
Valtin, Jan (Richard J. H. Krebs). Out of the Night. New York: Alliance, 1941.
Varain, Heinz Josef. Freie Gewerkschaften, Sozialdemokratie und Staat: Die Politik der Generalkomission unter der Führung Carl Legiens, 1890–1920. Düsseldorf: Droste Verlag, 1956.
Vieth, Ferdinand. Siebzehn Jahre Handelsgesellschaft Produktion m.b.H. zu Hamburg. Hamburg: Verlagsgesellschaft deutscher Konsumvereine, 1930.
"Vom Leipziger Parteitag bis zum Oktober 1923. Material zur Stellungnahme der Opposition der KPD gegenüber der offiziellen Parteipolitik." Sonderbeilage zu *Die Internationale,* Heft 10–11 (1924).
Wells, Roger H. German Cities: A Study of Contemporary Municipal Politics and Administration. Princeton: Princeton University Press, 1932.
———. "Partisanship and Parties in German Municipal Government," *National Municipal Review,* XVII (1948), 473–81.
Waite, Robert G. L. Vanguard of Nazism: The Free Corps Movement in Postwar Germany, 1918–1923. Cambridge: Harvard University Press, 1952.
Waldman, Eric. The Spartacist Uprising of 1919 and the Crisis of the German Socialist Movement. Milwaukee: Marquette University Press, 1958.
Wolffheim, Fritz. Betriebsorganisation oder Gewerkschaft. Hamburg: Willaschek, 1919.
Zeutschel, Walter. Im Dienst der kommunistischen Terror-Organisation. Berlin: Dietz Verlag, 1931.

Zwing, Karl. Geschichte der Deutschen Freien Gewerkschaften. Jena: Karl Zwing Verlagsbuchhandlung, 1926.

———. Sociologie der Gewerkschaftsbewegung. Jena: Verlag Gewerkschafts-Archiv, 1925.

PART II

[1] *Arbeiterrat.* Nr. 1. "Organisation, Entstehung und Entwicklung, 1919ff."

[2] ———. Nr. 2. "Pressemitteilungen, Jahresberichte, 1920–21."

[3] ———. Nr. 3a, Band 1a. "Sitzungsprotokolle."

[4] ———. Nr. 3a, Band 1b. "Sitzungsprotokolle, 1919–20."

[5] ———. Nr. 4. "Schriftwechsel (auch Tagesordnungen), 1920–33."

[6] ———. Nr. 6. "Mitglieder des Arbeiterrates, 1921–33."

[7] *Arbeiter- und Soldatenrat.* Nr. 1 Band 1–5. "Protokolle, 1918–19."

[8] ———. Nr. 6. "Beschlüsse betr. Massnahmen des A.u.S.-Rates."

[9] *Ausserordentliches Gericht des Reiches in Hamburg.* B 1/21. "Ziehl wegen Aufruhr in Geesthacht."

[10] ———. B 3/21. "Weber wegen Aufruhr bei Blohm und Voss."

[11] ———. B 89/21. "Riedel wegen Unruhen auf den Werften."

[12] ———. C 157/24. "Urbahns wegen Aufruhr und Hochverrat."

[13] ———. C 65/24. "Broweleit u. Gen. wegen überfall auf Polizeiwache 42."

[14] ———. C 476/23. "Aufruhr in Barmbeck."

[15] *Ausserordentliches Kriegsgericht in Hamburg.* B. "Verfahren gegen Verschiedene betr. Juniunruhen."

[16] *Bürgerschaft.* Stenographische Berichte über die Sitzungen der Bürgerschaft, Jg. 1919, 1920, 1921, 1922, 1923.

[17] *Familienarchiv Lamp'l.* Nr. 9. "Bürgerschafts-Untersuchungskommission betr. sog. Sülze-Unruhen, 1919–20."

[18] ———. Nr. 17. "Zeitungsausschnitte über Unruhen 1919–20."

[19] *Kriegsversorgungsamt.* 6.VIIIa. "Protokollmaterial; Stimmungsberichte."

[20] *Plankammer.* "Flugschriften und Plakate, allgemeine, 1919–25."

[21] ———. "Reichstagswahl, 1920."

[22] ———. "Reichstagswahl, 1924."

[23] ———. "Bürgerschaftswahlen, 1921 u. 1924."

[24] *Polizeibehörde, Abl. 38.* Bestand 9 Nr. 52–55, "Politische Lageberichte, 1920–23."

[25] ———. Bestand 13 I/10. "Gewerkschaftsbewegung, 1918–19."
[26] ———. Bestand 13 I/11. "Linksradikale Parteien, 1918."
[27] ———. Bestand 13 I/19. "Demonstrationen in Hamburg."
[28] ———. Bestand 13 I/26. "Spartakistische Umtriebe."
[29] ———. Bestand 13 I/20. "Arbeitslosigkeit und Notstandsarbeit, 1918–19."
[30] ———. Bestand 13 I/36. "Rätesystem, 1919."
[31] *Polizeibehörde, Abl. 45.* Liste 2 Nr. 38. "Kapp-Putsch, 1920."
[32] ———. Liste 2 Nr. 40. "März-Unruhen, 1921."
[33] ———. Liste 2 Nr. 61. "KPD-Informationen, 1921–22."
[34] *Pressestelle I.* B.I. "Ermordung des Reichsministers Rathenau, 1922–28."
[35] ———. B.VI.12 (Mappe 2a). "Politische Angelegenheiten."
[36] ———. B.VI.13 (Mappe 4a). "Politische Angelegenheiten."
[37] ———. B.VI.25. "Vorgänge in Bayern im Sept., 1923, in Hamburg im Okt., 1923."
[38] ———. B.VI.26. "Reichstagswahl, Mai, 1924."
[39] ———. B.VI.29 (Mappe 1 u. 2). "Politische Angelegenheiten, 1922–29."
[40] ———. B.VI.30. "Reichstagswahl, Dez., 1924."
[41] ———. D.I.1b. "Tod des Bürgermeisters Diestel, 1924."
[42] ———. D.I.1d. "Neuwahl des Senats, 1924."
[43] ———. D.I.2b. "Bürgerschaftswahl, 1924."
[44] ———. D.II.2. "Politische Attentate in Hamburg, 1922–24."
[45] ———. D.II.5 (Mappe 1 u. 2). "Politische Angelegenheiten."
[46] ———. E.II.4. "Correspondenz- und Nachrichtenbüro 'Corma,' darin: Bericht über KPD, 1922."
[47] ———. L.I.19. "Faschistenbestrebungen, Putschpläne, Skagerfeiern."
[48] ———. L.I.20. "Antifaschistentag, Unruhen in Hamburg und im Reich, 1923."
[49] ———. L.I.22. "Putschpläne der Kommunisten, 1924."
[50] ———. L.I.25. "Politische Lageberichte."
[51] ———. M.IV.3d. "Gehalts- und Lohnstatistik."
[52] ———. M.IV.3f. "Streiks und Aussperrungen, 1924–29."
[53] ———. M.IV.3h. "Gewerkschaftsgutachten über Verhinderung der Verelendung, 1923–24."
[54] *Senat.* Cl.I Lit.T Nr. 1 Vol. 21b Fasc. 30. "Erwerblosenstatistik für Deutschland und Hamburg, 1919–25."
[55] ———. Cl.I Lit.T Nr. 1 Vol. 58 Fasc. 1–26. "Wahlen zur verfassungsgebenden Nationalversammlung."

[56] ———. Cl.VII Lit.Bd. Nr. 45 Vol. 17. "Wahlen zur Bürgerschaft, 1919."
[57] ———. Cl.VII Lit.Bf. Vol. 1 Fasc. 45. "Wahlen zur Bürgerschaft, 1921."
[58] ———. Cl.VII Lit.Bf. Vol. 1 Fasc. 47. "Wahlen zur Bürgerschaft, 1924."
[59] ———. Cl.VII Lit.Lb. Nr. 28a2 Vol. 206. "Antrag Urbahns, die Überwachung von Arbeiterorganisationen durch Spitzel zu verbieten."
[60] ———. Cl.VII Lit.Me. Nr. 12 Vol. 24 Fasc. 1–18. "Unruhen in Hamburg, 1919–21."
[61] ———. Cl.VII Lit.Me. Nr. 12 Vol. 26. "Bekämpfung innerer Unruhen und Überwachung der KPD, 1919–24."
[62] ———. Cl.VII Lit.Me. Nr. 12 Vol. 30–32. "Unruhen, Verbote, Ausnahmezustand, 1919–24."
[63] ———. Cl.XI Gen. Nr. 2 Vol. 66b. "Streikbewegungen, 1919–24."
[64] ———. Cl.XI Gen. Nr. 2 Vol. 188 Fasc. 1–3. "Sozialisierungsfrage, 1919–20."
[65] *Senat-Kriegsakten*. Xd. "Bericht der Marinebesichtigungskommission über die innere politische Lage in Hamburg, 1919."
[66] ———. Xo. "Eingriff des Arbeiter- u. Soldatenrates in die Tagesordnung der Bürgerschaft, 1919."
[67] ———. Xq. "Wahlen zum 2. Rätekongress, 1919."
[68] ———. Xw. "Polizei Verhältnisse, 1918–20."
[69] ———. Z.III.n. "Berichte des Korps Lettow-Vorbeck über die politische Lage in Hamburg, 1919."
[70] *Senatskommission für die Justizverwaltung*. I.Eb.14a14 Vol. 1–4. "Belagerungszustand, 1914–24."
[71] ———. I.Eb.14d5 Vol. 1–2. "Unruhen, 1919–20."
[72] *Staatsarchiv*. "Handschriftensammlung Nr. 601. Verzeichnis der Bürgerschafts-Mitglieder." Collected by Franz Mönckeberg, 1959.
[73] *Zeitgeschichtliche Sammlung*. IV.3 "Amtlicher Polizeibericht über den Oktoberaufstand, 1923: 'Denkschrift über die Unruhen im Oktober 1923 im Gebiete Gross-Hamburg' (Zum dienstlichen Gebrauch)."

# Index